I DON'T LIKE THE BLUES

I DON'T LIKE THE BLUES

RACE, PLACE, & THE BACKBEAT OF BLACK LIFE

B. BRIAN FOSTER

THE UNIVERSITY OF NORTH CAROLINA PRESS

Chapel Hill

Designed by Jamison Cockerham
Set in Arno, Scala, and Egiziano
by codeMantra, Inc.

Cover photographs courtesy of Bradford Fair. Used with permission.

Manufactured in the United States of America

The University of North Carolina Press has been a member
of the Green Press Initiative since 2003.

LIBRARY OF CONGRESS CATALOGING-IN-PUBLICATION DATA
Names: Foster, B. Brian, author.
Title: I don't like the blues : race, place, and the backbeat of black life / B. Brian Foster.
Description: Chapel Hill : The University of North Carolina Press, [2020] |
Includes bibliographical references and index.
Identifiers: LCCN 2020018408 | ISBN 9781469660417 (cloth) |
ISBN 9781469660424 (paperback) | ISBN 9781469660431 (ebook)
Subjects: LCSH: Blues (Music)—Social aspects—Mississippi. |
African Americans—Mississippi—Social life and customs. |
African Americans—Mississippi—Social conditions.
Classification: LCC ML3918.B57 F67 2020 | DDC 781.64309762—dc23
LC record available at https://lccn.loc.gov/2020018408

TO THE FOLKS
WHOSE FOLKS
LIVE(D) WHAT
THEY SING

[A] stumbling block for those who would
like to exploit [the blues] as mere "entertainment,"
a mere ruse to keep the cash register ringing. Born
in passionate revolt against the unlivable . . . the
blues are the cries of a new society being born.

FRANKLIN ROSEMONT & CLYDE WOODS

Good mornin', blues
Blues, how do you do?
I'm doin' all right.
Good mornin'.
How are you?

BESSIE SMITH

I don't remember whether I sang them, but I know I never
liked them. . . . I still don't like the blues. Never have.

JAMES BROWN

CONTENTS

MAPS & TABLES

MAPS

TABLES

Demographic tables 2 through 11 appear in the appendix.

I DON'T LIKE THE BLUES

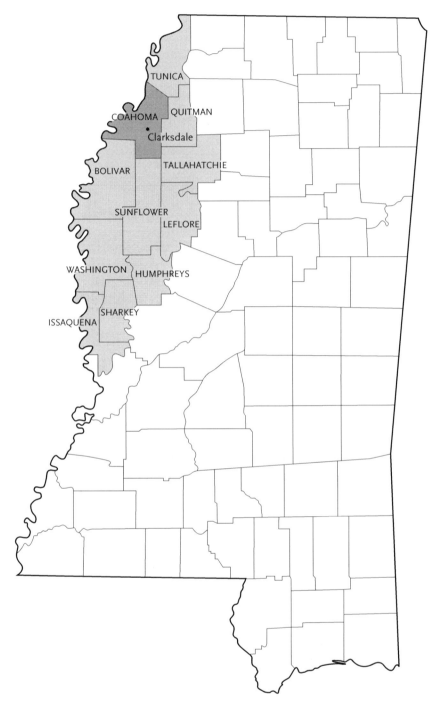

Map 1. Eleven counties of the "Central" Mississippi Delta region.
Source: Lynn L. Reinschmiedt and Bernal L. Green, *Socioeconomic Conditions:
The Mississippi Delta* (Starkville: Department of Information Services, Division of
Agriculture, Forestry, and Veterinary Medicine, Mississippi State University, 1989).

PRELUDE

I got it wrong from the beginning.

I think.

It wasn't that I had decided to move into the back bedroom, or that I had decided to move into the back bedroom of a house in the Mississippi Delta. It wasn't even that I had decided to move in the middle of the summer in the middle of the day. Well, I did get that part wrong; but I'm thinking of another kind of wrong, one that happened in the middle of that night, my first night in Clarksdale: July 23, 2014.

That night, I wrote in my journal, *I wonder if I'll be able to say something beautiful.* The entry didn't have many words or much weight but for that, but when you are wrong it don't take much of either.

I got it wrong from the beginning.

I had gone to Clarksdale to study the South, to talk to enough people and spend enough time to say something worth knowing about the Black folks who called the region home. I had gone to set the record straight. To say how, for Black southerners, the civil rights movement was less a period and more a comma. That the 1960s was not when life stopped for Black folks but when it paused and reconfigured itself. Making the old sound new or at last seem different. I had gone to Clarksdale to say how the rural Black South had changed.

I was wrong, but not because it hadn't, just that I had only gone to say how it had.

I had gone to Mississippi from the University of North Carolina at Chapel Hill (UNC), where I was working toward a PhD in sociology. I got there green and ambitious, ever reminded of what somebody had told me one time about UNC: it was a place that made "blue-chip sociologists." Ever reminded of what somebody else had told me another time about blue-chip sociologists: they don't go anywhere to "say." They go to "show, then tell," which is another way to say describe, then explain. Describe the thing that happened. Describe the expression on her face. Describe what he did with his hands. Then explain what the thing meant. Explain how she felt. Explain how he explained what he did. The best blue-chip sociologists show, then tell. I got it wrong. I only wanted to tell, or as I wrote *say something beautiful.*

I wanted to say something beautiful, I wrote in an earlier version of this story.

I wrote that *I wanted to write the thing that I had wanted and needed to read but could not find.*

I wrote that *I wanted to write about race and inequality in and from a place at the bottom of the margins.*

I wrote.

I wanted to give a retrospective on a place long thought to be left behind. I wrote that I wanted to write something *shiny* and *extravagant.*

That was not the blues.

I had gone to Clarksdale, Mississippi, the "land where the blues began," where Muddy Waters lived and Bessie Smith died, where the Crossroads lied (and folks lied on the Crossroads), where hundreds of people who played the blues played and hundreds of thousands of people who liked the blues watched; and I did not want to write the blues.

I did not like the blues. I wrote that too, for a time on just about everything that I could get my hands on. *I am not studying the blues.*

I did not want to be a blues scholar.

I did not want to be blue-chip.

I did not want B. B. King.

I did not like the blues.

So, I went looking for something else. Between that one middle-of-the-summer day in 2014 and another one in 2019, I lived, worked, and visited Clarksdale. I talked to hundreds of local folks. I went just about everywhere.

And, I found some things. In that same preface to that same earlier version of this story, I wrote *I found what the Census and Clyde Woods had foretold: arrested development; limited opportunity; and big mansions with big yards in the distance. I saw in plain sight the persistence of the color line, which followed, ballast-by-ballast and mile-by-mile, the tracks of the Illinois Central Railroad, literally and figuratively splitting the town in two.*

I wrote, *I also found, as Zora once urged us to see, Black folks leading ordinary lives. In the summertime, people liked to be outside. Children laughed and played like children do, with boundless energy and wide smiles, jumping in and over ditches, riding bikes, waving sticks, throwing balls through all manner of hoops. Women and men worked long days, cursed and went to church, drank beer, smoked weed, and played dominos on all manner of tabletops. Folks washed and fixed on cars, sat and cursed on porches, sweated and laughed on the backs of pickup trucks with their shirts off. In the fall, they went to football games, then raucous basketball gyms in winter, a holiday parade at Christmas time, somebody's dinner table on Sundays. They lit candles, released balloons, and sang elegies for lost loved ones and neighbors. They fought, married, lived, died, and had birthday parties.*

I wrote, *I found more of the same—the expected and ordinary—among the . . . people I met. . . . I heard stories of Civil Rights workers and Freedom Houses, Gangster Disciples and Vice Lords, guns, drugs, and dead bodies by the river. People talked about God and church, and reveled in their wildest dreams. They bemoaned politicians and sometimes other residents. They celebrated each other with laughter and flowers. Men bragged about sex and cars and their mommas. Women spoke of 100 days of peace. People sang to me, rapped their best freestyle verses to me, shared profoundly personal stories with me. They invited me into their homes, welcoming me with chicken and cheap liquor, "shit talking," and more love and trust than I could have ever earned.*

What I wrote that I found was not wrong. What I thought it all meant was. Or, *that* I thought it meant at all, was. I thought I had found no blues. That Black southerners were no longer blues people. Post-blues people? I thought the children and the dominos and the holiday parade and the 100 days of peace meant something beyond the blues.

That was a lie.

I *wanted* all of that to be beyond the blues.

So, I wrote it; and I thought I was writing exactly what Black folks in Clarksdale had told me, exactly how they told me too: "I don't like the blues" with a still face. "Fuck that blues shit" after hitting the blunt. "I've never even been to a blues show" before holding quiet. "I'm not a blues person" with an eye roll. "The blues just won't keep us standing."

I got it wrong.

I thought *I Don't Like the Blues* was about the rural Black South telling.

From the beginning, "I don't like the blues" was the rural Black South knowing.

Not liking a thing does not mean the thing is no longer a part of you, or its essence apart from you. If a tree loses a limb, it loses a limb but stays a tree. And, a boomerang should always come back.[1] And, the rural Black South is the blues. They just don't like it like (we think) they used to.

INTRODUCTION

"What's the guy, that sings 'Mom's Apple Pie'?" Mrs. Irene asked me, her voice like the morning, quiet and still and warmer than usual. "I like him. I looove him." We were sitting in her office, a front room in a funeral home on the backside[1] of Clarksdale, Mississippi.

"You're like mom's apple pie!" I sang, and as I clapped and carried on, Mrs. Irene smiled and rested back in her seat, a stiff chair behind a heavy desk. Her demeanor had been reserved and guarded for most of the morning—at seventy-one years old, she was like that most of the time—but our exchange about her favorite song had stirred something different: laughter, both hers and mine. A few moments later, something else stirred, a soft but unflinching glare from her to me, a moment of quiet, a thought that could not go unsaid. "I don't like the blues. It saddens me." Her voice was a whisper, somehow both tentative and absolute. "I guess I've never even been to a blues show."

I wondered. The guy who sings "Mom's Apple Pie," Tyrone Davis, is a blues singer. And, Clarksdale, where Mrs. Irene had lived since 1965, is a blues place. Muddy "Father of the Chicago Blues" Waters grew up on Stovall Plantation just west of Clarksdale. Bessie "Queen of the Blues" Smith died at the G. T. Thomas Afro-American Hospital, east of the Sunflower River in Clarksdale. When Robert Johnson "sold his soul" to play the blues, he is said to have been at the "Crossroads"[2] in Clarksdale. Today, when people want to travel to hear the blues, they often go to Clarksdale. Each year, the town's circuit of blues festivals, blues performance and entertainment venues, and blues heritage markers attracts some 132,000 visitors, more than eight times the resident population.[3]

I wondered. How could Mrs. Irene love a blues singer for his blues song, and live for so long in the world's most famous blues place, and still not like the blues?

I asked her. "What about Moonies?"[4] I remembered all the times folks had asked me had I been to one of the most popular blues clubs in Clarksdale. "Have you been to Moonies?"

"I've been," Mrs. Irene said, as if it were the most unimpressive thing she had ever done. She shrugged. "I went last [year]. My cousin, they gave him his seventieth birthday party there; and I've eaten there." In an instant, her voice and face tightened, like she had just tasted a sour thing, or remembered one. "I don't understand it. The floor is crooked. The tablecloths are crooked. The tables are leaning." I laughed at what she said. She didn't.

I sat at the funeral home with Mrs. Irene Sandiford for a long time that morning, long enough for outside to go from kind-of-hot to "too hot to be outside," long enough for two women who had been there when I got there to leave and come back before I left. We all moved at Mrs. Irene's pace. The morning seemed to too.

I asked Mrs. Irene about her family, and she told me a long story— something about some encyclopedias, some blues records, and an uncle that made her husband and two sons feel like all she ever needed. I asked her how it felt to come back to Mississippi after living in Pennsylvania for much of her early life, and she told me a short story—"This was such a strange place to me . . . coming back to the Country South." I asked her whether Clarksdale had changed at all over the years, and she told me no story at all. She stayed quiet for a little while, looked and nodded toward the downtown square.

"It has gone down here, it has," she said eventually, her shoulders following her words. "People used to have jobs . . . there are no jobs. The schools are down. The crime is up. We used to have businesses, lots of businesses, but not now. It's a mess. . . . If [our elected officials] have a plan, I would like to see it . . . because they don't show it." I laughed unsure. Mrs. Irene looked, unmoved. Then, perhaps thinking that an example would help me see what she saw, she said, "Look at Mound Bayou." She referenced a place—Mississippi's first independent all-Black town—about thirty miles south. "People have some beautiful homes there, but they don't have a store, they can't start a business, they can't get nothing going. They don't even have a decent restaurant."

Mrs. Irene's assessment of Mound Bayou was a matter of fact. The town was reaping what chattel slavery and 150 years of the Mississippi Delta's peculiar and exploitive regional development policies[5] had sown: it was a virtually all-Black town contending with a polarized and limited labor market and under-resourced social institutions, which had yielded poverty rates among the nation's highest and social outcomes among the nation's worst. "That's about to happen here." Mrs. Irene said, a prophesy.

It had already happened. In the years between the civil rights movement and 2014, Clarksdale had transitioned from an agricultural stronghold and formidable manufacturing outpost to a middling service economy. The transition made "good work" (i.e., jobs that offered worker benefits and paid above minimum wage) hard to find and, for the vast majority of residents, earning a living wage impossible. The town's public infrastructure underwent a similar decline. By the late aughts, the city and county school districts risked state takeover; the town's second-largest retailer closed; and the local hospital declared bankruptcy.

"It makes you tired," Mrs. Irene sighed. "You just keep asking, 'Okay, what is wrong, what has gone wrong?'" Her look demanded an answer. Her tone betrayed her look. "Look at the downtown. . . . It's just so much blues." She was alluding to the ever-growing network of blues places that filled Clarksdale's downtown square and colored most every other facet of public life in town.

Clarksdale's blues was not happenstance. It was the product of a new development vision in the state of Mississippi. Beginning in the late 1970s, as the Delta faced new and intensifying structural challenges (e.g., a mass of plant closures, the continued downsizing of the region's agricultural economy), state lawmakers and stakeholders looked to hospitality and tourism as promising solutions. For Delta towns like Clarksdale, that meant the blues: new blues festivals, new blues clubs and performance venues, new blues museums, new blues heritage markers; and a new state-sponsored Blues Commission to connect and oversee it all.

For some folks, the Delta's blues was cause for optimism. State lawmakers called it a "powerful" economic promise. Tourists called it a good thing. Folks like Mrs. Irene called it what it was: the blues. "The blues just won't keep us standing," she said, her face a glare unflinching and her claim a story—this one another long one.

BLUES (DEVELOPMENT), BLUES (MUSIC), AND THE BLUES (EPISTEMOLOGY)

Between 2014 and 2019, I talked to more than 200 Black residents of Clarksdale, Mississippi;[6] and many of them sounded like Mrs. Irene. They talked how she talked. They said what she said, often how she said it: like they knew. They said they loved some blues songs and blues singers, but that they did not like the blues. They talked about the blues as if it belonged to them but avoided Clarksdale's blues scenes—places like Moonies on the Square—like the scenes belonged to someone else. They were skeptical of Clarksdale's blues, suspect of the blues tourism development agenda that had come to shape the local (and regional) economy. "I hope it can do some good, it's got some potential," they would often say, before asking, "but is it for everybody?"

Heard one way, what Mrs. Irene and Black folks in Clarksdale said about the blues makes for a riddle. How do you "looove" and not like the same thing all at once? How can a thing belong to you and seem like somebody else's? How do you hold hope and doubt in the same hand, say "yes" and "no" at the same time? There are two ways to deal with a riddle: solve it or make it not be one. *I Don't Like the Blues* goes the second way, telling three related stories, all about not liking the blues, all asking you to hear not "one way" but "another," *on the backbeat*, where riddles ain't riddles, just the blues.

First, that Black residents of Clarksdale were skeptical of the town's blues scenes is a story about tourism and economic development. That story is a straightforward one. It is a long-standing finding in social science research that place natives are almost always critical of attempts at community and economic development that center on tourism.[7] There are questions about land use and resource allocation: Will the tourism system siphon space and resources from native communities? Who will be displaced? Where will they go? There are questions of public infrastructure and sustainability. Where will folks park? What about traffic? What happens if the tourism system goes away? There are questions about how tourism revenue will be allocated. Is it for everybody? More often than not, the answers to these and other questions translate to place natives in most places not liking tourism; and, in this case, translated to Mrs. Irene and Black folks in Clarksdale not liking the blues. That is the first story: a blues development story.

The second story that this book tells is about blues music and Black culture. When Mrs. Irene Sandiford and other Black Clarksdalians said what they said about blues music, they were repeating generations of Black Americans before them. They were suggesting that Black expressive traditions should be rooted in and responsive to the social, political, and economic conditions of Black life at a given time.[8] At the turn of the century, the "afterlife"[9] of slavery and early life of Jim Crow made the blues sound necessary. The early decades of the twentieth century made "Strange Fruit," jazz, and Mahalia Jackson sound important. From the 1960s to the 1980s, an ebbing then ended civil rights movement gave way to a new set of challenges and opportunities for Black folks, and again made Black life sound different. Then, as in the two decades before, older Black expressive traditions like the blues moved to soul and were paired with rhythm.[10] This break eventually set the stage for more contemporary cultural formations like R&B and hip-hop; and it at least partly sets the stage for *I Don't Like the Blues*.

Most of the Black Clarksdalians I spoke with came of age between 1950 and 1980. They were a bunch of civil rights and "Soul Babies,"[11] born in the aforementioned "break," at the height of Black folks not liking old-style blues music. Black Clarksdalians wanted (southern) soul. They wanted Stax or Motown. They wanted gospel. They wanted Tyrone Davis and "Mom's Apple Pie." Younger folks wanted trap and bass. Almost none of them wanted blues; which would make it make sense for almost none of them to want to go to local blues venues or want a local entertainment and economic apparatus anchored around a cluster of blues clubs and festivals. That is the second story: a blues music story.

Yet, for most of the Black Clarksdalians I spoke with, blues was about more than local tourism scenes and Black culture production. It was also about identity and lived experience. It was about race and region, Blackness and the rural South. Their blues was about knowing. While many people hear the blues as performance and play, Black residents of Clarksdale knew it to be flesh and bone, a spirit in the dirt. Their blues was a conduit. A map. A method. As the late geographer Clyde Woods documented and theorized in *Development Arrested* (1998), the blues was their (rural Black southern) epistemology, which is to say, it was how Black Clarksdalians claimed who they were, explained what they had been through in their lives, and hoped for what would come of it all. That is the third story that *I Don't Like the Blues* tells:

not just blues as development agenda or blues as music, but blues as social epistemology.

Take epistemology to be both our beliefs about what is true and knowable, and the logics that we rely on to justify those beliefs. If someone asks you whether fire is hot, what would you say? If they then ask you to explain how you know that it is (or believe that it isn't), what would you say? Both sets of answers constitute what we might call a "fire epistemology." A social epistemology, then, involves what we believe to be true and knowable about the social world, as well as how the social world shapes what we believe to be true and knowable.

Clyde Woods conceptualized "blues" as a social epistemology that Black folks in the Mississippi Delta had crafted in the years between Emancipation and Reconstruction. In this framework, "blues" was a distinct perspective on the world. It was present in patterns of political participation and organizational activity. It prompted collective action and shaped new intellectual and expressive traditions. It was how Black folks in Mississippi lived. It was what Black Mississippians and the Black South knew.

That is what Mrs. Irene Sandiford was doing that morning in her office. She was telling what she knew and how she knew it. She was reflecting back and projecting forward, remembering and anticipating. Her comments were about blues development and blues music, yes. But they were also the product of a blues epistemology. Her "I don't like the blues" was about racial identity and group belonging, an epistemological move that I take up in chapter 2. Her "I've never even been to a blues show" was about place, lived experience, and interracial interactions (chapter 3). Her "The blues just won't keep us standing" was about racial domination, community development, and the future (chapter 4). And *I Don't Like the Blues* is about it all, not just what Black residents of Clarksdale say and believe to be true about the blues (tourism or music) but what *what they say and believe to be true about the blues* says about what Black southerners believe to be true about race, identity, and lived experience in the United States.

The Backbeat

It is no coincidence that this, a book that takes the blues as its subject and theoretical framework, uses the "backbeat" as its primary analytic device. It must. Along with the "blues scale" and the I-IV-I-V chord progression, the backbeat rhythm is one of the defining features of the blues sound, especially of early styles like Delta blues.[12]

To "play a backbeat" is to emphasize the off, or "weak," beats in a music measure. For instance, take a song written in "common time," wherein each bar is composed of four beats, as in *one-two-three-four, one-two-three-four,* and so on. In the earliest forms of Western music (e.g., classical), the most common way to play such a song was to emphasize beats one and three, as in *ONE-two-THREE-four* or, for illustrative purposes, *CLAP-stomp-CLAP-stomp.* The blues sound reversed course, instead emphasizing the second and fourth beats: *stomp-CLAP-stomp-CLAP.*[13]

While backbeat emphasis has become ubiquitous in Western popular music, its roots lie in the expressive traditions of Central and West Africa. In *Blues People*, cultural critic Leroi Jones notes as much: "The most apparent survivals of African music in Afro-American music are its rhythms: not only the seeming emphasis in African music on rhythmic, rather than melodic or harmonic qualities, but also the use of polyphonic, or contrapuntal, [layered and diverse] rhythmic effects" (25). And also, by extension, the use of the backbeat.

That African, and ultimately Black American, music treated percussion as a paramount part of music composition was about more than music composition. It was about life. "Africans used drums for communication," Jones continues, "and not, as was once thought, merely by using the drums in a kind of primitive Morse code, but by the phonetic reproduction of the words themselves—the result being that Africans developed an extremely fine and extremely complex rhythmic sense, as well as becoming unusually responsive to timbral subtleties." Put differently, polyrhythmic percussion—including use of the backbeat—was, for its originators, a way to say, hear, and know.

As the rhythms of Central and West Africa became the blues of the Mississippi Delta, Black folks found new ways to make the backbeat do what it had always done; that is, stretch and subvert the status quo. Black blues singers used the backbeat to sing a song their own way—for instance, by way of ad-libbing or embellishment—and musicians used it to compel audiences to listen and move in a different way: not *CLAP-stomp* but *stomp-CLAP*; not a lean or a sway but move your feet, not sit and watch but hear the call and respond.

The backbeat makes music that is typically rendered one way be heard another. *I Don't Like the Blues* does that with Black life, shifting attention from the attitudes and behaviors that are most widely associated with Black culture and lived experience to those that are typically relegated to the background. Black folks find joy and pleasure in things, yes. *CLAP-stomp-CLAP-stomp.* But they sigh and roll their eyes at things too. *Stomp-CLAP-stomp-CLAP.* They move into, build up, and bring life to some places, and they say they've "never even been" to others. They are hopeful and skeptical, optimistic and sick and tired. They "looove," and they don't like.

Just as emphasizing the backbeat allowed blueswomen and bluesmen to mark themselves as makers of aesthetics ("not simply receivers"[14]), minding the Black backbeat is an attempt to show Black folks as arbiters of (their own) agency, as subjects with subjectivity, as human. It is human to not like a thing, even if you sometimes "looove" some versions of it, even as you can't remember all of its details. It is human to sometimes not want to go to some places, especially if those places don't impress you. It is human to hope, then guess, then doubt, then change the subject.

It is not quite a new thing to call Black folks human, at least not when Black folks have been the ones calling. That was W. E. B. Du Bois's call during his early work in the southern Black Belt, his landmark study in Philadelphia's Seventh Ward, and his later work on Africa and global imperialism. It was the call that Zora Neale Hurston was making when she wrote, "Negroes love and hate and fight and play and strive and travel and have a thousand and one interests in life like other humans."[15] The call was at the bottom of the opening line of Richard Wright's 12 Million Black Voices: "Each day when you see us black folks upon the dusty land of the farms or upon the hard pavement of the city streets, you usually take us for granted and think you know us, but our history is far stranger than you suspect, and we are not what we seem."[16]

Zandria Robinson made the call too, hers from behind the "third or fourth pew" in her allegorical essay about dying and attending her own funeral: "My death, like all the others, split me clean into the two sides I had been all along: those loud and quiet, out and in, A- and B-sides."[17]

Robinson's call for "loud and quiet" echoes the work of cultural studies scholar Kevin Quashie. In Sovereignty of Quiet, Quashie argues for a different, more wholistic way of reading Black life. Rather than limit Black folks to their most pronounced, assertive, and public sensibilities and actions—the "loud" that Robinson references—Quashie asks us to mind the other side, the "quiet" side. "Quiet . . . is a metaphor for the full range of one's inner life," he writes. "The inner life is not apolitical or without social value, but neither is it determined entirely by publicness."[18]

The crux of Quashie's argument is the foundation of mine: Black life is not just one way, and Black people are not just one thing. Knowing that is not as hard as racism would make it seem.[19] It just requires doing some things in a different way. Here again, Quashie is instructive, writing that "to notice and understand [the full scope of Black humanity] requires a shift in how we read, what we look for, and what we expect, even what we remain open to. It requires paying attention in a different way."[20] Here I say, it requires listening in a different way too, on the backbeat.

Why the Rural South?

If we understand the Black backbeat to be those elements of Black life which are usually not recognized or acknowledged, then there are backbeat places too. They are those Black places where Black people are thought to either only be one way or not be at all. They are those places that are often kept on the fringes of popular and scholarly commentary about Black life. For as long as all of the Black Clarksdalians I spoke with have been alive, the rural South has been a backbeat place.

Mrs. Irene Sandiford, the oldest resident I spent time with, was born in 1944; and since around then the prevailing empirical assumption about Black community life in the rural South seems to be that it is either (and only) a changing same or a wrinkle in time, more valuable for its connection to the past than for what insight it might offer about the present or future. The assumptions raise questions. In the former case, why give attention to a thing that can only be what it was; and in the latter, why study a thing in which the end is known at the beginning? *I Don't Like the Blues* does not necessarily aim to answer those questions, but rather to ask new questions of them: if Black folks in the rural South are a changing same, how have they managed the magic—to move while staying still, or the other way around? And if they are a wrinkle in time, what might we learn from the folds?

I know. It is a tricky proposition to argue that the primary reason for doing a thing is that the thing has not been done before; or if before, not recently; or if recently, not well. Yet that is partly what I am doing here. Folks have produced ethnographic accounts of Black life in the rural South before, especially in the decades between Emancipation and the Second World War; but, save some notable exceptions in literature and cultural studies, ethnographic work on the rural Black South has only occasionally been done recently; and, advisedly, but for the work of Karida Brown, Danielle Purifoy, Karla Slocum, and a few others, the recent work has not been done very well.[21] *I Don't Like the Blues* starts there—with the scarcity of contemporary ethnographic accounts of Black life in the rural American South that listen for the full scope of how Black people live in the rural American South. That is the tricky part.

In the social sciences, when justifying the utility of a research study, the "so what" question is important. Yes, the topic is interesting, but so what? Yes, the topic is invigorating and innovative, but so what? Yes, there are data that fit the research question, but so what? Conventional wisdom in the discipline says that the answer to the "so what" question should never only be, "Because no one else has done it." Sociologist Richard Lloyd gives voice to this perspective in a recent essay, noting that "a general neglect is in itself not a good reason for taking interest in any particular topic."[22] I mostly agree, but I might add a "most of the time." Most of the time, a general neglect is not a good enough reason to study a topic, except for the times when it is. Except for the times when the "topic" is people, and the people are living, and their lives are bearing the weight of historical trauma, cumulative disadvantage, persistent poverty, violence, development failures, and so on. In those times, neglect is not just a "reason" or a "gap in the literature." It is erasure. And, if the stakes are erasure, doing a thing because it has not been done (enough) is enough.

And studying the rural Black South ain't been done enough. The last time was at the turn of the twentieth century, when American sociology was in its infancy, and the American South was in flux. The Peculiar Institution had fallen. Reconstruction had come and was going. There were more than 4 million newly freed Black Americans moving to make life in the region. Understanding the determinants, contours, and potential aftermath of their movement and their lives quickly became one of the discipline's defining research agendas. Folks wanted an answer to the "southern question."[23] What was happening in the South—in its economic systems, its social relations, its cultural mores? How would the South adjust to the rupture sprung by the Civil War? Would the region adjust at all? Lurking just before or at least not long after each of these questions was another question—that of race relations. In many ways, that has always been what the southern question has been about. What is to become of Black people in the South, and what it is to become of the South in light of Black people?

"For many reasons, it would appear that the time is ripe for undertaking a thorough study . . . of the real condition of the Negro," wrote W. E. B. Du Bois in 1898.[24] He was trying to answer the southern question and had gone to the Black Belt town of Farmville, Virginia, to do the work. The study, "The Negroes of Farmville, Virginia," is among the earliest attempts to document and understand Black life in the rural South; and for Du Bois it was just the beginning. Along with a group of students from the Atlanta Sociological Laboratory, Du Bois went on to complete four additional monographs on Black southern life, including profiles of rural towns in Georgia and Alabama; a reflection on his time teaching at an elementary school in rural Tennessee; and an assessment of the condition of Black farmers in the Black Belt.[25]

Many scholars followed Du Bois, studying Black life in different ways and across time, but mostly listening for the same thing: What is to become of Black people in the South, and what is to become of the South in light of Black people? Where Du Bois had worked throughout the rural Black Belt, others focused on one place, the same place: Mississippi. Sociologists Allison Davis, Burleigh Gardner, and Mary Gardner went to the Mississippi Delta. So did John Dollard and Charles Johnson. So did Hortense Powdermaker. Beyond sociology, so did Charles Peabody and Alan Lomax. They found what Christopher Silver and John Moeser (1995) call "separate cities," Black and white folks living different lives in the same place. They found Black folks trying to make something from the nothing that 300 years of chattel slavery had forced on them. They found the perspective, ethic, and expressive tradition that came to be called the blues.[26]

By the 1940s, sociologists had quieted on the southern question. Black people had left the region's rural countryside en masse. Went to places like Chicago, Kansas, and Louisville.[27] As the nation's racial map shifted, so too did the scope and sights of sociological inquiry. The southern question became an "American Dilemma."[28] Mississippi became Chicago. And, all of a sudden folks weren't studying Black people in the rural South.

More recently, as millions of Black Americans "return" from their migration destinations and (re)settle in the South, a growing cadre of sociologists, historians, demographers, and political scientists have, too, returned to the southern question. They are studying an apparently "New South," asking an apparently new southern question. What of the sprawling suburban neighborhoods that spill from rapidly growing "New Urban South" centers like Dallas, Atlanta, Charlotte, and Washington, D.C.? What are the conditions of life for an ever-diversifying populace in "New Destination" communities in rural Texas and North Carolina? A few scholars have even pushed the southern question to Historic South cities—for instance, New Orleans and Memphis—chronicling the lifeworlds of both native Black southerners who have always called the region home and their once "migrating cousins" now returning.[29]

Heretofore, Historic South cities like Memphis are about as far as scholars documenting daily life in the newest New South (and scholars studying Black life in the South) have gone. Rural places like Clarksdale remain largely unchartered, save for historical monographs profiling a person or period from the region's past and humanistic accounts of the region's culture.[30] In a discipline enchanted with things that are changing and things that are "new," the rural South apparently is neither one of them enough. Some say it is "fading."[31] If that is the case, *I Don't Like the Blues* is here to bring it—the rural South and its people—back into focus, to put places like Clarksdale back on the map of social science inquiry, to call the new southern question home.

What does Black life in the rural South look like?

What does Black life in the rural South sound like?

"From First Street to Riverton used to be white," Mrs. Irene said on that same kind-of-hot-turned-too-hot-to-be-outside morning when she told me she ain't like the blues. She was describing the racial demographics of a neighborhood known by most residents as "Oakhurst." Sprawled across about two square miles in northwest Clarksdale, Oakhurst is the second-largest and most populous neighborhood enclave in town (The Brickyard is the largest and most populous). Mrs. Irene recounted the unrest and upheaval that played out "all over [Clarksdale]" when the city school district was forced, by court order, to integrate.[32] To her best recollection, it was the integration of the city schools and, eventually, all of the town's public places that drove neighborhoods like Oakhurst to "start turning." That is what several Black Clarksdalians called the piecemeal-then-rapid reshuffling of the town's racial demographics in the years following the civil rights movements: turning.

"[Oakhurst] was white when I first got here," she said. "All white . . . until it started turning, and now the Blacks have come in over there, and that's what it is now, Black."

What Mrs. Irene said about Oakhurst, the Census says too. In 1990, about 98 percent (n = 6,000) of Oakhurst's 6,100 residents were white.[33] In 2000, while the overall population was about the same, the proportion of white residents had declined by about 23 percent (n = 1,400). This trend—of a stable overall population amid precipitous white out-migration—continued through the aughts. In 2013, Oakhurst had the same number of residents that it had in 1990. The neighborhood's racial demographics were the opposite. Only about 30 percent (n = 1,800) of Oakhurst's 6,095 residents were white, a figure that represented a nearly 70 percent decline in white residents in just twenty years.

As Mrs. Irene had watched Oakhurst "turn," Clarksdale had watched its overall resident population shrink, topping out at 21,673 in 1970 and dropping to 17,964 by 2013 (see table 4 in the appendix), a rate (−18 percent) of depopulation that, according to Kenneth Johnson and Daniel Lichter,[34] likely means Clarksdale will never be as populous as it used to be.

In the span between 1970 and the late aughts, other things in Clarksdale stopped being like they used to be too. The town's once-robust labor market— anchored by a bustling agribusiness imprint and promising manufacturing outlook—became a precarious assortment of low-wage, service-sector jobs.

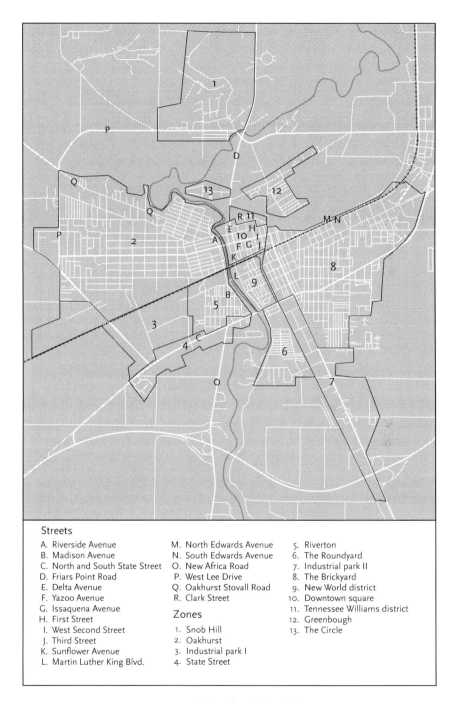

Streets

A. Riverside Avenue
B. Madison Avenue
C. North and South State Street
D. Friars Point Road
E. Delta Avenue
F. Yazoo Avenue
G. Issaquena Avenue
H. First Street
I. West Second Street
J. Third Street
K. Sunflower Avenue
L. Martin Luther King Blvd.

M. North Edwards Avenue
N. South Edwards Avenue
O. New Africa Road
P. West Lee Drive
Q. Oakhurst Stovall Road
R. Clark Street

Zones

1. Snob Hill
2. Oakhurst
3. Industrial park I
4. State Street

5. Riverton
6. The Roundyard
7. Industrial park II
8. The Brickyard
9. New World district
10. Downtown square
11. Tennessee Williams district
12. Greenbough
13. The Circle

Map 2. Clarksdale, Mississippi.

The town's public infrastructure suffered, as did the livelihoods and mobility opportunities of the town's residents, especially its most vulnerable ones: Black folks. The suffering was evident almost everywhere, in the recurring threats of consolidation and closure facing some of the town's most vital social institutions;[35] in the persistence and magnitude of poverty, especially among Black residents; and, eventually, in the growth of blues tourism spaces.

Blues tourism was supposed to help fix what was broken in Delta towns like Clarksdale. That is what state lawmakers and stakeholders said, anyway. Black residents like Mrs. Irene said other things.

"I think they call it the Blues Street," Mrs. Irene said, referencing Clarksdale's downtown square. "I think," she added for good measure. What she called the Blues Street was a five-block stretch of blues venues on the downtown square. In the early aughts, local officials named the area the "Blues Alley," the moniker a coronation and bookend to more than twenty years of blues tourism development in the town and across the Delta region. In that stretch, especially between 1980 and 2003, new blues venues had opened up, heritage markers put down, and state funds for blues development set aside. There came new museums and a string of specialty shops and boutique hotels, and along the way a longer string of blues festivals, concerts, and near-nightly live music showcases. "We play live blues 365 nights a year," became a chorus, repeated by local elected officials and stakeholders every chance that they got. The more venues and spaces that opened, the louder and clearer Clarksdale's development formula became: the answer to the town's (structural) blues would be the town's blues (history). The formula was a riddle, and for Mrs. Irene the riddle was exhausting. That is what was in her voice when she said, "Look at the downtown . . . it's just so much blues. . . . The blues just won't keep us standing."

Clarksdale's post–civil rights story is one of change, just like other new South places. Just like Charlotte, just like Texas, just like the "City Too Busy to Hate," but different. While the common New South story emphasizes growth, opportunity, diversity, and dynamism, Clarksdale's story emphasizes other things. Clarksdale's labor market is shrinking. The economic prospects of its residents are dimming. The town's social institutions are doing the best that they can, which for folks like Mrs. Irene has just not been enough. All of that is change. All of that is "new," just not new the regular way, and that is the rub.

I Don't Like the Blues is not about doing what has not been done (all that much) just for the sake of novelty; nor is it about doing what has not been done recently just for the sake of recency; nor is it about trying to do better what has not been done well just for the sake of false confidence. It is about doing the undone so that we can better see the often unseen, in this case demographic change in a place assumed to always and only be the same: the post–civil rights rural South. In seeing the unseen, we might then hear the as-yet unheard, the backbeat, what Black folks in the rural South are saying about it all.

And what they are saying about it all is the blues (epistemology).

What Is the Blues Epistemology?

The blues has long been a space and tool for Black southerners to talk about their lives and to make prescriptions about the world they want to live in. Geographer Clyde Woods said as much in *Development Arrested:*

> The elimination of state-sponsored segregation and re-enfranchisement were the beginning, and not the end, of the historic African American agenda in the rural South. However, there is more involved here than just a political agenda: there is a distinct perspective on who they are and where they are, on their predicament, and on who is responsible. Like other blocs in the region, working-class African Americans in the Delta and in the Black Belt South have constructed a system of explanation that informs their daily life, organizational activity, culture, religion, and social movements. They have created their own ethno-regional epistemology. Like other traditions of interpretation, it is not a monolith; there are branches, roots, and a trunk. This central tradition is referred to in this work as the blues epistemology.[36]

The blues is still a method of sense-making for Black folks, even as they don't seem to like it like they used to. Which perhaps raises a question: How? How is it the case that the blues epistemology is alive and well if most Black American audiences think blues music is dead, and if most of the folks I talked to in Clarksdale seem to want parts of the blues to be gone? On the one hand, the answer is in the question. The essence of the blues episte-mology is that Black southerners should, and will, do what they need to to preserve their selfhood, build community, and survive the violence of racial domination even if that means not liking the blues. That is what the blues epistemology is and has always been—a space for Black southerners to real-ize their own subjectivity by any method necessary. Put differently, it is just like the blues to not like the blues.

On the other hand, the answer to the above question is another question: What came first, the blues or the blues epistemology? The answer to that question is a lesson: the genealogy of the blues epistemology is rooted in the toils and snares of plantation life in the antebellum South and flows through each wave of development that followed the fall of the Peculiar Institution. In particular, Woods argues that as the Delta's planter class worked, at every development turn,[37] to protect and bolster its social and economic dominance, poor and working-class Black communities in the region crafted, in the torque, their own system of "social explanation and social action."

That system was the blues epistemology. It included collective action, family formation, and literacy. It was how Black folks came to see themselves, each other, and other people. The blues epistemology was Black southerners doing what they needed to do to get through the day-to-day, often singing, moaning, and wailing as they went. As Elijah Wald gives voice to in *Escaping the Delta* and Leroi Jones does in *Blues People*, "blues" was little more than an ad hoc, early twentieth-century attempt to name, commodify, and profit on the singing, moaning, and wailing.[38] The "blues epistemology" came first. The "blues" expressive tradition came out of, and thus after, that.

If you are drawn to metaphor, Woods's writing is again prescient. Imagine that the blues epistemology is a tree with "branches, roots, and a trunk." The roots of the blues epistemology, or the beginning point and anchor of the tree, are Black southerners' desires for "humanistic autonomy." That is, the desire to be seen and acknowledged as human, as agentive subjects, as deserving of an opportunity to make a life for themselves, as beings with the capacity to feel and need and not want and not like. The trunk of the blues epistemology, or the vessel that allows the roots of the tree to grow and give life, includes all of the methods that Black southerners have enacted in pursuit and protection of their autonomy. Individual protest and collective action are a part of the trunk. Interiority and community-building are a part of the trunk. Hope and despair are a part of the trunk. Expressivity and movement are a part of the trunk. And, just as trunks produce branches, the blues epistemology has produced many cultural and political traditions. One of those traditions is blues music.

In the same way that a tree can sometimes reject or be robbed of a branch—perhaps the climate is not quite right, or the seasons have changed, or a family needs firewood—Black folks can be moved to not like the blues. Losing a branch does not mean the tree is no longer a tree, just that it now needs to grow something new. That is what has happened with Black folks in Clarksdale. The blues does not register the same way, and blues music does not sound like it used to; so they don't like it (like they used to).

Introduction

1 HARD . . .
MAKE IT EASY

A woman and man stepped from the entrance of Janky's Art Boutique in downtown Clarksdale. They talked and laughed, then stepped into a shaded area to gather themselves. She pushed a small bag into a bigger bag draped over her shoulder. He returned something to his back pocket. Hand-in-hand, they walked toward a wide blue sign jutting from the sidewalk in front of a boarded building beside Janky's: "WROX, Clarksdale's first radio station, went on the air on June 5, 1944, from studios at 321 Delta Avenue."[1]

The couple had come to Clarksdale for the Juke Joint Blues Festival, joining some 5,000 other out-of-town visitors (and approximately 2,000 locals) for a weekend of blues performances, southern food, and carnival fare. It was the Tuesday after, and most of the festivalgoers had gone, but the couple remained.

Across the street from them and Janky's, local blues singer Penro "Pooh Baby" Dorsey and I sat in front of Dank's Music Store. Pooh Baby had pulled a folding chair and his amplifier near the edge of the sidewalk, his normal busking setup. I sat up on a bench behind him.

"I been going too much lately, I feel like," Pooh Baby told me after taking a deep pull from a cigarette, releasing the smoke and an echoing guitar riff at about the same time. At twenty-seven, he was one of the youngest musicians playing in Clarksdale, and, if his weekend schedule was any indication, he was as busy as any of them. "Played T-Bone's Friday night," he said. "Set up over by Mac's [Consignment Shop] Saturday day, and I was at the Blues Spot Saturday night." His gigs were a source of pride—and income.

"You was on the go!" I said.

"Shiiid, that's money," he said matter-of-factly. Then, after turning a few nobs on his amplifier and adjusting the tuning pegs on his guitar, he began playing a song in full. I watched him. Then, both he and I, almost at the same time, watched the tourist couple start watching us, first from where they stood in front of the WROX marker, then as they crossed the street in our direction.

"Sounding good!" said the man, who told us his name was Himmens [him-ins] White. As he and the woman—Shelbie—got closer, Pooh Baby played louder. "See, honey, he's a real blues player," Himmens told Shelbie while flashing a thumbs-up to the clouds, while Shelbie danced a two-step to a beat all her own. Then Himmens told Pooh Baby, "Man, if I could play that thing like you, I'd be all right!"

"Mane, if I could leave this motherfucka [Clarksdale] today, I would," Pooh Baby told me, not long after Himmens and Shelbie told us they were getting ready to "hit the road back [to Georgia]." I had asked him what he "saw for himself moving forward." His "motherfucka" was a definitive answer, each syllable like blues chords, echoing louder than the one before it, blending together in distress. "Unless, I could find just a real good-paying job, or get my own business. I want a family, I want a kid, but not here. . . . Can't do shit for 'em here."

I asked where he would go if he left.

"A'lanta. New York. Anywhere. You go to a place like A'lanta, you know they hiring . . . They'll hire you to do anything. Down here, it's not jobs like that. . . . The last, like, three years been rough for me. No funds. No crib. Working this job." Pooh Baby had not had regular work since being laid off a year prior. At the time of our conversation, he was working when and where he could—playing an unreliable, if at times frantic, schedule of small gigs in North Mississippi; playing backup drums for a small church in the area; and, as he put it, "playing himself" by working a temporary construction job for small money in a neighboring town.

Pooh Baby told me he was tired—tired of small, tired of "real blues player," tired from the weekend, tired of hard. He said that last one a lot. "It's hard here. . . . Everything here hard. The school system here is bad, all the

high poverty . . . and the jobs are doing more firing than hiring. It's hard. . . .
Take my momma and my dad, they worked they whole life and still struggle,
you know. . . . Go 'round here [Clarksdale] one day and you go'n see what
I'm tal'bout. Go around here and you go'n see just how hard it is." Pooh Baby
pulled his guitar closer to him, leaned and held his ear downward, like he was
listening for something he ain't want nobody else to hear. "Put it like this, you
born here, you live here, you been through the blues for real. . . . I ain't just
gotta play the blues. I don't have to. But, how hard it is here . . . make it easy."

Both Pooh Baby and the tourist couple tell a blues story. The couple's
story represents what Mississippi lawmakers and stakeholders in the Delta
region have promised about the blues since the 1980s: that it could be a
source of positive attention and economic revitalization for a place in need
of both. Pooh Baby's story is that story's foil. His story shows where the
promise of blues tourism has fallen short, where, for Black folks, the blues
has not been a solution to a development problem, but rather a sign that
a problem remains. In the couple's story, coming to Clarksdale is exciting
because real blues players sound good. For Pooh Baby, a real blues player,
playing the blues is easy because Clarksdale is hard. From those stories—the
couple's and Pooh Baby's—this chapter moves to tell two more: the story of
the Delta's post-1960s development agenda, and the story of some of what
Black residents of Clarksdale have faced in its wake. Long story short: both
are the blues.

BLUES DEVELOPMENT IN THE MISSISSIPPI
DELTA AND CLARKSDALE

When Haley Barbour became Mississippi's sixty-third governor in 2003, the
Delta was in its fifth decade of a development crisis that had created a matrix
of problems on top of problems for the region's residents. There was the
problem of a polarized and precarious labor market; which intensified the
problem of poverty, especially among the region's Black residents;[2] which
compounded the problem of a fragile, underfunded public infrastructure;
which accelerated the problem of population loss. Barbour saw the problems
and offered a solution: reimagine what "development" could look like for the
region. To Barbour's eye, the Delta had more than agriculture and manufacturing, two shrinking economic sectors.

"The Delta has the blues," Barbour said on the day he signed legislation
reconstituting the Mississippi Blues Commission in 2004. "[The blues gives
us] the opportunity to take something of which we are very proud and turn it

into a genuine economic development."[3] The eighteen-member commission was to "study, deliberate and report to the Governor and to the Mississippi Legislature by January 15, 2004, a plan for marketing the blues, including a tourism program, that features the historical, cultural, musical and business elements and opportunities of this 'Bluesland.' The marketing plan will be designed to attract tourists, conferences, music performances, filmmakers and others for the purpose of economic development of the blues, the region and the state."[4]

The Blues Commission had been more than two decades in the making. In 1978, Mississippi Action for Community Education, a small, Delta-based grassroots organization, partnered with blues enthusiasts and musicians near Greenville, Mississippi, to organize the Mississippi Delta Blues Festival, the first modern festival in the region.[5] Spurred in part by a national revival of commercial interest in the blues that spanned from the late 1970s to the early 1990s, the Delta quickly became internationally known as ground zero for all things blues. In 1983, just five years after its establishment, the Mississippi Delta Blues Festival attracted some 30,000 attendees, making it the largest blues festival in the country. Its popularity was a sign of things to come.

By 1990, the tourist traffic generated by the Delta's growing circuit of blues festivals and entertainment scenes started to catch the attention of elected officials and business owners in the region. "I think [the blues is] an incredible resource," said Howard Stovall, a Memphis businessman and blues enthusiast who had grown up on his family's plantation just west of Clarksdale. "A local festival can be the equivalent of one or two new industries in the amount of money put into the local situation."[6] Stovall would eventually serve as director of the Blues Foundation, co-owner of Clarksdale's Ground Zero Blues Club, and head of the Sunflower River Blues Association.

Elsewhere, Clarksdale native and Delta Blues Museum founder Sid Graves noted, "It's exciting to see so many people from all over the world making the pilgrimage to Highway 61 and the cradle of the blues."[7] In 1993, Clarksdale mayor Henry Espy referred to blues tourism as "a seed waiting to be germinated."[8] Officials put these optimistic pronouncements into action too, taking the moment to approve the formation of tourism commissions across the region. The moment culminated in 2003, when Ronnie Musgrove, Haley Barbour's immediate predecessor as governor, announced plans for a state-sponsored Blues Commission.

In 2006, two years after endorsing the Blues Commission, Barbour visited Holly Ridge, a small Delta community in Sunflower County. The day marked the unveiling of the first Mississippi Blues Trail marker, a tribute to Delta blues legend Charlie Patton. Now comprising nearly 200 markers between Memphis, Tennessee, and the Mississippi Gulf Coast, the Blues Trail was a part of the commission's founding vision, and the inaugural interpretive marker was viewed as a sign of promise. "The blues are a powerful part of Mississippi's heritage and America's musical history," Barbour said after the unveiling, his remarks echoing what he said when he formalized the commission. "The creation of the Mississippi Blues Trail is an appropriate way to capture this distinct part of our history and culture, and also will undoubtedly serve as an economic development tool."[9]

The Blues Commission signaled a new social and economic development agenda in the Delta and spawned a wave of excitement and, perhaps more important, organizational infrastructure and resource mobilization. Over the next ten years, local tourism commissions partnered with chambers of commerce and private investors to organize and expand the already-bustling yearly schedule of blues festivals. State and local budgets earmarked money for planning, organizing, and marketing the state's multiplying blues scenes. Billboards promoting the Delta's blues history sprang up along highways and byways in the region. Media profiles, travelogues, and tourism brochures touted the Delta as the "Land of the Blues," and folks flocked to and through the region by the hundreds of thousands, to see what all the fuss was about. Most of the region's blues travelers were like Himmens and Shelbie White—white bohemians, drifters, and blues enthusiasts excited to drive the real "Blues Highway," to hear real blues players play real blues, and especially excited to stop or stay in Clarksdale.

Almost since day one, Clarksdale has been the center of the Delta's blues tourism system. In 1979, the year after the Greenville festival, Clarksdale native Sid Graves outfitted a small wing in Clarksdale's Carnegie Public Library with items from his own collection of blues memorabilia.[10] A year later, Jim O'Neal, who had moved to the area from Chicago, founded Rooster Blues Records, a middling record label that operated out of rented space near the downtown square. Riding this momentum, a group of local blues enthusiasts introduced the idea that Clarksdale could host its own blues festival. While some residents and local organizations, including the Downtown Merchants Association and Chamber of Commerce, supported the idea, some public officials had reservations. Was it wise to promote public alcohol consumption? What about all the tourists who would see all the "Black parts of town"?[11] Reservations notwithstanding, by 1988, the idea had garnered enough support that Clarksdale hosted its first blues festival, the Sunflower River Blues and Gospel Festival.

The Sunflower River Festival was evidence enough for some local stakeholders and enthusiasts that the blues had not just staying power but economic potential. There was money in it. "When we came here and tried to tell some of the local civic leaders about some of the tourism possibilities of the blues, they thought we were crazy," said Jim O'Neal, reflecting on the early momentum in Clarksdale around the possibilities of blues tourism. "There was a time when they just ignored the blues, but you can't ignore it when people are coming from Belgium. . . . This is the place where devoted blues fans want to come."[12] Sid Graves echoed O'Neal's enthusiasm: "I think the people in this town are taking notice. They're asking, 'Why are all these people from Europe, Japan and elsewhere coming here?' Recently, we've had the city fathers pass a resolution in honor of Muddy Waters and the blues. We're talking to them about having musicians play on the sidewalks, and there are live blues shows already in several outdoor locations.'"[13]

The growth of blues tourism in Clarksdale in the 1980s was bookended by the news of a $100,000 gift to the Delta Blues Museum by the Hard Rock Café.[14]

In the early 1990s, Clarksdale began to garner more public attention for its relationship to the blues. Local establishments appeared in travel and lifestyle magazines. The town became the backdrop of film productions and the subject of documentaries and books. And more and more tourists streamed in. In 1991, the Sunflower River Festival, then in only its fifth year, attracted some 7,000 visitors, and the Delta Blues Museum expanded its memorabilia collection.[15]

By the end of the 1990s, the blues had not just made Clarksdale sound different. It had made it look different too. In 1998, local developers completed a renovation of Clarksdale's Hopson Plantation, retrofitting it as a set of bed-and-breakfast-style cottages that opened as "The Shack Up Inn."[16] Hopson had been one of the largest plantations in the region in the early decades of the twentieth century and spearheaded the Delta's move toward farm mechanization when, in 1944, it became the first plantation to produce a cotton crop without the use of manual labor. The Shack Up Inn positioned itself as a gateway to that past, offering "blues lovers making the pilgrimage to the cradle of the blues . . . the unique opportunity to experience Hopson Plantation . . . virtually unchanged from when it was a working plantation."[17]

In 1999, through a combination of its own regional popularity and the conjoined efforts of public funds and private donations, Clarksdale's Delta Blues Museum opened in its own space, moving from the local Carnegie Public Library to the newly renovated Freight Depot Station on the downtown square.[18] By 2000, local officials and stakeholders in Clarksdale were essentially fine-tuning what had proved to be a well-oiled commerce machine. Seeking to further reify the town's branding as a quintessential blues place, officials renamed several spaces on the downtown square to emphasize their connection to the blues. During this time, a five-block stretch of Delta Avenue on the downtown square became the "Blues Alley," a side street was dedicated to local bluesman John Lee Hooker, and a spring of clubs (re)opened all around the downtown square: Club Vegas became the Delta Blues Alley Café, the Blues Station Café opened in the lobby of the old Greyhound station, and developers completed renovations to an old cotton warehouse on the downtown square, enabling the opening of the Ground Zero Blues Club.[19]

Indeed, what had been a remarkably successful, nearly uninterrupted, rise for Clarksdale's blues tourism apparatus essentially since the inaugural Sunflower River Festival in 1987 became a blues boom in the early 2000s. Some officials remained skeptical, especially about how the town would manage its commercial growth and sustain its economic prospects, but the prevailing narrative was one of optimism. Nationally, the blues was as popular as ever—Congress had declared 2003 the "Year of the Blues"—and as I have noted, state legislators had given their full endorsement with the constitution of the Blues Commission.[20]

In the late aughts, local officials and stakeholders took a more intentioned approach to blues development. The first sign of this commitment was the establishment of Clarksdale Revitalization Inc., a nonprofit, "Economic Development (Community Improvement, Capacity Building)" organization with a guiding mission "to facilitate collaborations; promote and support community efforts to enhance the quality of life of its citizens; to be an information resource for business and community; and to serve as a conduit for assistance, private and public, to be utilized efficiently in the preservation of area architecture, history and culture."[21] That same year the town hired a development and research firm (Economic Essentials) to draft an economic action plan for downtown Clarkdale. The purpose of the plan was twofold: assess how much the town's blues tourism system had grown over the years and identify best practices for ensuring more growth over more years.[22] The firm documented, among other things, sixty businesses, buildings, and other entities on the downtown square that shared some relationship with the blues, and noted that blues-related businesses accounted for half of all downtown commercial activity (the other half coming from antique shops, tailors, hairdressers, law firms, accountants, and insurance agencies).[23]

Today, blues tourism continues to attract attention and generate revenue in Clarksdale. Recent estimates suggest that the town attracts some 132,000 visitors (more than seven times the number of local residents) and that its tourism revenue amounts to $46 million annually.[24]

"Blues is our greatest export," a local official told me on an afternoon in the main office of his insurance practice on Clarksdale's downtown square. "It's probably our greatest export . . . " I had been sitting with him for nearly an hour, especially interested in his perspective on the local economy. "The economy, generally around this area, is still driven by agriculture. That's a shrinking industry, but I don't think it'll ever die away. So you've got agriculture and the related businesses to agriculture. Then, after that, you probably have casinos. . . . But, somewhere down the line, you get to tourism, these out-of-town visitors," he gestured with his hands, as if impelling me to imagine a room full of people. "[Tourism] is a segment that's green and creative and easy and doesn't take infrastructure. . . . It doesn't take new buildings and factories and all that. Tourists come in and spend their money, and that's very helpful."

The elected official told me what Himmens and Shelbie White had told me on that Tuesday after the Juke Joint Festival, his words matching theirs almost word for word. "We come in on Tuesday [before the weekend of the Juke Joint Festival]," Himmens told Pooh Baby and me, while retrieving his wallet from his back pocket, just before dropping a five-dollar bill into an empty coffee tin that Pooh Baby had placed beside his amp. "It costs to come down [from Georgia] and stay like we do, but a place like this, you don't mind it. . . . Shit, we come here every year, come here just for the blues."

"When we first started coming, it wasn't a big thing like now," Shelbie said. She had stopped two-stepping and started talking to me. Pooh Baby had kept playing but stopped looking at them, down at his guitar instead. The square had stopped being so hot—clouds passed over—but kept being empty except for us. "Every year we get more surprised at how many people come in for it. The blues . . . "

"That is what this place has that's different from anywhere else in the world, is the blues," Himmens said before Shelbie finished. "From anywhere else," he said again to make sure.

What Himmens said had an echo, almost like Pooh Baby's blues riffs, almost like the downtown square had a few nights before, almost like something I heard from other folks, Black residents of Clarksdale.

"That's all they [Clarksdale's local elected officials and stakeholders] got is blues," said fifty-four-year-old Pastor Alfa McKinney as we, and a half-dozen others, waited our turn in a barbershop.

"Is that all it is that's here, the blues? Is this all that we have, that we can stand up publicize?" asked fifty-six-year-old native Tempie Mayfield as we stood in the parking lot of the local Walmart.

"That's all [that is] around here, the blues thing. Their blues thing. That's all they want. That's all they want to come," said thirty-one-year-old native Sharmetria [SHär-mē-tē-a] Smith, us sitting with a few other folks in her apartment.

LIFE AND OPPORTUNITY IN CLARKSDALE

"One thing you will learn quick after you live here is the blues. . . . That's all we got, all, every time you turn around it's a blues show or a blues festival . . . and you got somebody here from Amsterdam, Australia, California, somebody here for the blues." Native resident Eddie Kane Jr. always talked like everything he said was common knowledge. This was no different. He had just picked me up from my house in West Clarksdale with a promise to "show me around [his] city." And, for four hours on a summer afternoon, that is what he did. We taxied through each of Clarksdale's seven major neighborhood districts, passed most of the town's major social institutions, and stopped at the used-to-be high school and a used-to-be carwash in between. What we saw that day—and what I would go on to see many other days—made what I had heard about the promise of the blues ring hollow.

"You want me to describe Clarksdale? It's the Great Depression. The damn Great Depression." Eddie, thirty-seven, slid his hand along the steering wheel of his sedan, his sarcastic laughter interrupting the steady hum of the air conditioner. "When I say Great Depression, this what I mean by that. Clarksdale had 'bout 20,000 people or more when I was coming up [in the 1980s] and, back when I was here, 'bout five [or] six factories. I'm talking industries. Real jobs!" He hit the steering wheel with the side of his loosely clinched fist, then lightly hit the brakes at a stoplight. A rickety pickup truck passed through the intersection in front of us, turning from the First Street Bridge, left, onto Riverside Avenue. After the light changed, we turned from Riverside, left, onto the First Street Bridge. "Now? All that just dropped off the map."

Between 1970 and 2000, following trends playing out across the Delta region, Clarksdale's agricultural economy shrank to a fraction of itself. Crop yields declined, as did agriculture-related revenue, as did agriculture-related jobs. In 2010, agriculture accounted for less than 3 percent of Clarksdale's labor force. The town's manufacturing foothold also slipped. Between 1980 and 2010, following a rash of layoffs and plant closures, manufacturing declined from 15 percent to less than 10 percent of the local labor force.

The rapid and ongoing decline in agriculture and manufacturing effectively reduced Clarksdale to a service economy. Today, the vast majority (84.6 percent) of the local labor force works across three sectors: "education, health, and social services" (34.3 percent); "retail trade" (11.7 percent); and "arts, entertainment, recreation, accommodation, and food services" (14.5 percent). The town's largest employers include the city and county school districts (as well as three private schools and a public charter K–8 school), a community college, a hospital, and a string of fast-food restaurants and retail stores along State Street stretching across the southern border of town. Beyond these, Clarksdale's largest employers are beyond the city limits—the Isle of Capris Casino about twenty-five miles northwest of Clarksdale in Lula; a cluster of casinos about sixty miles to the northeast in Robinsonville (Tunica County); and the Tallahatchie County Correctional Facility about fifteen miles south in Tutwiler.[25]

A long-standing finding in sociology and economics is that service economies beget income polarization—that is, when a place's labor market is filled primarily with service-sector jobs, a lot of that place's residents will be limited to working for low wages (at the bottom "pole"), decidedly fewer of that place's residents will have access to higher wages (at the top "pole"), and almost none of that place's residents will find their way to the middle (class).[26] That is Clarksdale, except the bottom pole is fatter than the top—not an hourglass or a peanut but a pear. Most workers in Clarksdale earn less than $10 an hour, with many earning just barely above minimum wage ($7.25).[27]

A straightforward explanation for Clarksdale's labor market dynamics would cite both supply (i.e., human capital) and demand-side (i.e., labor market) factors. For demand-side: an opportunity structure with limited job opportunities is a problem of demand. People cannot work in jobs that are not there. A labor market in which jobs offer few promotion and salary advancement opportunities is a problem of demand too. People do not want to work in low-paying jobs in which low pay is all they can ever expect.

Some say supply-side problems also ail Clarksdale's labor market, the "problem" of resident human capital chief among them. Like most Delta towns, in Clarksdale, there are more people with no high school diploma (21 percent) than there are with a four-year college degree (18 percent) (see table 4 in the appendix). Including two-year degree holders (8 percent) helps the math, but not by much. Given this, the rationale for supply-side arguments is straightforward too: Why would jobs locate to a place that is unable to provide a skilled labor force? It is a trick question.

Like so many other things in the South—its history, its people, the blues—the Mississippi Delta's supply-and-demand equation is not straightforward, at least not the supply side. First, scholars have documented the peculiar calculus that led to the inability of Delta towns like Clarksdale to attract and keep large-scale industrial employers after the brief manufacturing uptick in the 1970s and early 1980s. There was the long tail of the civil rights movement, in which industrial promoters and business leaders worried about boycotts by Black workers, not a lack of worker human capital, and thus saw the region as a risky place to locate future plant sites. There was the question of hiring discrimination among industrial employers, in which some business and development leaders saw Black workers as undesirable, not because of their educational profile but because of—their Blackness. There was also, as always, the question of planter interests, in which the region's power elite acted as gatekeepers, effectively deciding which companies would and would not be complimentary to the region's agricultural economy. The calculus was peculiar but precise.

By 1990, what had been a promising forecast for manufacturing in the region was reduced to a remnant. Rendered in this way—wherein an entire sector of the labor market is skirted away from a place for reasons (e.g., racial anxiety and animus) beyond the purview of that place's labor force—what might first register as a supply-side problem all of a sudden sounds a lot like demand. People cannot want to work in jobs when the jobs are too anxious to show up.[28]

Second, at least since 1970, Delta towns like Clarksdale and rural places across the country have struggled to produce and keep college graduates.[29] "Most young folks, the first chance they get to leave, they leave," Eddie told me as we circled around the downtown square. It was a thinly veiled, if unintentional, reference to his own story. Eddie was born in Clarksdale in 1977, graduated from the county high school in 1993, and, riding the strength of his own "just what I felt I could do," became the first person in his family to go to college. That fall, he enrolled at the University of Mississippi. "I just never came back," he told me as he turned onto Delta Avenue, just a couple of blocks north of where Pooh Baby and I had sat in front of Dank's. "It just don't make sense [to come back]. When you in a place where nothing is going on, nothing positive anyway, it beats you down mentally."

Eddie's story was a lot of people's story—resident leaves home to attend this college or that university, while away realizes the place where he or she grew up is in one way or another not a desirable place to keep growing, and ultimately opts to never return. A part of a place's desirability is its labor market. Can residents who left for college find work with the credentials they went to get? In places like Clarksdale, more often than not, the answer is no, and the "no" has gotten louder in the last thirty years. Again, what might first register as a question of supply is, at its root, a problem of demand. People will not want to work in a place that does not offer a place for them to work.

However dressed, Clarksdale's opportunity structure problems have begotten lived experience problems. In 2010, the town's median household income was $24,700, just under half of the national average ($51,000) (see appendix table 4) and about 70 percent of Mississippi's average ($37,000), which itself ranked behind all fifty states and Guam. The progression works the same for virtually every other metric of economic well-being. Mississippi faces a wealth of challenges; Clarksdale and the Delta face more than that; and Black residents of Clarksdale and the Delta face the most of all. To extend what forty-five-year-old resident Urschel [ur-shuhl] Dilworth told me, "What you say once for Mississippi, say it twice for the Delta; and if you say it twice for the Delta say it three times in Clarksdale." And if you say it three times in Clarksdale, say it four or five times for Clarksdale's Black residents, or whatever makes the metaphor work.

In 2010, Black households in Clarksdale had an average median income of $19,000, about 73 percent of Clarksdale's average and far less than half (40 percent) of the average for white households in town ($46,669). The implications of that disparity are jarring. For example, in 2017, 91 percent of Clarksdale residents who lived below the poverty line were Black.[30] That is the rub. Clarksdale's opportunity structure problem is especially problematic for the town's Black residents, a reality reflected in every single economic metric for which reliable data exist.

"That's the shit that make it so rough out here," said Shundrick Bledsoe, a twenty-eight-year-old native resident, coughing through a haze of smoke, echoing Eddie and other Black residents I spoke to. "Niggas ain't working, ain't got no jobs, and that's the bad part. It's really crazy, bruh. If niggas had some jobs, I think it'll be better." Shundrick was born in Clarksdale, and at the time of our conversation he lived in Clarksdale with his mom, but only some of the time. Most of the time, he was either at a friend's house in a neighboring town—which is where we met to talk—or he slept in the backseat of his car. "It just depends on where I'm at and if I had to work that night," he explained. "I drive two hours one-way for my job, so sometimes I don't feel like just being out there on the road like that."

Where Shundrick and Pooh Baby navigated Clarksdale's opportunity structure by traveling beyond the city limits, twenty-seven-year-old native resident Latoya "Toya" Johnson did her best in town. We met for our initial conversation at a chain restaurant, one of two where she worked full time. She had told me the interview "can't take that long" because she was "working a double" that day, and the first shift would start soon. In that conversation, and several others, Toya painted a clear picture of how hard Clarksdale can be for Black residents. Toya had two daughters, Lashiya, five, and Shalaya, seven, both of whom were "[her] everything," both of whom motivated her to "do everything [she could] to take care of them." That was a lot. "I work two full-time jobs," she told me, which meant anywhere from seventy to eighty hours a week. "I leave one job, I'm going right to the other. . . . And, seem like I get one check and I'm looking right for the next one. It's just not enough."

What Toya said was basic math. One job paid her $7.25 per hour, and the other paid $7.35. She had four paydays a month. Presuming a forty-hour workweek, which she told me was the least she typically worked each week, on the first and third Friday, Toya netted (i.e., earned after taxes and deductions) $506 from the first job. On the second and fourth Friday, she netted $512 from the other. At the end of each month, she had earned $2,036 ($506 + $515 + $506 + $512). Rodrick, the father of Toya's daughter Shalaya, worked at a furniture manufacturing plant in a central Mississippi town, earning approximately $11.00 per hour. Each month, Toya received about $180 in child support from him. Toya also received about $400 in aid from the Supplemental Nutrition Assistance Program (SNAP, better known as food stamps), dispersed via an electronic benefit transfer card.[31]

In total, Toya relied on $2,616 ($506 + $512 + $506 + $512 + $180 + $400) to cover a month of expenses for her, Lashiya, and Shalaya. That would equate to earning about $16.35 per hour if she earned the full amount from a single full-time job. In Mississippi, the living wage for a single-adult household is $11.04 per hour.[32] For households with one adult and one non-working child, the amount is $21.07. For Toya's household—a single adult with two non-working children—it is $23.75. What Toya made ($16.35/hour) was just not enough.

"When you give people work, you give people something to work for. You give people something to live for," Eddie said. We had circled the downtown square, passing Dank's on Delta, passing the Delta Blues Museum Stage on Third, passing the few banks and insurance offices scattered in between, eventually shuttling to his parents' home in the Circle, a small residential area nestled between the winding tributaries of the Sunflower River in the north central part of town. Both of Eddie's parents were in their sixties. His mother, Pearline [per-leen], was born inside the city limits. His father, Jimmy, was born in a small, unincorporated place on Clarksdale's rural periphery.

After sitting with Mrs. Pearline and Mr. Jimmy for a while, which really meant me sitting on the couch while Eddie walked and talked with them from backroom to backroom, Eddie and I retraced our route to the First Street Bridge, passing through the same intersection where we had seen the rickety pickup truck. This time, we took the route the truck had taken, turning left onto Riverside, picking up where we would have if we had kept straight earlier.

"Ride down here by the old high school," Eddie said under his breath. Then, leaving little room for my input, he continued talking. "My folks been in this town forever. I'm try'n'a get 'em out before it get just too too bad, but they don't wan'a leave. Then, their house is run down. I should've showed you the tree that done fell out there in the back[yard]." Eddie raised his hand from the center console and extended his open palm slightly in my direction. "So, I'm at a debate, you know: do I put money into the house to fix it—redo the outside, fix the yard up, all that—or do I take that money to [help them] move." He sighed and lowered his hand. "But, then, that's a hard debate too because you kinda feel like you leaving your past behind. [Clarksdale] is home . . . " He let the thought linger. "Sometimes you just . . . love it and hate it at the same damn time."

Eddie had been driving slowly all day, but as we approached what I had learned was the old city high school, he slowed even more, eventually stopping in the middle of the road. To our right, about 100 yards away, were the remnants of a remnant of a remnant: the abandoned structure of what was once Clarksdale's all-white Bobo Senior High School, which had once been a plantation before it was a school.[33] The bricks were a dull red, the cement foundation darker than gray, almost black. There were three rows of windows. Each window on the bottom row was completely boarded up. The windows on the top two rows were a combination of boarded, broken, and

Hard . . . Make It Easy

some indistinguishable in-between. It looked exactly as one might expect an "old high school" would, save for the headstones, on a small north lot, marking the graves of several members of the Bobo family.

"That's where you went?" I asked Eddie.

"No. . . . I went out to 'The County,'" he told me, his shorthand a reference to Coahoma County High School—located about two miles west of where we were. "This was the city school. . . . This was where the whites went up 'til the 1960s, 1970s. They said it used to be a pool out there." We both sat watching the vacant schoolyard—trees, grass, and a few light poles the only thing watching us back. I imagined what it must have looked like when full of young people standing and talking, laughing and plotting. Eddie interrupted me. "[They] say that when the Blacks started out there, they filled it [the pool] up with concrete. Now, I'm saying!" He raised his voice, but quickly stopped himself, resigned to shake his head with a laugh that sounded like it wasn't nothing funny.

It is funny—in most every Delta town, Black residents began calling for school desegregation years before the *Brown* decision made it law, and many white residents and officials resisted the *Brown* decision for as long as the law allowed. In Clarksdale, the former began in the late 1940s and reached a head in 1951 when two Black women residents, thirty-five-year-old Leola Tates and twenty-two-year-old Erline Mills, each accused the same white man—E. L. Roach—of rape. Initially, three justices of the peace dismissed the charges "based on alleged discrepancies and conflicts in the victims' testimonies."[34] However, after a massive organizing effort in which Black residents raised $10,000 to secure the legal representation of a well-connected local attorney, the case was presented before a grand jury. Roach was indicted on charges of kidnapping and "pointing a pistol," but he was found not guilty of the kidnapping charges. He ultimately walked without being convicted of anything.

That was that: Black residents who had organized on behalf of Tates and Mills had lost. However, the loss on one front sparked a movement on another: the fight for school desegregation. That Black residents had been able to coordinate such a large fundraising campaign and mobilize in a way that forced the hand of the local white establishment was momentum. That momentum carried local Black folks through two decades of movement-building.

If 1951 was the year Black residents of Clarksdale began challenging the local status quo on the cause of school desegregation, 1970 was when the status quo actually gave in. After a five-year legal battle that started when Black residents filed a lawsuit to admit Rebecca Henry to all-white Clarksdale high school, the U.S. District Court for the Northern District of Mississippi ordered the immediate integration of the city's school district. Yet, as is often the case with the status quo, giving in a little did not mean giving in all the way.

By the time Black students began enrolling at Clarksdale High School in the early 1970s, white parents had already begun enrolling their children elsewhere—Lee Academy, a K–12 private school that a collective of white residents, many of them members of the local branch of the Association of Citizens Councils of Mississippi, had helped establish in 1968.[35]

"I was in the seventh grade when integration came in," recalled Mrs. Classic Mae "Classi'Mae" Agnew, a sixty-year-old Clarksdale native. I had joined her at her home in the Roundyard, a community of about 575 residents spanning 0.15 square miles in the southeastern corner of town. "They pulled us from Lyon [on the rural outskirts of Clarksdale] and sent us to Higgins— you had all the Blacks, you know, who attended Higgins [Junior-Senior High School]—and you saw some whites over there, but those [white students attending Higgins] was mostly poverty-stricken children, you know."[36]

Mrs. Classi'Mae had an encyclopedic memory of what she called Clarksdale's "integration years," the years roughly between 1970 and 1980. "Then, you had at that time, Black students started going to Clarksdale High," she continued. "And, when that started to happen, the whites pulled out like that," she snapped her fingers, "and started going to Lee [Academy]." She found something in her memory funny. She laughed and smiled and laughed. "That swimming pool right by the old high school, when Black kids started going out there, they filled it up with concrete. That's the truth. It's right there to prove it." She said what Eddie had said, and as Eddie and I continued to sit and talk in front of the vacant building, he returned the favor, saying what she had.

"All in this area, by the school, back [that way]," Eddie pointed back in the direction that we had just come from, "all that, this whole block, was nothing but white, but then, they [white residents] started running out."

"Where did they go?" I asked.

"Most of 'em? Most of 'em left!" He laughed. "They would go to Oxford [Mississippi], or to Olive Branch [Mississippi], even down to Cleveland [Mississippi].... You do still have some whites that's here [in Clarksdale]. In a minute, I'll ride you over by what we like to call Snob Hill." He was talking about an area stretching along the northern border of town that was, as the name might suggest, Clarksdale's wealthiest neighborhood enclave. The Census proves Eddie right about Snob Hill. Of the seven major enclaves in town, it has the largest share of white residents (68 percent in 2013).

Eddie's observation that "this whole block was nothing but white" was also right. The "whole block" that he was referring to was the same "from First Street to Riverton" that Mrs. Irene had mentioned that morning in her office, both a reference to a neighborhood that most local residents called Oakhurst, one of the town's largest neighborhood enclaves. In 1990, the two-square-mile area in northwest Clarksdale had been home to about 6,100 people; after peaking at about 6,500 in 2010, it had settled again to around 6,100 in 2013.[37] The observation that Oakhurst's resident population had shifted from virtually all-white to predominantly Black was one of the most widely repeated that I heard. Young and old folks told me. Black and white folks told me. Elected officials told me. Historical accounts and the Census told me too: between 1990 and 2013, while the overall resident population of Oakhurst remained about the same, the proportion of white residents dropped from 98 to 30 percent, which translates to a loss of more than 4,000 people.

The racial turnover in Oakhurst was part and parcel of an equally pointed pattern of demographic change that had been happening in the entire town for the better part of fifty years. In 1970, 45 percent, or about 9,500, of Clarksdale's residents were white. There were 11,703 Black residents (54 percent). By 2013, the number of overall residents in Clarksdale had declined by about 18 percent (about 17,725 people), and, of those who remained, 19 percent (3,332) were white and 80 percent (14,135) were Black. If the Oakhurst neighborhood tells, on a micro-level, a part of Clarksdale's macro demographic story—one of a steady and drastic reshuffling of the town's racial demographics—Clarksdale tells, in three acts, the post-1970s story of the Delta writ large. One act is an encore. The other two are new.

First, the encore: numerous scholars have noted that the Delta has experienced some degree of population loss every decade since the expansion of farm mechanization (and, by extension, sharecropper evictions) in the mid-twentieth century.[38] Since 1950, the eleven counties comprising the "central" Delta region have lost about 48 percent of its resident population. For Coahoma County, the figure is 46 percent. Until 1970, Clarksdale and other Delta towns of similar size (e.g., Cleveland, Greenville, Greenwood, and Vicksburg) were the exception, each demonstrating consistent, substantial growth.[39] For instance, between 1940 and 1950, Clarksdale's resident population grew by 35 percent, from 12,168 to 16,539; by 28 percent from 1950 to 1960; and by 3 percent from 1960 to 1970. That growth slowed, then reversed itself in the 1970s, bringing Clarksdale back in line with the Delta's prevailing demographic story of population loss.

Two aspects of Clarksdale's post-1970s demographic landscape do not fit with the Delta's enduring patterns of population change. People have always left, yes; one thing that is different is who. In the early decades of the twentieth century, most of the people who left the Delta were Black. There were "pull factors" like the prospects of economic opportunity and the hope of escaping the violence and discrimination of the Jim Crow South. There were push factors too, namely, the mass evictions of farmworkers by white planters.[40]

Since 1970, out-migration has shifted from a product of Black sharecropper eviction to one of "white flight." On the one hand, the impetus for the town's unprecedented rates of white out-migration is straightforward. If you think the building is on fire, you leave as quickly as possible. For white residents, Clarksdale's porous and limited opportunity structure, rising poverty rates, and ever under-resourced public infrastructure is fire enough. Leaving makes sense. On the other hand, that out-migration did not materialize until the 1970s raises a different, or at least an additional, possible catalyst: race. The spike in white out-migration corresponds to the time when Clarksdale's schools and other social institutions were integrating. Mrs. Classi'Mae summed up the sentiments of many of the folks I spoke with. "We [Black residents] came in—I guess it was in there in the [1970s]—and right when we got in . . . seem like that's when the whites got out!"

The second way that Clarksdale's post-1970s demographic story differs from decades prior is not just who is leaving, but who is growing: Black residents. While the number of white residents in Clarksdale has declined by 66 percent since 1970, the number of Black residents has increased by 21 percent. This emergent trend is notable for two reasons. First, it points to the enduring reach of the blues epistemology in the ethics of Black Delta communities. "We have to grow where we are planted," Clarksdale native Ms. Kathereen Ford, fifty-one, told me when explaining her belief that the best thing one could do to boost Clarksdale's structural profile was "stay right where we are."

Second, that the Black resident population is not only *not declining* but growing adds credence to the sentiment expressed by Mrs. Classi'Mae and dozens of other residents that white out-migration has been driven at least partly, if not primarily, by racial anxiety. In a place where the opportunity structure is enough of a push factor to cause such substantial out-migration in one part of the resident population, one might expect stagnation, at best, in the population that remains. With the exception of the span between 1980 and 1990, stagnation has not been the case. Clarksdale's Black population has shown unfettered growth for the last fifty years.

"I guess you say, I better gone and drive," Eddie said as he eased off the breaks, and we inched forward. The old Bobo Senior High School was a landmark of one type. It made older Black residents remember, and younger ones wonder, how things used to be. Further along Riverside Avenue, Eddie and I passed under a viaduct, an overpass that supported the old tracks of the Illinois Central Railroad running along the top, splitting the town from west to east. It was a landmark of another type. It made everybody know.

"You know what that is, don't you," Eddie asked. "Railroad tracks. . . . The great divide! That side is Oakhurst. . . . This side is coming into Riverton." Prior to 1970 every neighborhood district North of the rail tracks—Oakhurst, Snob Hill, the Tennessee Williams district—was predominantly and in some cases exclusively white. Every enclave that was south of the tracks, including the Black commercial district known variably as "Black Downtown" and the "New World," were virtually all Black. Again, the town's racial calculus was precise.

After passing under the viaduct, Eddie and I passed a looming structure, another remnant of a remnant, what remained of what had been a 500,000-square-foot cotton compress.

Further along, as Riverside turned into Madison Avenue, Eddie and I approached another building that looked to have at one point been something else. "That carwash ain't been a carwash in a long time," Eddie said, again easing on his breaks as we got closer. The building still bore signs of what it used to be. The name, "Shine-and-Go," was still visible from the road, painted bright red.

"Most of your issues you run into here [in Clarksdale] are because people are poor or because people can't have access to things they need. You look at these right here." He pointed to a set of duplexes on one side of the road. "Probably in the last ten years—or, I guess it's been longer [ago] than that—they built that carwash into some apartments and put it in with these right here." We were passing a set of four duplexes. "Look like folks still living in 'em too!" As we neared the end of Madison Avenue, he again referenced Clarksdale's public infrastructure. "You live here, and some of the most basic stuff you can think of, people don't have."

Eddie had extended his commentary beyond Clarksdale's opportunity structure and demographic profile to include local social institutions like the city's schools, health-care facilities, and services. What he had said, so many residents had already lived.

"When I had [the stroke], they didn't even know it until five days later. Five days!" Dottie Peoples, forty-nine, had suffered a massive stroke and fallen unconscious while working her normal swing shift at an area manu-facturing plant. "If I'd've went [to a hospital] somewhere else, like Oxford, like Southaven, even Cleveland, they'd've caught it. They would have saw that I had had a stroke, and I wouldn't be in the shape I was in." She scoffed at her initial treatment regimen. "The doctor [would] come in, all they do is give me shots, hook me to a IV, and every morning he come there, he'll feel my right ankle, and boom, he would leave."

Mrs. Dottie was three years removed from the stroke when we talked. She still walked with a limp and at times had trouble talking. While she was insured through a meager benefits package at the local plant where she worked, she often had to arrange travel outside of Clarksdale for treatment. When we talked, she was preparing for two months of intensive speech and physical therapy, cause for both excitement and dismay.

"[When] I get done with that [therapy], you ain't go'n be able to tell me nothing!" She laughed; then, as her face settled, she explained that because Clarksdale's Northwest Mississippi Regional Medical Center (NMRMC) offered no such services, she would have to travel to Cleveland, a 100-mile drive roundtrip. "I got to get family to take me because I can't drive that far by myself. . . . I tell you, it's just hard for us down these parts sometime. Hard."

Mrs. Dottie's experience is one symptom, and but a small one, of a more extensive health-care crisis in Clarksdale and the Delta. First, there is the question of quality—can residents expect competent, ethical treatment from local health-care providers. The answer to that question seems to be, "maybe, maybe not." In 2015, the U.S. attorney for the Eastern District of Arkansas announced that sixteen hospitals, including the NMRMC where Mrs. Dottie received some of her care, had agreed to pay nearly $16 million "to resolve False Claims Act allegations that the providers sought and received reim-bursement from Medicare for services that were not medically reasonable or necessary."[41]

Second, there is the question of access—can residents get the health services and medication they need. The answer to that question seems to be, "at least for now." In 2018, Curae Health, which owns the NMRMC, filed for Chapter 11 bankruptcy and warned local officials that the NMRMC was losing money (operating expenses top $5 million per month) at a rate it could not sustain. The closure of the NMRMC would drastically hamper health-care availability for residents of Clarksdale and Coahoma County. The nearest health-care institutions of similar size and capacity are in Helena, Arkansas (about thirty miles from the NMRMC), Charleston, Mississippi (forty miles), Batesville, Mississippi (forty miles), and Memphis, Tennessee (about ninety miles). The closure would also impact the approximately 500 employees of the NMRMC.

As Eddie and I approached the intersection where Madison Avenue stops at State Street, he joked, "You seen enough yet?"

The light turned green, and Eddie turned left. The cross-linked blue guitars of Clarksdale's "Blues Crossroads" monument came into view, reminding Eddie and me (and all who passed by) the promise of the town's blues, the promise that Himmens and Shelbie and Janky's and Dank's and Juke Joint and the WROX marker all embodied, the promise that state lawmakers and stakeholders all promised, the promise that blues tourism was the Delta's answer to its development crisis.

All that Eddie and I had passed before the Crossroads monument reminded me of what the promise had missed. It reminded me of the town's polarized labor market, nearly unparalleled rates of poverty, inadequate public infrastructure, and steady stream of residents leaving with aspirations for more.

It reminded me of Pooh Baby. He lived around the corner from the Crossroads marker; in the New World district,[42] an area just south of the downtown square. Before 1970, the New World was the epicenter of commerce and entertainment for Black residents. Back then, it was the only such place for Black residents in town. Clarksdale's downtown square, which sat north of the tracks of the Illinois Central Railroad—the same tracks that Eddie called "The Great Divide"—was for the white folks. If Black folks were seen on the square, they faced both formal and informal sanctions: harassment from white residents, violence at the hands of local police, blacklisting from local businesses and financial institutions, and arrest. So Black residents mostly stayed off the square. They met south of it in the New World. They opened a string of businesses—boutique shops, funeral homes, laundromats, and restaurants—alongside a handful of Black churches right beside a small Black community. As of 2013, about 700 people, virtually all of them Black, lived in that community. Including Pooh Baby. Sixty percent of residents in the New World neighborhood lived below the poverty line. Including Pooh Baby, his momma, and his dad. Every day, Pooh Baby crossed the tracks to busk, usually in front of Dank's, leaving the blues to play the blues.

The Delta's blues development agenda made Pooh Baby's blues seem good and exciting, like a festival. Pooh Baby's life made the Delta's blues development agenda seem like a lie.

"Seem like, it's you take two steps forward and one step back," Pooh Baby said on that Tuesday after the Juke Joint Festival. "That's all it is around here . . . seem like you stuck." We had sat out in front of Dank's and talked for about two hours. Pooh Baby played his guitar just about the whole time. I listened. "I just see myself out of here one day!" he said while packing away his amp and guitar. "Out this motherfucka!" His words were something like defiant and hopeful, frustrated and amused. "I don't know if it's go'n be the blues that help me do it or something else, but I'm out!" The sun was too. It had come back from behind some clouds. Himmens and Shelbie were not anymore. They had already left. "Out this motherfucka," Pooh Baby said again, to make sure.

2 WE AIN'T THAT NO MO'

"I done lived the blues," Mac said to me. His voice made it sound like he knew things other folks didn't, or couldn't. We were sitting in the main office of his consignment shop. I was looking around and listening to him. He was doing what he always did when we talked—answering my questions with questions of his own, then not giving me time to respond.

"How do you define the blues?" I asked him.

"How do I define the blues?" he asked me back. "You define the blues by what you been through. Somebody else might define it different from me. I had a friend who writes music, and he was go'n tell *me* what the blues was. He said you gotta have some many notes, so many beats." On cue, Mac started stomping a foot and rapping his knuckles on his desk to the rhythm of an imagined song—*stomp-CLAP-stomp-CLAP*. Then he dismissed the story and act altogether. "Whatever that meant," he said.

Allen "Mac" McIntosh, forty-five, was born and raised in Clarksdale. Let him tell it, he had "seen it all." He had watched the town make itself into a blues tourism destination between 1980 and the aughts; and before that he had critiqued the town's piecemeal move toward school desegregation in the 1960s; and he had heard how, before that, his sharecropping parents had navigated the aftermath of farming mechanization in the 1940s and 1950s. If anybody knew the blues, it was Mac, or at least that's how it seemed from how he talked.

"I'll tell you what the blues is. My best friend died in 1997. I lost my job in 1997, got a divorce in 1997, dropped out of [college] in 1997, and you see that bus up there?" Mac shifted his attention to a framed Polaroid hanging above and to the side of his desk. "I moved in that bus in 1997."

Mac's office was full of stuff—stuff stacked and tacked against walls, piled across his desk, and pushed into corners. Most of it was indistinct. It ran together. But the framed picture was set apart. It hung on a wall to itself.

"Can I look?" I asked.

Mac looked at the picture for what seemed like a long time. It seemed like he was waiting for it to say something. "Go 'head."

The picture showed an old school bus, its tires flat, its underbelly tangled, its back door hinged open. "When it was ninety degrees outside, it was 115 in that bus," Mac told me. "I would have to go hang out in the club . . . or [the pool hall] until it cooled down. Then I come home right there to that bus."

"That was a tough time," I said.

"It was a tough time," Mac repeated me, his voice like his office, full of heavy things. "It was a lot of thinking time too. But you learn from those struggle times just like you do the high times, and that's the blues. That's why when you say, 'How do I *define* the blues?,' I define the blues as, to me, going through them hard times back in the day—going through 'em, and learning from 'em, and getting out of 'em before they get too deep on you." I could not tell whether Mac's tone was born of reverence and appreciation or melancholy, or if perhaps it was some combination of them all. "Do we wan'a remember [the hard times]?" he asked. "Yeah," he answered. "We made the best of [those times]. . . . We learned from [those times], living that country life. We all had it like that. We all had to go through that, you know. But do we wan'a remember [the hard times], being poor, struggling, and doing bad like that? Naw. We ain't the blues no mo'. We ain't that no mo'."

I first met Mac at Woodlawn Coffee on the downtown square. He was leaving a lunch meeting with a community group. I was there reading and people-watching. "Anytime you see a Black man in a place like that, doing something positive," he later explained, "you stop and say something to 'em." That initial encounter spurred several subsequent conversations. Over breakfast, at civic meetings and community events, and in his office, Mac and I talked about his life, his family, and his hometown, a place that, he told me, he had come to love and hate.

Love and hate was also how Mac talked about the blues. Mac appreciated the blues that symbolized the "struggle times" that he had overcome in his life. He did not like the blues that played on the downtown square to masses and small crowds of tourists. He told me it seemed fake, stripped bare of its history and cultural resonance.

For Mac, the blues was many things. It was both a soundtrack and a memory, familiar and strange. It was all of these things, seemingly at the same time, and seemingly all informed by the same thing: race. Throughout our conversations, Mac both suggested and said outright that Black folks in Clarksdale, and Black southerners more broadly, had a unique relationship with the blues.

"Blues is different for the Blacks here [in Clarksdale]." The way Mac's face went before "blues" made the day seem serious, and his office a church, and his desk missing, and his voice the truth. "It's not the blues that the people that come here, the whites. . . . and you got some Blacks too, but it's mostly whites [that] come. It's not the blues that they go listen to. They go listen to blues, and, that's all it is. Really? Is that all it is?" he asked; but this time he didn't answer. He let the question sit.

Mac's logic had two tenets. Tenet one: to know the blues, one must have lived the blues; and, conversely, if one had not, one could not. In a later conversation, again in his office, he made this claim directly. "People think they know the blues, all them folks that you see around out there [the downtown square]. They think they know blues. *Think* they know blues. But what they been through? Is that real blues?"

Mac's second tenet: to know the blues was to not like the blues; and to not know it was to like Clarksdale's (i.e., the town's blues development agenda and entertainment scenes). Mac made this claim directly too. "You won't see too many of us [Black folks] at the blues festivals, at Moonies or T-Bone's," he continued. "We have more or less pushed that old blues out. . . . We just don't want no parts of that. We don't want no parts of that."

Lots of Black Clarksdalians followed Mac's logic. They told me what he told me, often like he told me too: like they knew. They told me that the blues was something they had lived, something that belonged to them, something they took pride in. They told me the blues was a part of who they were. They also told me, "We ain't that no mo'." This chapter chronicles the ways Black Clarksdalians use such claims to accomplish a distinctive Black southern identity.

What Mac and other Black residents of Clarksdale said about the blues highlights the constitutive relationship between Black folks and affective dispositions like desire.[1] Desire does not always manifest as an unbridled affinity for a thing. It is not always presupposed by feelings of attraction and delight. It is not always happy. Sometimes desire registers on the backbeat, as what I call "negation," as a sense of ambivalence about a thing, as loving a thing but not all the way, as "I done lived the blues" but "we ain't the blues no mo.'" Ultimately, this chapter posits that Black Clarksdalians like Mac used this discursive move—moving from loving something to not liking it and back again—as an epistemological tool, a "small axe,"[2] as it were. It allowed them to do work, to craft and protect their own constructions of identity and selfhood, till and mark the boundaries of racial group membership, and carve out space to reify and celebrate racial group bonds along the way.

I-THEY-WE: RACIAL IDENTITY, BOUNDARY WORK, AND NEGATION

When I asked Black Clarksdalians to "define" or "tell me about" the blues, they typically started by talking about music. They named singers and songs. They mentioned people, mostly men, playing instruments, mostly guitars. They said things like "roots of all music" and "foundation of every music genre." Music was only part of the story though—and a small part. The bigger part was how people lived. That is what the blues really was: lived experience, and not just any lived experience, but lived experience of hardship, or "struggle," that was in some way tied to the region's and nation's racial history. The blues was "struggle times," and "back in the day when people was struggling," and "it came out of the struggle." Black residents of Clarksdale told me the blues was selfhood and kinship. It was both a pillar of their own identities and an important symbol of where Black Americans had (had to) come from. It was this sense of shared history and "linked fate"[3] that foregrounded what Black residents said about the blues, and it played in the background of comments like "We ain't the blues no mo.'"

The more folks told me what the blues was (and whose it wasn't), the more familiar what and how they said it became. Like the I-IV-I-V chord progression in old-style blues, our exchanges had a predictable cadence and sequence: "I"-"They"-"We." First, Black Clarksdalians implied that they had a unique individual relationship with the blues. They told me, "I done lived the blues," and "I have had the blues," and "I know the blues." They said, "I believe the blues is" this, and "I say the blues is" that, and like Mac, "I define the blues as, to me" this other thing.

It is possible to hear people's "I" clauses (e.g., "I define" and "I say") as partial claims, indeed as a way to say that something is so without presuming that that something is necessarily true. "I define" is usually a hedge. It usually portends and precedes a tentative claim that, by its nature, allows for alternate interpretations. Black Clarksdalians were not so straightforward. They used "I," and the ways that talking about "I" made them feel, differently—not as an admission of subjectiveness but as a nod to subjectivity. "I" allowed Black Clarksdalians to take ownership and claim legitimacy. It marked their efforts to name themselves as the owners, arbiters, and holders of the blues, which they defined both as a personal sensibility and cultural form.

Second, Black Clarksdalians distinguished between what the blues was to them and how it had come to be used by other people. This is where "they" came in. If "I" was how Black Clarksdalians positioned themselves as the lead authority on the blues, "they" was how they doubled down. If "I" legitimated what Black residents said, "they" codified it. Black Clarksdalians told me "they" could (try to) play the blues, but "they" could not know the blues; that "they" could have the blues, but that "they" had not lived the blues. "They" were the people who were most likely to spend their days at the Juke Joint Festival, and to shop and stop at places like Janky's and Dank's, and drink and dance at places like T-Bone's Blues Club. Most of the time, "they" were not from the South. Almost all the time, "they" were white. Almost all the time, "they" was a cloak. Black Clarksdalians used it to talk about race and class stratification when they did not want to make such claims directly or overtly.

Finally, Black Clarksdalians positioned the blues as a repository of Black (southern) history and culture. To them, the blues was everything that "we," by which they meant Black southerners and Black Americans, had made, sang, and overcome. "We" came near the end of what Black residents said about the blues and was often accompanied by gestures of sincerity[4]—a sigh, a cry, a distant gaze, a smirk. Mac smiled when he told me, "We ain't the blues no mo'," his voice full with the sound of accomplishment. Boyce Shumpert (chapter 3) chuckled when he told me of the predominantly white crowd at a local blues club, "We don't be out there," his laugh the sound of unconcern. Black Clarksdalians almost always said "we." "We" was important to them. "We" was purposive. "We" forged bonds between Black residents' "I's" and helped mark the social and symbolic boundaries that separated them from "they." "We" was how Black Clarksdalians honored what had been, while clearing space for what would (and what they hoped would not) be moving forward; and when it came to the blues, Black Clarksdalians believed "we ain't that no mo'."

If blues music typically moves between I, IV, and V, how Black Clarks-dalians talked about it moved between I, They, and We.

"I Have Had the Blues in My Life": *Claiming (Subjectivity with) "My" Blues*

"I have had the blues in my life," Hessie [hez-ē] said, then hesitated. The pause was not long, but it was long enough. I wondered if he was done talking, if maybe I should repeat the question—"Do you like the blues?"—or move on to something else. He had already told me what he thought the blues was: "the roots of all music." He had also suggested where I could go if I wanted to hear it. "Soul, funkadelic, rock-and-roll, R&B, you listen to any of that, and you listening to the blues. You go to church on Sunday? Listen at some of the songs. That's blues too." In both cases, his voice echoed through his living room with gravity, not a hint of doubt or a thought to second-guess himself.

I met Hessie Trice, fifty-four, early during my time in Clarksdale and sat with him often over the next few years. In that time, I took note of, and came to admire, his gentle but confident demeanor. He wore suits a lot, always pressed and slightly oversized. Sometimes he added a hat, sometimes a vest, always a colorful pocket square. He sat near the front on one side of the church that he went to. His wife, Mrs. Laura Lee, sat right behind the "mourners bench" (the front pew) on the other. When I saw him out in town, he was always talking to somebody about something that seemed both funny and deathly important. He was not loud, overly gregarious, or overbearing, just talkative—except when I asked him if he liked the blues.

"I can't say if I like it," he eventually answered, finally reaching the end of whatever long division he had been compelled to do. "I see the blues as living in hard times . . . and I can't say I want that. Sometimes you have to [live through hard times]. You just get down; but you never want that, I wouldn't think. A lot of people don't know what the blues is. They get the blues, and they can't handle it. I want to say the blues is hard time living—no food, struggling to pay rent, you get put out your house, evicted, the lights get cut off. Me, I have had all that. I have had to put up with all of that. That's why I say, I have had the blues."

"And, when you have the blues, what do you do? What did you do with your blues?" I asked.

"Just lived," he said, like I should've known. Like everybody should have. "That's all you can do, try to live through it, work up out of it. You'll be down for a little while, but then you find your strength. . . . and going through blues, it makes up what come of you."

During our exchange about the blues, Hessie reflected on growing up in a small rural community just east of Clarksdale. He told me he had lived in a five-room "sharecropper house" with both of his parents, his three sisters, four brothers, and no indoor plumbing. "We had a outhouse and a well," he explained matter-of-factly. "We would have to go out there and roll the water out of [the well]. . . . we had a rolling pin with a rope on it, and we had the rope tied to a bucket; and you let that down in the well, scoop up the water, and roll it back up." He acted out each step, briefly pushing to the edge of his recliner. "The water would be clear as the sunshine and cold like you just got it out of the refrigerator. The best water you ever had!" He laughed.

"How do you feel about that time now?" I eventually asked him.

"You know," he spoke quickly, then paused, waiting for his thoughts to catch up to him again. "I think back to then a lot. It hurt me to think about that time, but I always say without going through that, I wouldn't be the person I am. I wouldn't know like I know now. . . . That time taught me every-thing I know, you know. It did. That is who I am." He said the last part with some combination of confidence and satisfaction, a resolution. "If I had to, you know, go back and do it again, I would never go back."

Hessie seemed to be talking about different blues. One blues was im-portant. It was indispensable to Black American culture. It was the roots of all music. It made him talk like he was proud. Another blues was different. It made him hurt. It made him not want to think, not want to go back. That blues was his life. And, there was another blues, the blues that Clarksdale was making. That blues was not worth much attention.

"I don't too much listen to the blues," he told me in one conversation.

"I never been out there for the Juke Festival," he told me in another.

"Really, never?" I asked.

"I never been out there. I don't have no interest in it. And Laura, she don't care nothing 'bout that kind of thing." Hessie and Mrs. Laura Lee pre-ferred gospel music. They went to church every Sunday—and Wednesday and most Saturday afternoons, and some Friday nights. On one occasion, when I asked what music they liked, Mrs. Laura Lee gestured toward a di-sheveled stack of compact discs, most of them, she told me, featuring gospel acts like the Canton spirituals. On another occasion, when I asked if they ever "got out of the house on the weekend," they told me about "choir days" and "quartet nights" at churches and civic centers in the county.

For Hessie, there was more to the blues than music, though; and there was more to how he felt about the blues than dislike. Beyond music, there was lived experience; and beyond dislike, there was pride and reverence. Hessie situated the blues as a constitutive part of his identity, both a set of experiences that he had overcome and a way of being that he had come to know. Whether he liked the blues or not, he talked about it as if it belonged to him, his words peppered with feel of importance and the language of selfhood and ownership. "I have had the blues." "I can't say if I like it." "I have had the blues." "I just lived." "That is who I am." "I would never go back."

The way Hessie talked about the blues is the way many other Black residents of Clarksdale talked about the blues. He and they positioned it as a style and sound of music and claimed it as a part of who they were. When they talked about the music part, they rarely talked a lot. With Hessie, a grand statement about the importance of the blues to American music, and a few passing comments about not really listening to it much, was enough to convey the idea. With folks like thirty-seven-year-old Cherlyn [SHə'r-lin] Bibbs, singing a line from a song made the point. "Ain't no love in the heart of the city, ain't no love in the heart of town." Younger folks like twenty-nine-year-old Daisha [day-sha] "Ms. Dee" Fields said even less—"old folks' music."

When folks talked about the blues as lived experience, they said more. They said the blues was personal. Mac said the blues was 1997. Hessie said the blues was ten people living in a five-room house with no running water. Sixty-year-old Evester [ē-vester] Huddleston said the blues was the unexpected death of her husband. They all also said "I."

"I" was personal. It allowed Black Clarksdalians to speak freely, without apology. It was how they told what had happened in their lives, how they felt about it; and how what had happened and how they felt mattered for who they were. No one could question them, because who can question what "I believe" or what "I say" or what "I don't like" or how "I define the blues"? By framing their claims as subjective, and therefore unquestionable, Black Clarksdalians gave themselves space and time to talk about the blues—which is to say, to talk about their lives—freely. And, by making their claims with a deep sense of reverence and pride, Black Clarksdalians infused their claims with a sense of importance and import, authority. What they said must be right and real and the final say because listen to how they said it.

"I" legitimated what Black folks in Clarksdale said and how they felt. It allowed them, not necessarily to speak truth to power, but to speak truth without power really knowing, and cosign what they said without power needing to notarize, or legitimate, it. "I" was the language of self-determination.

It was how Black Clarksdalians took ownership of the blues and took pride in having lived it—even though they did not like it.

"I" allowed Black Clarksdalians to say and do other things too—like talk about "they."

"They Crazy about Some Blues": Marking (Group Difference with) "Their" Blues

I knocked on the door, then took a few steps back.

"Who is it?" I heard Dorothea [dohr-thē-a] "Thea" Goolsby, fifty-one, say from the other side. Her voice was sturdy, like the house was hers, like whoever was knocking better hurry up and answer.

I did quickly. I told her my name, reminded her who I was—"the one you met at Daisy's [Laundromat]"—and that she had told me to stop by.

Soon I heard the unlatching of locks. She opened the door, smiled, welcomed me in, offered me a seat, and returned to hers all before I had time to step fully inside the house. It felt like that anyway. Before I had time to fully rest into a low-sitting couch in her living room, she returned to doing what I suspect she had been doing before I got there: a word-search puzzle.

"I have lived here my whole life," Thea told me after I told her what other people had been telling me since I had arrived in Clarksdale. "People talk about crime here, but it's crime, you can have bad crime, everywhere. People talk about the bad schools here, but it's bad schools everywhere."

"The blues is a big thing here too, I see," I said.

"The blues is big here," she repeated me. "They have really built it up into this great big ole thing where you have people coming from everywhere. . . . Australia, New York City, and they come here to go out to a blues festival? I tell you, they crazy 'bout some blues. I don't get it. I really don't; but I guess you can say they don't bring that in for me no way." She forced a quick, fake laugh for effect.

"Wait, why you say that?" I asked, quick-fake-laughing like her.

Thea looked up from her word-search puzzle. "They don't! I look at it as this, the blues is old-timing music, okay. It takes you back to that struggling time, okay. Now, tell me why people want to be hooked on that? What is the blues? The fact that people were in the cotton fields? And they sang about the oppression, depression, and the things they had to live with? The outside toilets? The shabby houses, the very little money? You look here and you see struggle. You look over there and you see struggle. Is that what they want? What you want the cotton field back for?"

"And the blues is, taking you back, or going back, to that time, to the cotton field?"

"That is what it is. That's what it is to me anyway. I guess people can say whatever the blues is according to them. Everybody ain't been through what everybody been through. They can come in and say the blues is something else . . . I guess. They see the blues as entertainment. We see the blues as hard, as," she searched for the word, "struggle. The blues is that *struggle* from the past, from what Blacks were going through back in the day. We all grew up with very little. We had to scratch for everything."

"Black people." I said.

"Black people. And, that ain't to say that other people had it easy, but you know coming from sharecropping, Blacks didn't have much. We didn't. My family, it was twelve of us. My momma raised twelve of us! Back in a time when people had to scratch for everything; and just about any Black person you talk to will tell you that same thing. . . . Now, that's the blues." She paused to laugh, this one dry and shallow, contempt. "*Hmph*, now that's the blues. . . . I think those times help you learn, though. They help you grow, and . . . I thank God. . . . I have learned to be thankful for the hard times, thankful for the blues, I guess you can say. . . . But I don't want to keep holding on to that."

Thea felt many ways at once. She did not like the blues, and she did not want to "hold on" to the blues, but she was thankful for the blues. She understood why the blues occupied such a central place in Clarksdale's cultural terrain, but she was puzzled why so many people wanted it to. Each feeling informed the other. Thea believed that the blues was "what you been through," and in her own life, she had been through a lot, which she described as having to "scratch for everything." Thea had lived the blues, and that reality engendered in her a sense of authority over what the blues was, what the blues meant, and whether the blues should still be. Like Hessie and Mac, she brokered this authority in first person. That is to say, she frequently started with "I." "I call the blues." "I look at it like." "I think those times." "I have learned." "I don't want to keep holding on to that." Thea used "I" claims to claim the blues. What she said evoked a sense of pride and gratitude, and the pride and gratitude guaranteed what she claimed.

Even as Thea allowed for alternate definitions of the blues—"People can say whatever the blues is according to them"—her "I guess" let me know whose definition counted the most: hers. The blues was hers. Other people could have a say, but she had the final say. That is where her puzzlement came from—others seemed to think the blues was one thing, while she knew it to be another. She knew the blues to be lived experience, and not the good kind. She knew it because that had been her life. The blues was a part of who "I" was.

When talking about the blues, Thea said more than "I." She said "they" too. Thea's "they" was a chorus of people. It included the approximately 132,000 visitors who came to hear and see Clarksdale's blues from forty-four states and thirty countries each year.[5] It included the local public stakeholders and decision-makers whose efforts and interests had led the agenda to center blues tourism in Clarksdale's approach to economic development. "They" also included a group of people who, Thea reasoned, could not understand the blues how she did, because if "they" did, "they" wouldn't be so "crazy" about it. Thea made clear both in what she said and how she said it that she did not like the blues that "they" liked.

Like Thea, Black Clarksdalians used "they" as both a descriptor and a tool. In the former case, it was a stand-in for people and groups, both actual and imagined—white people, visitors, local public officials. In the latter case, "they" helped Black Clarksdalians differentiate. They used "they" to draw attention to a matrix of social (and symbolic) boundaries distinguishing them from other people. Just as lived experience formed the bedrock of how Black Clarksdalians defined the blues and saw themselves, it was the rubric that they used to determine who was like them and who was not. "They" was validation for the bedrock and the rubric. "They" were not like them. "We" were.

"We Are a Blues People": Celebrating (Group Belonging with) "Our" Blues

"I'm a blues musician to my core." Juwell [jü-well] told me, pressing her clinched fists gently near her heart and holding them there. We were sitting in a cramped booth at De Casa, a popular Mexican restaurant on State Street. "Blues is what I do. It's what I always knew I would be. I've been playing guitar for thirty-five years. . . . I do tambourine. I've done djembes and tumbas since I was fifteen. I've been playing drums on set I guess for about seven years now. I sing here and there too; and I'm an artist."

I laughed at Juwell's growing list. "Wow, all that!"

Juwell laughed at my laughter. "I've had a wild life, man. A wild, beautiful life."

Juwell Turner, fifty-four, had lived her whole life "here and there," as she put it. She lived in Chicago until she was fourteen years old, between a handful of cities in the Midwest in her early adult years, near New Orleans until Hurricane Katrina, and in Clarksdale ever since.

"I came here to play the blues," she told me; and after I asked what had inspired her to play the blues, she told me, "Church . . . I grew up in the Pentecostal Church, and when you come up like I did, in that Pentecostal world, you were really coming up with the blues."

"Really?" I said as I thought about what she said.

"Yeah, man! Especially hill country!"

"Wait, so tell me about hill country?"

"You don't know about hill country? It's different from other blues! It's got that deep percussive sound, and I love it!" I sensed a growing excitement in Juwell's voice, a growing disconnect between her and our surroundings—the nearby tables of people talking and laughing, the wait staff dodging families and large groups coming and going, some faint, indistinguishable music giving a soundtrack. Juwell was in another place. " . . . Holly Springs [Mississippi]. Hill Country is out of Holly Springs and really just North Mississippi. It's a folky, country blues."

" . . . Like church," I repeated her.

"Like Pentecost! Oh my gosh! Oh my goodness. The Pentecostal Church is all up in there! It's very distinct." Juwell began humming a rolling bass line, stomping and clapping as she went. "Doomdoom, doomdoom, doomdoom, doomdoom." Occasionally, she stopped to keep talking. "You got your drums, the piano . . . You know when the shouting music comes on. Everybody know shouting music. Eeeeverybody know shouting music. You almost feel like you're in church; and we stay it on stage. This is Mississippi Juwell, and we go'n go to church now, y'all." She continued her baseline. "Got my tambourines! Doomdoom, doomdoom, doomdoom." I started to stomp and clap along with her—"Boomboom, boomboom, boomboom." We eventually burst into laughter. "And, you got all that rolled up in [hill country blues]."

"So, that's what the blues is . . . " I said.

Juwell leaned in and returned to her normal, fast-talking self. "Here is what I tell folks about what the blues is," she started, then stopped and thought, then started again. "The blues is Black folks—Black folks coming home from church, from work, from out, and they chillin'. We chill on the weekend, you know. Momma 'n'em get in the kitchen and get to cookin', and that's if they didn't already [start cooking] on Saturday night. You got your greens, hotwater cornbread, pot of beans, or maybe you got some barbecue, you know, potato salad, Momma's specialty. Somebody go'n' make spaghetti. It's always go'n be some spaghetti in there, some kinda way. Folks in the kitchen. Folks on the porch. You know Black folks go'n' talk shit. Folks in the big room. Music playing—Eddie Mayfield, some Al Green, some city-slicker [blues], whatever. Somebody break out a deck of cards. Somebody go'n' start playing spades or dominos. It's predictable. It's got a beat. . . . And, that's how I talk about the blues—it's the beat, it's the sound, it's the feeling. . . . It's our culture, and that's what you love about it."

In some ways, Juwell was different from other Black Clarksdalians I talked with. She did not grow up in Clarksdale; in fact, she had not grown up in the South at all. She loved and played blues music. She was an encyclopedia of blues history. She was a fixture on Clarksdale's blues scenes. In other ways—many, many other ways—Juwell was not so different.

"I'm Mississippi," she said in a different conversation in a different restaurant in Clarksdale. "I'm Chicago. I'm a Chicago girl, but I'm a Mississippi girl. My family is from East Mississippi, and I call Chicago Mississippi North." She laughed. "I grew up in Chicago, but I stayed in Mississippi. I was in Mississippi a lot . . . and allll my parents used to talk about was Mississippi." Her voice was in two places at once. One place was remembering—remembering her parents, remembering Chicago, remembering Mississippi, remembering how much her parents compared Chicago to Mississippi. The other place was realizing—realizing that they knew what they were talking about. "The food is better in Mississippi. We had tamales in Chicago, but they weren't like Mississippi tamales. . . . The music was better in Mississippi."

The most striking similarity between Juwell and other Black residents of Clarksdale—especially given the differences—was the way she talked about the blues. As I have noted with Mac, Hessie, and Thea, Juwell said "I" a lot. "I'm a blues musician to my core." "I play the blues." "Blues is what I do." When Juwell said "I," she was talking about her *self*. She was making a claim about her identity, taking time along the way to honor earlier experiences in her life. When she said "here is what I tell folks the blues is," she was doing what Mac was doing when he said, "I define the blues as, to me"; and what Hessie was doing when he said, "I want to say the blues is"; and what Thea was doing when she said, "That's what [the blues] is to me anyway." She was disguising a definitive claim as a subjective clause. She was talking about more than the blues. She was drawing on what she had been through in her own life to make a claim about herself and about Black people more broadly.

Like many other Black residents of Clarksdale, Juwell's concluding thoughts about the blues centered a collective—"we." For all that Juwell had to say about the sound of blues music, she said more about the feel of blues living. Juwell's blues was what "we" do, and what "we" have done. Juwell's "we" was Black folks—and not always an unnamed collective of Black folks. "L. C. Ulmer, R. L. Burnside, Junior Kimbrough." Juwell reflected on some of her favorite hill country blues singers, placing herself right alongside them, as she should have. "I played with all of them. Played with their kids." And Juwell placed them all alongside other looming figures in Black history, as she should have. "That was a time where you had Martin Luther King, Malcolm X, the Black Panther Party was strong . . . and I was into all of it. I was reading the [newspapers] and playing the blues. . . . That's why I have tried here in Clarksdale to bring the blues back in with the Blacks here, to get the young people to see how *we* did the blues back in our time. . . . It's our culture!"

Juwell said "we" as if it were the most important word she knew, her conviction matching what I heard from thirty-six-year-old Clarksdale native Early Anderson one Friday night at Johnson Chapel. Early was a pastor. Johnson Chapel was a church. The Friday night was two days before Easter.

"I'm on my way, I'm on my way, I'm on my way!" Pastor Early glided from behind the pulpit, stopping near a corner of the front pew in a side section. I sat on the edge of a pew near the back. "And, when I get to Heaven, I'mma kick off my shoes!" He shuffled back toward the center of the church, stopped, and whipped his right leg forward, sending a shoe tumbling down the aisle. He repeated himself. "I'mma kick off my shoes!" Then, repeated himself. *Kick.* His second shoe went flying, falling not far from the first. His voice rose above, then fell flush with, the cry of organ chords and the *crash* of cymbals, and the echo of "Amen's." A snare and bass drum too.

Pastor Early Anderson grew up in Clarksdale; and after leaving to earn to his BA at eighteen, he did something that not many other residents like him had: he came back—"home" he called it. When we first met, he had been pastoring a local church for about four years. The night I saw him kick off his shoes, his church had joined several others to observe Good Friday.

"Gon' put on my robe!" Pastor Early looked over the congregation, removed his suit jacket, and numbly let it fall to his side. As I watched with some mix of conviction and amusement, I thought about several earlier conversations when he had joked that his wife had joked that he could sometimes "do the most" when he preached. He was keeping true to form, "whooping" and hollering, "tarrying"[6] and carrying on.

Pastor Early preached on. "This city ain't dead 'cause if it's dead you gotta bury it!"

"Amen!" A cry from the congregation.

"And, after you bury it, it's gone."

"Say it!"

"And we got too far to go to be gone!" The following day, I met Pastor Early in the "pastor's study" (his office), a small room in the corner of his church. He joked with me about his wife joking with him about the scene from the previous night. I asked him why he preached how he did.

"I want to be able to meet people where they are," he told me, his voice missing. "I use modern cultural things. . . . but at the same time, I want [people] to at least know where we come from. [Spirituals and old hymnals] play a part in our African American history and culture . . . just like . . . blues."

"I wanted to ask you about that, the blues. What is that? What is the blues?"

Pastor Early looked down at his desk. I decided not to restate the question or filibuster. I just waited. After a little while, he looked up. "The blues is struggle," he finally said, his words quick, his voice like Juwell's "we." "The blues is, 'You went through that too?' The blues is, 'I just came home from a sixteen-hour shift and found my wife in the bed with my brother, and when she left me, she took my dog.'" What he said could have been a joke. How he said it suggested it wasn't.

"The blues," he took a shallow breath then released a deep sigh. "My granddaddy died at forty-six, my daddy died at fifty with a 90 percent blockage; I'm thirty-six, and we [my dad and I] got the same heart condition, so I gotta set my clock backwards. Time run backwards for me, see." After an exchange about some of the lifestyle changes that his heart condition had forced on him and his family, he went back to talking about the blues. "The blues represents the strivings from the valley. What you was going through at yo' darkest hour, when you thought you wasn't go'n make it, when you thought the battle was lost, and gospel . . . is what we turn to when we get to that point where we sick of being down and we tired of being out."

In a later conversation, Pastor Early drew on familiar language positioning the anticipation of hardship as an essential part of Black sensibility. "Everybody has had the blues at one point in they life. Probably every Black person can say they have had the blues at least once. I say, we are a blues people. . . . To me, that's where gospel comes in. Gospel comes out of the blues, or the blues comes out of gospel one [way or the other]. . . . The blues say, 'I'm going through.' Gospel say, 'I'm pressing on.'"

Like other Black Clarksdalians, Pastor Early's first mention of the blues was couched in a comment about Black expressive culture. His blues was at least partly music, in particular music that was central to Black history and lived experience. Yet, after Pastor Early's quick remark about blues music, he shifted to a much more expansive and impassioned account of blues living. "The blues is struggle," he said. His words echoed like they had on that Good Friday night at Johnson Chapel.

Pastor Early's belief that the blues was struggle manifested in two ways. On the one hand, he believed "blues" was an experience or encounter with hardship that was decidedly personal and individual. That blues was *his*, and he made that clear by saying "I say." On the other hand, Pastor Early believed that the "blues" was a collective and communal experience, a rite of passage even. That blues was Black folks, or like he said, "*We* are a blues people."

Like Juwell, Pastor Early situated the blues as an elemental, or expected, part of Black American life. He said as much—"probably every Black person can say they have had the blues at least once"—his words sure, like he knew. What he knew was the gospel truth. He also hinted at as much, again appealing to metaphor. Relying on the rhetoric of many Black religious traditions, Pastor Early imagined Black life as a trek through the wilderness, replete with valleys, "strivings," and mountains, the former two being references to personal hardship and the latter representing the resolution of, or at least survival after, said hardship.

Black Clarksdalians like Pastor Early and Juwell depict the blues as both, and at the same time, personal and communal, individual and collective. Whether their blues came in a discrete event (the death of Pastor Early's father), helped frame a set of memories (Juwell's memories of food and fellowship), or unfolded over some undefined period of time (what Mac, Hessie, and Thea said), Black Clarksdalians talked about the blues as an endemic and immutable feature of Black consciousness and lived experience, like "we."

PARADE

"It usually go through right over there," the man told me, pointing along the sidewalk of Clarksdale's downtown square in the direction of Mac's consignment shop. Eventually I saw Mac himself go through, his truck behind another truck that had been outfitted with a holiday wreath and in front of a float for the County Youth Outreach Program. There were other floats too, most of them draped with glowing string lights, many of them carrying people who carried bags of candy to throw toward the waiting hands of children and other people watching. There were local and area high school marching bands filling the night sky and dim sidewalks with rhythm. There was a dazzling group of Black adolescent girls smiling and high-stepping in front of a truck boasting of the Delta blues. It was Clarksdale's annual Christmas parade, an event that brought residents to the downtown square.

"Now, I like that," I heard one woman say as the high-stepping girls stopped high-stepping, fell into a coordinated dance, then started their march again. In time, a float for Desiree's Salon and Boutique passed, followed on foot by a church group, then the owners and associates of a childcare center, then several cars representing local businesses, then the color guard and band for the nearby community college. A group of children jumped up and down in front of me, excited to see the band and flags go through.

Clarksdale's holiday parade was as spirited as it is instructive: Black American life is a parade—a steady procession of people boasting in themselves, claiming what belongs to them, and celebrating ties of kinship and affiliation, all while going through a terrain that dips, turns, and is sometimes too dark. Despite the darkness, Black folks have gone (and go) on anyway, moving forward and sometimes resting in place both on their own terms and in response to the things behind and ahead of them. When they go through, they go with rhythm, even if there is occasionally some blues.

"Going through," a Black idiom for experiencing personal hardship, is a constitutive part of Black identity and (blues) epistemology. That is to say, Black people look to lived experience to help them navigate and make sense of daily life; and when that lived experience features hardship, its resonance and utility compounds. It becomes an emblem of self-determination and a source of motivation and resilience. That is what lived experience was for Clarksdale's native and noted civil rights organizer Vera Pigee, who was known for insisting that people address her formally. "I am Mrs. Vera Pigee, a wife, a mother, political prisoner, business and professional woman," she said after being arrested for leading a boycott of Clarksdale's downtown department stores in 1961. "Wherever I go, even if I am brought in handcuffs, my name is still Mrs. Vera Pigee."[7]

Lived experience was courage and conviction for Pigee, just as it was for another forbear of the Delta's Black Freedom Struggle, Fannie Lou Hamer. In 1964, Hamer testified before the Credentials Committee of the Democratic National Convention. She began with who she was. "My name is Mrs. Fannie Lou Hamer." She followed it with what she had been made to go through. "It was the 31st of August in 1962 that eighteen of us traveled twenty-six miles . . . to try to register to become first-class citizens." In this chapter, Black Clarksdalians like Mac, Hessie, Thea, Juwell, and Pastor Early offer another way to think about Black identity and lived experience—one that centers not just what Black people go through, but also how they feel about it.

This chapter began with the almost-whispered words of Allen "Mac" McIntosh, "I done lived the blues." We were sitting in the office of his consignment shop, and while I looked around and listened to him talk, I heard and felt what, at first, seemed like a contradiction, a riddle. He talked about the blues as if he loved it, except how he talked made it seem like he didn't. He protected the blues like it belonged to him, but carried himself as if he did not want it. He seemed to revere the blues, yet he dismissed it without doubt. He said it was a part of who he was, then said, "We ain't that no mo." Other Black Clarksdalians followed suit, suggesting that they appreciated the blues, while saying they did not like it. I listened, I wondered, and eventually I asked them to explain themselves. What they said made sense: they felt many ways about the blues because they understood the blues to be many different things—music, lived experience, Black culture, Black history.

To return to Clyde Woods's metaphor (discussed in the introduction), Black Clarksdalians understood the blues to be a tree with many different branches, rooted deeply in the earth. They understood some part of themselves to be the roots ("I done lived the blues"). They knew they had survived and grown into the trunk. They were the tree. They did not like what had happened to some of their branches (the blues music that "they" were "crazy 'bout"). They wanted to break away from them, or to break them away, whichever came first. Black residents knew their roots could not be moved, that they were theirs ("We did the blues"). They believed what Hessie said: "I always say without going through that [some difficult things when I was growing up], I wouldn't be the person I am. I wouldn't know like I know now. . . . That time taught me everything I know, you know. It did. That is who I am." Yet to know one's past is indispensable, and to value and talk about it as such, is one thing. To want to return to that past and relive, resuscitate, and replay it? That is something altogether different. Would a tree want to retreat into the earth? "Naw."

Woods's metaphor helps, but people's lives are people's lives—not trees—and so what Black Clarksdalians said ultimately tells the story whole. Though they talked about the blues like it was many different things, they generally did the talking in the same way. They started with "I," dismissed "they," and celebrated "we." Mac said, "I done lived the blues," then said, "They think they know the blues," then said, "We ain't the blues no mo." Thea

We Ain't That No Mo'

said, "I look at [the blues] as . . . " and "they crazy about some blues," and "we all grew up with [the blues]." Juwell said, "[Blues] is what I always knew I would be," then ultimately "we did the blues."

When Black Clarksdalians said "I," they were speaking the language of subjectivity and self-determination. They were positioning themselves as the owners of the blues, and they were positioning the blues as a stand-in for past life experiences. "I" made the blues theirs, giving them license to love it, not like it, and dismiss it on their own terms, sometimes at the same time. When folks said "they," they were referencing an often-unnamed contingent of people who had not shared the types of blues experiences that they had. "They" was the language of distinction. When the Black Clarksdalians I talked to said it, they were typically pointing to the town's (and region's and nation's) enduring lines of racial difference. "They" typically meant white folks, and if "they" were white, "we" were necessarily Black. Black Clarksdalians used "we" not just to further demarcate racial boundaries but to celebrate the side on which they fell and planted themselves.

Black Clarksdalians' I-They-We claims were not just about racial identity and racial group membership. They were also about desire—or, rather, desire on the backbeat. That is negation, or moving between multiple affective dispositions, even when those dispositions are set on the same thing. When Mac said, "I done lived the blues," his voice was both somber and reverential. When he said, "They go listen to blues, and, that's all it is. Really?" His voice was a scoff, dismissive. When he said, "We ain't the blues no mo'," he was proud, both about the blues that Black folks had made and gifted the world and about the prospect of having gained a foothold in the world despite the blues he had been given. Hessie, Thea, Juwell, Pastor Early, and other Black folks in Clarksdale talked about the blues the same way—as a thing that they loved but just did not like.

3 THAT'S FOR THE WHITE FOLKS

"I gotta take momma to revival. I'll meet you at T-Bone's when I get done out there." Boyce [bȯiz] Shumpert, a twenty-seven-year-old native of Clarksdale, had promised to meet me at T-Bone's Blues Club after church.

"It's cool. I can just wait for you," I said.

"Go on. I'll hit you up." He was insistent.

It was the first night of Juke Joint Weekend, just a few days before Pooh Baby and I had talked with Himmens and Shelbie in front of Dank's (chapter 1). Known by locals and familiars as "Juke Joint," the festival had grown to be one of the most popular of the year, attracting blues acts, street vendors, 5,000 out-of-town visitors, and some 2,000 local residents to the downtown square for four days of live music, street vending, heritage tours, and southern eating.

According to the Juke Joint schedule, T-Bone's was the premier opening night venue and would feature a night-long lineup of local and visiting blues performers. I knew that meant the small, multipurpose storefront would likely be standing-room-only, so I decided to do what Boyce had told me.

"Headed out," I texted him. "[Let me know] when you headed that way."

I arrived to the downtown square at dusk, early enough to squeeze into a parking space just a few paces away from T-Bone's but late enough that people had already begun to crowd along the sidewalk and near the entrance. I pushed through the crowd slowly, scanning for familiar faces and ducking through stale clouds of cigarette smoke.

"Just five [dollars]," said the stubby bouncer, his extended hand prompting a group of middle-aged men to step aside and allow me to pass through. Inside, women and men moved between the cluttered dining room and the primary performance area, which had been clumsily arranged with mismatched chairs, a bar, and a scatter of sound equipment. Rather than make my way to the back of the room where a few empty seats remained, I decided to stand along the wall near a small speaker by the stage.

"How ya doin', mane?" I turned to find a mid-thirties man, wearing a bright-orange "Staff" T-shirt, leaning near my ear. I shifted my weight away from the wall, anticipating that he would ask me to move. "If you need anything, I got'chu. You need a drink or anything, don't worry 'bout it."

"Aight, I 'preciate that," I answered, struggling to decipher if his insistent tone was a cue that we had met before. We locked hands, and he rushed away, ducking under the arm of a twenty-something woman, also wearing a bright-orange shirt, before disappearing into the kitchen.

The performers carried on with a contained energy. The lead singer of one of the feature acts rattled an oversized tambourine as she twisted, offbeat, from side to side. Her partner strummed his guitar with a singular focus, patting his foot deliberately, not bothering to look up at the crowd. A burly man rocked in his seat. A woman did her best to sing the lyrics—"Tambourine! Tambourine!" People walked back and forth, clutching beer bottles, occasionally pausing to clap, then stomp, then sway in place.

After the show, as I retreated to the dim sidewalks outside, I swiped through a string of notifications on my phone. Boyce.

"Casino?"

Within minutes, I was dodging potholes and creeping over speed bumps at Boyce's apartment complex. He and I had become friends since I had moved to Clarksdale. We went to the same gym during the week, talked local politics and made friendly wagers on sports games on the weekend, and occasionally, like that night, we tried our luck at the casinos in nearby Tunica County.

As we drove, I fake-fussed at Boyce for standing me up at T-Bone's. "Man, I thought you was coming to the show!" I said, half-shouting, half-laughing.

He half-smiled. "I told you I was going to revival with momma." Then, he half-looked at me but really just kept looking at the road, his face like it was, still. "We [Black residents] don't be out there, mane. That's for the white folks."

Boyce had explained, with impressive efficiency, something that I had noticed at virtually every event during the Juke Joint Festival. I had walked past about thirty people in the Blues Alley on the way to T-Bone's, squeezed through a handful of men at the door, and pushed through about fifty more people inside. They had all been white. Earlier that day, I had watched people watch sidewalk shows and busking musicians—a man playing a suitcase-turned-guitar outside of Woodlawn Coffee on Yazoo Avenue, another playing a full drum set across the street. The musicians and all the people passing and watching them had all been white. Earlier that week, I had watched as the festival's first arrivals overtook patio chairs and benches along the two main downtown streets, unfolding maps and snapping photos with green excitement. They had all been white. By the end of the weekend, I had mingled in concert crowds and eavesdropped as people reviewed their festival plans over lunch and dinner. I had watched vendors haggling with would-be patrons over everything from harmonica keychains to life-sized prints of B. B. King. With few exceptions, they had all been white.

Black festivalgoers had been rare, their intentions for being at the festival specific, and the duration of their stay almost always short and predetermined. There had been thirty-one-year-old Shaunice [shə- nēs] McGee, calling to her two shirtless sons, Tyreek [tī- rēk] and Tyshaun ['tī-shən], as they ran spryly toward a dunking booth near the Delta Blues Museum stage. "Child, it's just something for them to do," she told me, her tone as relieved as it was dismissive. There had been Big Danny, fifty-six, who joked that the only reason he was out amid the festival crowds was to go on a date with, Ms. Kathereen Ford, fifty-one, also a Clarksdale native. "I told her I was go'n buy her a milkshake," he had said grinning. There had been Pooh Baby, the blues singer with whom I would sit for one of his regular busking sessions the following week, gripping my shoulder while bragging about his upcoming performance at Ground Zero. "I'm the best doing it right now," he laughed before winding through the milling crowd. And there had been the myriad service and civic workers: the stubby bouncer and bright-orange-shirt-wearing bartenders at T-Bone's, the wait and kitchen staff at Ground Zero, the police officers patrolling the streets on and near downtown. What I saw and heard from each of them confirmed what Boyce explained as we rode through the night toward Tunica.

"Black folks will come out every now and then. With us, you got people out working, you probably got family members of somebody that's playing a show. People our age will come out here late night. . . . Basically, it gotta be something for us in it to get us out the house."

The scene at T-Bone's Blues Club matched those at other blues venues in town. Nearly everywhere I went, no matter when I went, I saw predominantly white crowds singing and dancing to old-style blues, with a few Black patrons and Black service workers scattered among them. The crowds that I saw during Juke Joint Weekend were common too, matching what I saw at virtually every other festival on the town's yearly calendar—a Black blues musician playing here, a pair of Black children running there, white festival-goers nearly everywhere else. To me, these demographics seemed curious, questionable even. Clarksdale was a mostly Black town with a mostly Black blues history. Why, then, was it so rare to see local Black folks at local blues scenes? To the local Black folks I talked to, the racial demographics were what one should expect: of course, Clarksdale's blues scenes were mostly white. They were "for the white folks." This chapter traces this shorthand claim to its epistemological source: vigilance, in particular the vigilance with which Black Americans approach the prospect of interracial interactions.

As sociologist Zandria Robinson concluded after talking with hundreds of Black residents of Memphis, Tennessee, Black southerners approach interracial interaction encounters with the expectation that white people (when the encounters involve them) might say or do something racist.[1] That is, Black southerners reason that where one or two white folks are gathered, racism shall (or could) also be in the midst. To Black residents of Clarksdale, then, the all-white crowds and audiences at local blues scenes were a congregation of racist possibilities—awkward glances, offensive comments, unfair or discriminatory treatment—and that reality called for vigilance.

One way that Black folks have enacted racial vigilance is through "Black placemaking,"[2] that is, by creating their own spaces of belonging, sustainment, and comfort, sometimes in the midst of violence and the threat of violence. Black Clarksdalians show another way to be vigilant, a backbeat way: "place-unmaking,"[3] that is, by withdrawing and staying away from a place that may seem threatening.

SEE, KNOW, TELL: RACE AND PLACE-UNMAKING

That Black residents avoided local blues venues and events was not necessarily, or always, about the entertainment value of blues music. That people would come from all over the world to sing and dance the blues in the Mississippi Delta was a point of pride, even celebration. Beyond guitar riffs and drunken two-steps, though, Black Clarksdalians told me that the local blues venues and events were home to another type of song-and-dance—one centered on race. According to them, the town's emphasis on blues tourism benefited white elected officials and business owners at the expense of Black music and musicians. Local blues scenes catered to white audiences with little regard for the tastes and interests of Black residents. Even the boarded storefronts, renovated commercial spaces, and outside performance venues had a racial character. They were white, just like the typical crowds of concert- and festivalgoers.

Lest they be accused of "playing the race card,"[4] Black Clarksdalians almost always supported their claims about Clarksdale's blues scenes with proof, what some younger folks called "receipts." They described what they saw at local blues scenes; they recounted what they knew about Clarksdale's place history; and they insisted on telling what they had experienced when they had gone to a local venue or event.

For some Black residents, identifying the intended audience of Clarksdale's blues scenes only required that one look and see who was in the audience the most. For them, seeing was believing. Thus, only seeing white patrons at the town's slate of blues events translated to believing that those events were "for the white folks." This belief manifested discursively as follows: Black residents would make a definitive declaration about Clarksdale's blues scenes, as in, "that's more of a white folks' thing." Then, almost immediately, they would supplement that declaration with a descriptor, as with "all you see out there is white folks." In some ways, such statements position race as a performative social category, the rationale going something like: whiteness is what white people do, and white spaces are where white people go. Framed in this way, Black Clarksdalians' racialized characterizations of Clarksdale's blues scenes functioned as a type of ethnographic report.

Yet Black Clarksdalians did not rely solely on performative, whiteness-is-as-whiteness-does assessments of race and place to assess the character of Clarksdale's blues scenes. They also took messages from Clarksdale's racial past. Here, seeing—that is, going to or passing by a blues show or festival event—had made folks believe, but history helped make them know.

Black Clarksdalians knew the town's racial history. They had read decades of tea leaves about the specter of race in Clarksdale. They were historians. They were versed in the town's history of neighborhood and school segregation. They knew the town's stories of racial exclusion and violence—confrontations between Black civil rights organizers and white vigilantes, church and house bombings, police harassment, public embarrassment. They had been told about them. They had read about them. They had lived them. Black folks knew, and this knowingness often informed not just how they viewed different places around town but also whether or not they went to them.

Most of the time, Black Clarksdalians were absent from Clarksdale's blues scenes, but not always. Some Black folks had spent time on the blues circuit. They had gone to shows at Ground Zero, T-Bone's, and Moonies. They had visited the Delta Blues Museum. They had gotten coffee or lunch at Woodlawn. They had spent time at the Juke Joint and Sunflower River Blues Festivals. They went for different reasons, sometimes as part of a work-group outing (remember Mac from chapter 1), some for a date (remember Big Danny and Ms. Kathereen), others to celebrate a birthday or personal accomplishment (remember what Mrs. Irene said about her cousin's 70th birthday party in the introduction). No matter why they went or how long they stayed, though, most Black Clarksdalians had a story to tell. They went to this blues venue, and somebody had said something that made them feel threatened. They went to that bar beside this other blues club, and somebody had done something that made them feel uncomfortable. They went to this one blues festival this one time, and somebody had looked at them in a way that made them feel out of place. The Black folks I spoke with almost always attributed the saying, doing, looking, as well as the feelings that it all engendered, to the racial demographics of the crowds or the racial character of the places. And they told me that's why they didn't go much or at all.

"That's about All You See over There Now": Whiteness Is Where White Folks Are

"Me, myself, I'm not a big blues person," said Cookie Echols, a forty-six-year-old native resident. Like several Black Clarksdalians, Cookie had agreed to sit and talk with me with the stipulation that we do it at her house and only after she cooked "a little something" for me to eat. I obliged. "I'm just not," she continued. "I won't say I never listened to it, but I don't listen much now." Her voice was muzzled by the *flush* of running water, as she lifted and rubbed two fistfuls of uncooked chicken over a bowl in her sink.

"So, have you ever been to one of the festivals?" I asked, part of me already knowing the answer.

"You know, I don't think I have. I'll pass by out there sometimes. . . . To be honest, sometimes I'll forget they [blues festivals] going on, but I'll be out on a Saturday morning, on my way to the store or somewhere, and I'll see all the cars lined all up and down the street. Then you remember that it's something going on . . . but I don't keep up with it. I go to work. I look after my two grandbabies. . . . I just mind my own, you know."

On cue, two adolescent girls burst through a side door, announcing themselves with a flourish of footsteps and laughter. Without turning or looking up from the sink, Cookie instructed them to introduce themselves and then go get started on their homework, promising that they could watch TV when they finished. When the girls were out of view, Cookie explained that their father, her son, was incarcerated at the Mississippi State Penitentiary, and that they were living with her until their mother could "get back on her feet."

I spent more than three hours over Cookie's house that day, watching as she made her kitchen into a symphony of *pops*, *sizzles*, *clangs*, and soul food. Much of our conversation centered on her family. She regretted that her son had gotten "caught up with the wrong crowd" and hoped that "the Lord would shake him to his senses." She bragged about her granddaughters' grades, even calling both of them from the back room so that they could announce how they had done on a recent progress report. Talk of the blues was brief, as was her interest in the town's blues scenes. While her home sat neatly on a street corner just a few miles from the downtown square, she could only talk vaguely about local blues festivals and venues there—with one exception.

"I can remember going to Red's," she said. Red's Lounge was Clarksdale's oldest continually operating blues institution and the town's last-remaining "original" juke joint. "That was when I was younger. We would go out there, me and some of my friends would go out there, but not now. The clubs is something I just don't do now. For one, I'm good and old," she chuckled to herself. "And it's different over there now."

"What's different?" I asked.

"Back then, Red's was where you went to show off. You would get dressed up—your dress, your heels, some jewe'ry [jewelry]. You would show off. If you wanted to dance, you could dance. If you just wanted to sit back, you could do that. . . . Now it's a different thing. It's more of a white thing. That's 'bout all you see over there now. . . . It's the same with the festivals. Anytime I have ever passed by out there, that's all I see. White folks. And you know the businesses are owned by whites. . . . And where do you think that leaves us?"

Cookie's comments seemed straightforward enough. She was ambivalent toward blues music and, thus, not all that interested in Clarksdale's slate of local shows and festivals. Yet the more she talked, the more she revealed race to be a factor in how she thought about the town's blues scenes. For her, venues like T-Bone's and events like the Juke Joint Festival were more than down-home places for singers, musicians, and fans to meet and celebrate the blues. They also carried racial meaning. "They were white," a designation that, I would learn, was intended as much for the demographics of the singers, musicians, and fans themselves as it was for the spaces and structures where they sang, played, and tried to dance.

Later, I asked Cookie to describe where people lived in Clarksdale. She again read race onto various places in town. "I live in the Brickyard . . . which is Black. Then, you got the Roundyard, which is Black. Pretty much, Clarksdale is all Black except out there, we call it Snob Hill . . . and out downtown. That whole area [downtown] is white. The businesses are white-owned . . . Sometimes I think they would paint the streets white if they could."

Cookie's comments echo those from many other Black Clarksdalians I spoke with. To start, folks often said they did not like the type of blues music that was most often featured at the shows and festivals in Clarksdale. The music was boring and repetitive. The performers were "stale" and "not good." Older residents preferred more contemporary blues subgenres like southern soul or, more often, gospel, soul, and rhythm and blues. They named names like Luther (Vandross), Marvin Gaye, Patti Labelle, Sir Charles Jones, the Williams Brothers, and the Brown Singers. Younger residents gravitated toward popular rappers—Drake, Nicki Minaj, Moneybagg Yo, 2 Chainz.

Still, as much as folks maintained that they did not like the blues, they did not typically explain their lack of interest in Clarksdale's blues scenes as a matter of music or entertainment. Rather, like Cookie, Black Clarksdalians referenced the atmosphere and character of the club and festival venues. In some cases, these references came alongside short, but telling, observations. According to Mrs. Regina Gladney, a forty-two-year-old native resident, "White people do a different kind of blues than we [Black residents] used to. . . . I don't like that." According to Thom [tōm] Henry, forty-four, "White blues and Black blues is different. We don't want that that they got going on out there [on the square]." Where such depictions evaded them, Black Clarksdalians resorted to shorter, simpler ones—"That's for the white folks."

Not going to Clarksdale's blues scenes was a decision that came easy for Black residents. It was something that they were sure of, and that assuredness came across not just in what they said but also in how they said it. Cookie had described the white crowds at the unnamed blues festival that she had passed on the way to an unnamed store on an unspecified Saturday morning as calmly and matter-of-factly as if she had been explaining what day of the week it was. She did not raise her voice when describing the white club scenes either. She was unbothered, content to simply keep seasoning her chicken. For her, avoiding the local show and festivals was not cause for special attention. It was not exceptional. It was her way of "minding [her] own [business]"— that is, opting out of a thing that seemed to be for somebody else anyway.

I heard and observed sentiments like Cookie's from other Black residents. Kizzy Isby, a thirty-one-year-old native resident, explained, "We [Black residents] not really big with the blues stuff, we got our own thing," before working her way through a short list of establishments patronized by Black residents. She then quickly revised her assessment. "Well, really, to be honest, it ain't nothing for us [Black residents] around here, unless you want to ride to Memphis. . . . Really, we have to make something to get into ourself." Gary Wilson, a twenty-nine-year-old native resident, echoed Kizzy. "We [Black residents] make our own fun. . . . We don't go out there [the downtown square], we just don't. . . . And, with how it is here, you better off just minding yo' business, keeping to yourself."

"We Knew They Didn't Want Us over There": Racial Intuition

"We knew they didn't want us over there," Janice "Auntie" Green, fifty-nine, remembered about being confronted with the reality of racial segregation when her family moved to Clarksdale from a neighboring town in 1968. Auntie was thirteen years old when they moved, but her memories of that time were bright and clear in her mind. She remembered fights with her older sister and brothers down to what they were wearing and where the fights started. She remembered her momma's cooking and her daddy's cursing, how the family knew Saturday was for the blues. She remembered, and scoffed at, having to lock the doors at night and put bed sheets over the windows for privacy—measures that the family hadn't had to take when they, as Auntie put it, "lived out in the country." And just as much as Auntie remembered, Auntie knew. "We knew when we came in . . . downtown, Oakhurst, wasn't nowhere over there for us . . . and that was something you just knew."

I had been sitting with Auntie for much of a summer afternoon, time enough for her to explain the intricacies of picking cotton and "trumping trailers" (i.e., as explained by Auntie, "when you put your cotton in the trailer, and you get up there, and you step on it"), time enough for her niece Teryeia to stroll through the door without knocking and get fussed at and dismissed with a laugh, time enough for Auntie to finish approximately one and a half cans of Coca-Cola. As we talked, Auntie situated the downtown square as a particularly important racial landmark in town. "The Blacks wasn't touching nowhere on that square, hear! Nowhere. . . . It was just that bad."

Spanning roughly eight square blocks (~0.11 square miles) just east of the Sunflower River, Clarksdale's downtown square was, for a time, the epicenter of local commercial life. As was the case with many small- and medium-sized southern towns in the early and mid-twentieth century, the square offered patrons a range of civic services, entertainment options, and commercial and retail spaces—everything from the city hall and county jail to an assortment of movie theaters, doctor's offices, hotels, and department stores.

As Auntie suggested, the downtown square also served a social function, to help mark Clarksdale's color line. Together with the tracks of the Illinois Central Railroad, which ran east and west splitting the town's land area in half, the square was a landmark demarcating public life for Black and white residents. Prior to the mid-1970s, white residents lived in a few neighborhood enclaves north of the downtown square and railroad tracks and had direct access to downtown businesses and civic institutions. Black residents lived south of the square and did not.[5]

"Downtown was white, and all over there through Oakhurst was white," Auntie rested back into the thin sheath of plastic covering her lily-white sofa. "When I tell you, they didn't even allow black cars on the streets over there [downtown]!" I laughed. She smiled and continued. "[They] didn't wan'a even see no black cat on the ground. They was just that prejudiced."

I asked where she went back then, where did Black folks go to shop, to meet friends, to do some of the things that their white neighbors were able to do on the square. She answered by referencing a small assortment of stores, night clubs, churches, and Black-owned businesses just south of the downtown square and railroad tracks, what she called the "Black Area." Auntie was talking about the "New World"—an area that some Black residents call "Black Downtown."

"We just did our own stuff," Auntie explained. "It was like, we was in our own little world. Just our own stuff." She paused and, as if to offer the most shining example of Black residents' self-determination, shifted the conversation to her own family. "My family lived—I wouldn't say a rough life—but we was in poverty, but we lived comfortable. Daddy made sho [sure] we was satisfied, you know. We had gardens and hogs—we ain't have no cows— chickens, and things like that. So, we really wasn't bothered 'bout going to the white man for nothing." Auntie seemed to take pride in her family's ca- pacity to survive and find happiness, to "make do" as she phrased it, even in a place where opportunity and mobility seemed limited to the other side of the tracks.

When Black residents did stray from the racial codes of the day, whether by attempting to rent or buy a home in the wrong neighborhood or being seen north of the tracks—on the downtown square or in the white Oakhurst neighborhood—after a given time, they risked backlash from the local white establishment. In some cases, the backlash came at the hands of elected officials and stakeholders. Local banks and lending institutions would deny a Black family credit or insurance. White planters would refuse to gin the cotton of a Black sharecropper. Local police would harass and arrest anyone proven, or even just rumored, to have broken the code.[6]

The late Frank Ratcliff, longtime owner and proprietor of the historic Riverside Hotel on Sunflower Avenue, remembered the local curfew. "[Black residents of Clarksdale] had a twelve o'clock curfew during that time [the 1940s and 1950s]. This town here, at twelve o'clock, baby you had to be off the streets. If you didn't have a job, you'd go to jail . . . if you were Black. That's how strict it was."[7]

Ratcliff's recollection of the local curfew came up often, both in interview accounts from civil rights workers in the 1960s and from Black residents I spoke to directly. Banner Sandiford, the thirty-one-year-old son of Mrs. Irene, relayed a story about his late father (Mrs. Irene's husband]. "You [would] go to jail for being over there in [the white neighborhood]! My daddy got locked up for walking across the bridge—the First Street Bridge right damn over there—to Oakhurst because no Blacks was allowed over there after a certain hour. [They] made a law called the 'dog law.' No niggas [were] to be seen after twelve midnight over there. Period."

In a separate interview, Mrs. Irene confirmed what her son had said. "I remember [my husband] said they come and got him in the morning. . . . [He] said it was two [police officers] that came banging on the door. They gave him some crazy reason for taking him, but it had got out that he had been over in Oakhurst. That's what was going around anyway." In our interview, Mrs. Irene also shared a story that showed how the enforcement of Clarksdale's racial code often extended beyond the reach of local stakeholders and elected officials, falling at the feet of white vigilantes. Mrs. Irene had started spending time in Clarksdale in 1963, when she started working as a secretary at her uncle's funeral home—Sandiford & Sons Memorial.

Mrs. Irene's arrival in Clarksdale had come at the height of an ongoing movement to desegregate the town. "It was a time to be alive and in Clarksdale. My, my, my! I had never seen anything like that time," Mrs. Irene remembered. That summer, Clarksdale became a landing site for dozens of civil rights volunteers, including workers for Mississippi's Freedom Summer campaign. "There was a house across the street from the funeral home," Mrs. Irene went on to explain. "It was a Freedom House. I can remember some civil rights workers who came. They were staying in that house. The Freedom Riders, that's what they were called. . . . I was over at the funeral home, and my uncle runs in, I can remember him running in and pulling me across to that house. He yelled to us to 'get on the floor, get on the floor!' He pushed us to the back and told us to sit down. And we were all hunched over, didn't know what was going on. All you could hear outside was cars and yelling and [gunshots]. . . . My uncle never told me what happened, but you always heard that he had gotten into it with some whites because he had sat in at the lunch counter downtown."

Black businesses were not exempt from harassment and intimidation. On May 5, 1963, there was an explosion at the Fourth Street Drug Store, owned and operated by Aaron Henry, who had helped found the Regional Council of Negro Leadership and served as president of the Mississippi branch of the National Association for the Advancement of Colored People (NAACP) in 1959. Henry and several others were having dinner in the back of the store when a bomb exploded near the main entrance. In his autobiography, *The Fire Ever Burning*, Henry recounted the events from the Saturday evening in July. "We saw a blue flash and felt a concussion that I thought would bring the store down on our heads."[8] While Henry's store was technically located in the New World district, its proximity to the downtown square—it was located just two blocks from Main Street—made it an easy target for white locals wanting to send a message about the town's racial boundaries.

In addition to Henry's drugstore, there was the beauty shop of Vera Pigee, former branch secretary of the local chapter of the NAACP and advisor to the state's Youth Council. Pigee was as important a figure in the local movement and as vocal a critic of the white establishment as Henry. She used her shop to host movement meetings and often left the shop doors unlocked in case Black residents or movement organizers needed shelter.[9] Yet Pigee's shop was never attacked. Historian Françoise Hamlin cites the location of the shop—on Ashton Avenue in the heart of the Black business district—as one reason why. Being surrounded by other Black businesses and the watchful eyes and arms of other Black residents served as a powerful deterrent. Pigee was once asked whether she was concerned that white vigilantes would someday target her shop. Her response was quiet, like her temperament, but sure. "They [white agitators] knew better than to come down here!"

Having come of age in Jim Crow Clarksdale, Pigee knew where the town's racial lines fell. For the Black folks I spoke with, most born at least thirty years after Pigee, time had not done much to fade or move those lines. In the 1970s and 1980s, a development crisis and the growth of big-box retail along State Street on the southern edge of town left the square commercially devastated, a string of boarded storefronts and empty buildings. Beginning in the 1980s, spurred by a statewide heritage tourism campaign, a small group of blues enthusiasts, investors, and elected officials began to buy the unused properties as part of a "revitalization" campaign centered on the blues. By the 1990s, Clarksdale had become a full-fledged blues tourism place, and the downtown square was ground zero, replete with blues-related lodging options, historical markers, museums, specialty shops, and an assortment of blues clubs.

Where some elected officials and opportunistic entrepreneurs saw the blues, local Black folks continued to see white. They maintained that the square was the sum of its racial history, that the color line that had been etched onto its sidewalks by custom and violence in the past were still there for all to see in the present. Given this, Black Clarksdalians said, they had little interest in visiting the town's blues scenes.

"This is what I know," said Ruberta [roo-burt-a] "Rube" Ivy, a sixty-one-year-old Clarksdale native. After several failed attempts to meet in person, we had both agreed that a phone conversation would "do just as good." We didn't talk for that long, but it was long enough for her to make her point. "This is what I know." It was her trusted, do-it-all refrain, suitable for beginning a new thought, emphasizing an old one, or addressing any apparent or potential challenges to what she said.

Mrs. Rube was insistent. She insisted that the prevalence of blues venues and events on the square was merely a crafty sleight of hand, a way to "fool" residents into forgetting about the town's history of segregation and racial violence. She also insisted that she knew better than to fall for the trick. "This town is funny . . . They want you to look out there [downtown] and see all the blues—the restaurants, the clubs, Ground Zero, this and that, and you supposed to go and give them your money. I remember when it was a Woolworth [department store] . . . where Woodlawn is now. Me and my sister would beg my momma to take us out there, and she wouldn't. Never would take us out there. . . . See, when I was young I didn't know. When I got older, though, I started to see it, the racism in this town. . . . It's right there for you to see."

"You Telling Him about That Night?" A Bought (Racial) Lesson Is the Best Kind

I was walking with Terrence "Thickie" Partlow, thirty-two, and Dashawn [də-SHən] "Deuce" Ivy (cousin of Mrs. Rube), also thirty-two, across the dusty gravel of a park near the northern edge of town. We had just finished a series of pickup basketball games and were discussing plans for the night. Thickie pulled a bottle of Gatorade from a small duffle bag and offered me a drink. Deuce cracked open a can of beer—and offered me a drink.

"So, that's really what you 'bout to do." Thickie said to Deuce, pretending to be fed up. Before responding, Deuce took a long drink.

"You know me, I get started early. . . . This ain't shit, just a beer." He said with a swaggering confidence, before taking a second drink and swiping through his phone.

"I ain't talking about you drinking," Thickie joked. "I'm talkin' 'bout you drinking some damn Budweiser." I had met Thickie through a mutual acquaintance and Deuce by way of Thickie. We had all met that day at the park at Deuce's invitation. During the games, we laughed and cursed and complained about bad foul calls. In between games and after, our conversations settled on Clarksdale, what it was like for them to grow up there, and how things had changed in the years since. Before parting ways, I suggested that we meet for drinks at the Brickhouse, a bar on the square, later that evening. Thickie quickly and casually declined. "We can drink, but I ain't try'n'a go out there."

Thickie went on to tell the story of a previous outing in which he, Deuce, and a few of their friends had gotten into a heated exchange with a patron outside of the bar. According to Thickie, the group had decided, against their better judgment, to go to the bar for drinks. "One time, we said we go'n' go out and watch the game. Usually, we go to the Mexican restaurant . . . but this one time, we said we go'n' go drink with the white folks, we go'n' get white-boy wasted, so we go to Brickhouse. Something we don't never do, but tonight we say fuck it, we go'n' go, right." Thickie explained that they had passed another group of patrons as they neared the main entrance. "White folks, you already know," he said reflexively. "The next thing, I hear, they go'n' say some, 'Y'all play nice tonight,' or some bullshit like that."

Deuce, who had been walking a step behind Thickie and me, took a break from his phone conversation to interject. "You telling him about that night at [the bar] we was 'bout to scrap them white boys."

Thickie continued, "I think [the white guy] said he was go'n make a joke. He with a female, of course he go'n try to be funny, okay," Thickie continued. "But that's something you don't just up and say to somebody you don't know. They know how it is around here . . . We didn't even go in. I swear to God. We stopped right there and had some words with them or whatever . . . we had words, [we] said what we said, then we left."

"All of us said the same thing," Deuce said. "Shouldn't've even went out there in the beginning."

"This town racist," Thickie said. "If you Black, and you live in this town, you best off keeping to yourself."

"Y'all been out there since then?" I asked.

"I won't even drive by that place. . . . It's like this, you go out there, and you pretty much know they already don't want you there. They already wan'a say something. Off top. You go, you say you go'n give it a chance, then they come with some bullshit."

When Thickie, Deuce, and their group of friends were deciding where to go watch the game, they were doing so with a particular racial map of Clarksdale in mind. In their view, the town was racist, which meant that they had to be thoughtful and selective about where they went and when. There were certain places that would be amenable to them, where they could meet, eat, drink, and laugh together without worry. There were other places that they knew to avoid, where "some bullshit" was bound to happen. The unnamed Mexican restaurant was the former. They had been there before, and they retreated there after the incident. The Brickhouse was the latter. It was a white space—for Thickie, Deuce, and their friends, a place where white people seemed to always already be, and where a particular type of whiteness seemed to always already be happening.

That the patrons that Thickie and the group passed outside of the Brickhouse were white was a truth so self-evident that Thickie insisted that I should "already know." Going to drink at the Brickhouse was, by definition, "going to drink with the white folks," which itself connoted a particular set of behaviors and expectations (getting "white-boy wasted"). Again, for Thickie and the group, as it had been for Cookie, Auntie, and other Black residents, whiteness was what white people did, and white places were where white people went.

Yet casting the Brickhouse as a white space was not just about seeing and describing. It was also about knowing and telling, which is to say it was about epistemology. Thickie and his people knew that by going to the Brickhouse, they would be viewed in a particular way and, therefore, would likely also be subject to a particular type of treatment. When they outlined this set of expectations, they were not speculating. They were not supposing. They were knowing. When this knowledge was proved true, Thickie and his friends responded in two ways. They addressed the other group of patrons directly. They "had words." Then they withdrew from the place altogether, deciding to go where they knew they could enjoy themselves bullshit-free.

Further, for both Thickie and Deuce, the experience at the Brickhouse was about more than the Brickhouse. It was not an isolated incident. It was not an anomaly. Rather, it was part and product of a broader racial reality about Clarksdale. "This town racist," Thickie had pronounced matter-of-factly. For him, that meant that there were some places that Black people could go and be free from discomfort, and there were other places like the Brickhouse, places Black people should not even venture to drive past.

Other Black Clarksdalians who spent time at some of Clarksdale's blues scenes told the same story that Thickie and Deuce had told. Different characters but the same plot: go to a venue or event that is typically, primarily patronized by white people. Be skeptical of said decision in the process. Have experience that confirms skepticism. Profess to have known said experience would likely happen, citing initial skepticism as proof of said knowledge. Count confirmation of initial skepticism as additional evidence that the venue or event is, in some configuration or another, intended and reserved for white people. Finally, resolve to avoid said white place for the foreseeable future. Sometimes this logic emerged, as with Thickie and Deuce, from experiences at places that were only tangentially related to the blues. The Brickhouse is located near the downtown district known as the Blues Alley and opened in the same period when the downtown square was being made into a blues place. It was a blues place by association. Other times, as with forty-three-year-old native resident Travis "Big Lap" McGowan, Black Clarksdalians' racial discomfort emerged more directly in Clarksdale's blues places.

"I'm a big talker," Big Lap had said, offering a light-hearted warning to start our winding conversation about race and politics in Clarksdale. "I want you to get all this now." He went on, nodding and gesturing toward my voice recorder. "You can get all this now." We had met in his office, a nondescript building south of the downtown square. The first order of business was to rehash a few things that we had already covered in a conversation a few weeks earlier. I told him I was from a small town in Mississippi. He reminded me that he was a "country boy to the bone." I told him I was writing a book about Clarksdale. He assured me that he could tell me "any- and everything" that

I wanted to know. I told him some of the places where I had been spending my time since we last talked. He fussed at me.

"You can't write no book without the real story," he said, with only a slight allowance for my nervous laughter.

Playing to his humor, I asked. "Tell me the real story, Lap. What's the real story?"

"This place is as racist as the devil. My hometown! I'm telling you. I'm telling you. This is a town where it's white folks . . . who got all the power . . . and not just the mayor. It's everybody up under the mayor too." He named names and offered examples, eventually setting his focus on the downtown square. "Who you think own them businesses out there [on the downtown square]? And, why you think it ain't nothing for us [Black residents] to do. Nothing to do. . . . Let's say I have some people here, and they ask, 'Where y'all going? We go'n' follow y'all.' Ain't nowhere to go! Nowhere to go."

"You mean if you want something to do on the weekend or something like that?" I asked.

"Just period. I say it all the time. I say it like this. Black folks got nowhere to go. . . . You gotta make everybody feel comfortable. Give me a nice-looking bartender, you know. Give me some good music. Give me a good jazz place! Invite some of the Black artists down from Memphis. Not that what they play out there now. Treat everybody right, not catering to this certain group or this certain clique or this certain type of person." When I asked Big Lap who he felt like local venues catered to, he responded by telling a story. "I can give you a couple [of] experiences. I had a lady come down here—a friend—and we was at Moonie's. [It was] me, her, my wife, and some mo' folks, and we was go'n' try to patronize Moonie's. But, the waitress [a white woman]," he paused midsentence. "I have to say this. I tip. I tip well. But [the waitress] act like she," he paused again. "I just need the same respect as an individual in there as the whites get. My wife . . . kept telling me, 'We ain't going back in there no mo.'"

"So, what happened?" I asked. "Was it bad, was it poor treatment?"

"We got poor treatment, nasty talking, just rude, you know, but what made it good for us is that we can laugh and talk and interact well with [anybody], no matter what crowd we in. Even that crowd," he said, laughing. "We laugh and talk and carry on, so a lot of good people come over, but as a whole, just bad, bad treatment. As a whole, just bad."

In a later conversation with Big Lap, the experience at Moonie's came up again. "Do you remember what happened?" I asked. "I remember you said

That's for the White Folks

that you felt like y'all were treated differently, but do you remember, like, what happened?"

"I'll tell you. I'll tell you what happened. We got there early to eat. We were going to eat and just sit around and talk, probably have a drink, do all that. We get there early, and the first thing you see is that some of them folks be there looking at you, cuttin' they eyes at you like you not supposed to be there. Me, I'm used to it. . . . But, you got my friend in there, might don't know how to take that. . . . Then, the waitress, it seem like she didn't want us to be there either. You know the way the place is set up, you don't have somebody just coming to your table all the time. . . . You call if you need something extra. You know. She came to our table one time," Big Lap hit the table softly. "I counted one time."

"When was this, have you been back since?" I asked.

"This gotta be two, three years ago. I can't tell you how many times I been back. I don't think we been back since."

Big Lap had warned me right. He was a talker. We—and, all told, mostly he—talked for two hours in his office that day, and still longer in more than a dozen subsequent conversations in the weeks and months that followed. Topics related to race were his wheelhouse. Like Thickie, Big Lap did not just claim or believe that Clarksdale was racist. He "knew" it was. "When you come in this Delta, this a different type of place," he had explained another time that we talked. "Whoooowhee, it's a different place. Like going back in time. We got a patent on that. Going back in time . . . back to the plantation time," he added with a laugh. "That's how racist it is."

Sometimes Big Lap resorted to creative exercises to make his point. At a local community meeting he asked a group of residents, "On a scale from one to ten, how racist do you think Clarksdale is?" After surveying the room, he offered his own answer, dramatically raising each of his fingers to the count of "one, two, three," and so on. When he reached "ten," with all of his fingers raised, he leaned back in his chair and started raising and lowering both of his feet, as if to suggest that he needed to use his fingers and toes to reach the appropriate number. Everybody laughed.

Humor helped Big Lap make sense of what, to him, was a discouraging reality about race in Clarksdale—that Black residents had "no place to go." He said that often, often pointing to Clarksdale's blues scenes as the most telling example. To him, the town's blues venues were not Black places. The food wasn't right. The music wasn't right. And the people didn't "treat everybody right." This latter claim was, in part, a critique of local community politics and cliquishness, a dynamic that he summed up succinctly with the following: "Here it's like this. Sally don't like Sue because Peter friends with Paul. It don't add up."

Big Lap's "treat everybody right" was not merely an indictment of community tribalism, though. Rather, at its root, it was a racial call to order. Big Lap could have responded to my follow-up question about who received preferential treatment in a number of ways. He opted to tell a story, one with a familiar tone and tenor as other people's stories, and with the same culprit working behind the scenes. Big Lap had "decided to patronize" a local blues venue with his wife and a group of friends. Where some folks, like Thickie and Deuce, remembered tense and uncomfortable encounters with fellow patrons of local blues venues, Big Lap's "bad, bad treatment" came from the blues venue itself, a club waitress. Beyond the direct affront by the waitress, the club had also engendered a sense of discomfort among some members of Big Lap's party, in particular his unnamed "friend" from out of town. Being uncomfortable, often accompanied by some reference to the feeling of being watched—people "cuttin' their eyes," as Big Lap noted—was a common feeling among Black Clarksdalians who had spent time at the town's blues scenes.

I met Pacious [pā-SHəs] "Bugg" Rogers, thirty-one, at a fast-food chain restaurant for a short conversation, our second in as many weeks. She had agreed to meet briefly, before the start of her afternoon shift. Bugg had grown up in Clarksdale with her mother and four older sisters. She talked about the town with both pride and disdain.

"This my city. Yeah, you get tired of it. The gangs and the senseless killings, but . . . it's like when you got a family member that do something stupid, you know. . . . Like, we can talk about Uncle Ray, but you can't talk about Uncle Ray," she laughed. "It's like that." The restaurant was empty, save for the occasional fit of laughter from behind the counter. A person at the register called for somebody named "Chill Will" to come look at a video on his phone. Chill Will came speed-walking from the back of the kitchen, snickering. A Black woman that they called "Tee-Dy" came slow-walking right behind him, holding something in her hands and the look of "Y'all got one mo' time" on her face.

Bugg and I sat and talked. I asked her what she liked to do in her free time, if she had ever been out in Clarksdale.

"Have you been out?" She returned the question to me with a sarcastic laugh. "For one, if you go out to the places Black people go to, they go'n get to shooting, or somebody go'n get to fighting. I ain't got time for that kind of drama. I got two kids. I got two kids to raise," she said, her face kind of

That's for the White Folks

like Tee-Dy's. When I asked if she could talk more about the "places Black people go to," our conversation shifted to a familiar back-and-forth, the same plot from Thickie's, Big Lap's, and other folks' stories. First, like other Black residents I spoke with, Bugg outlined a short list of establishments that Black residents regularly went to, none of which had any overt relationship with the blues. Neither "blues" nor "juke joint" were a part of the establishments' names, and none of the venues were located on the downtown square. Then, when I asked if she could name any other places that Black residents went or activities that Black residents liked to do, she concluded that her "best bet" was to "just ride to Memphis . . . or ride to the casinos [in Tunica County]."

"Have you ever been to any of the blues stuff here," I asked, as I often did, when it became clear that Bugg did not consider Clarksdale's blues offerings to be places "where the Black people go."

"I have been to that club, Moonies. One time. And I'll never go again, never go again."

Laughing, I followed up. "Why is that?"

"It's just, it ain't for me. . . . For one, you feel out of place. You just feel out of place. I ain't prejudiced or nothing like that, but just having to be around all them white folk. . . . They be looking all upside yo' head. Take me, I like to wear color in my hair. I like to wear colors, like reds, blues, purples," she grabbed and flung her thick ponytail, styled with purple highlights, over her shoulder. "You would've thought I had a sign on my head that said, 'Look at me, look at me, look at me.' I ain't like that."

"Did anybody say something to you?" I asked.

"Pshh. Now you know they wasn't go'n do that."

"You just noticed them looking."

"You know how you can just feel people looking at you. It's was more that . . . and you just feel out of place. Then, the music. I like the blues, but sometimes you want them to mix it up, to play something more up to date." We shared an exchange about the types of music she preferred to listen to—Moneybagg Yo and Drake—then, again, I returned the conversation to Clarksdale's blues scenes.

"And, the festivals. Like Juke Joint Festival . . . do you go to any of that?"

"Now, I will go out to that," she said, the pitch of her voice high like she had just learned something new about herself. "I'll take my kids out there anyway. They like to eat them funnel cakes. They like to get wet. They like all that, so I'll let them do that."

Bugg did not see Clarksdale's blues scenes as places for Black residents to go. A part of that conclusion seemed to be rooted in the same logic of racial performativity that Cookie, Boyce, and so many other Black Clarksdalians had used to explain the all-white crowds at local shows and festivals. Clarksdale's blues scenes were not places where Black people went *because* they were for the white folks. Her rationale was also informed by personal experience. She had been to, by most accounts, the most popular blues club in town and had left unimpressed, and not just unimpressed but also uncomfortable. Her discomfort was rooted in both the striking racial imbalance among the club patrons—"all them white folk"—and in the way those patrons interacted with her. "They be looking all upside yo' head." Bugg felt like a spectacle, and, in her view, it did not help that she had a sense of style that many of the white patrons at Moonies were unfamiliar with. Based on that experience, she had reached a familiar conclusion. "I'll never go again."

Bugg felt out of place at Moonies when she went. Big Lap, Thickie, and Deuce remembered being treated as if they were out of place when they went to the Brickhouse. Auntie, Rube, and Cookie claimed to know that, if they had taken the time to go to the downtown square or a local blues show, they would be out of place too. Their perspectives played different parts of the same tune: Black residents of Clarksdale saw the town's blues places as white places. On the one hand, this meant that the clubs and performance venues were, in one configuration or another, owned, patronized by, and intended to cater to white people. On the other, it meant that these spaces had historically been off-limits to Black people, or contemporarily were the possible site of unfair treatment.

CHURCH

"Come and go to that land! Come and go to that land!" It was the night after the Juke Joint show at T-Bone's Blues Club, and I was at Boyce's momma's church, sweating and clapping as the choir and congregation sang in unison. "Come and go to that land where I'm bound!" Boyce had asked me to come with him to the closing night of spring revival services for the week. "Don't you wan'a go to that land!" I was glad that I had come.

"I was glad when they said unto me, let us go into the house of the Lord" the pastor recited a scripture from memory, then compelled folks to clap and sing. "Come and go to that land!" Folks clapped and sang. "I wan'a go to that land."

The song was as spirited as it is prophetic: Black Americans have always been coming and going, "searching for places to be free, safe, and Black [Promised Lands] since Europe's enslavement and colonization of Africa."[10]

Coming and going—or moving and resettling—are integral ingredients in the Black American story. After the Civil War, Black "Exodusters"[11] moved from the South and settled for Kansas. Through the first half of the twentieth century, Black southerners moved from rural towns like Clarksdale and settled in cities like Chicago, Louisville, and New York. Since the 1970s, Black Americans have been moving and resettling back in the South. Black folks have always been coming and going, placemaking.

Black people make Black places as both a way toward their own self-sustainment and a stay against the racism that they expect to encounter en route. Clarksdale native Vera Pigee made her beauty shop into a place where Black folks could meet, eat, sleep, hide, and organize during the height of the local Black Freedom Struggle in the 1950s. Black Clarksdalians today make their front porches into backrooms, hidden in plain sight, where friends and family share laughter and secrets. These placemaking practices have become recurring subjects of scholarly and popular discourse, and rightfully so. Poverty, "urban renewal," and gentrification have proved themselves to be enduring features of American life, hampering and threatening to disappear Black spaces, from Inglewood to Cabrini-Green to Harlem. Yet where racism and the possibility of displacement loom, Black folks linger, "shapeshift,"[12] and resettle. Boyce, Cookie, Auntie, Thickie, Bugg, and other Black residents of Clarksdale show that while a part of that shifting and settling is about moving into new places, another part is about withdrawing or staying away from old and misused ones.

This chapter began in the dingy shadows of a show at T-Bone's Blues Club during the Juke Joint Blues Festival, Clarksdale's most popular blues event. The club featured chicken wings, amateur and professional blues singers, and an all-white crowd of patrons. Most of the weekend's festivalgoers were white too. In fact, with only a few exceptions, the only Black people I saw the whole weekend were some of the musicians playing shows and virtually all of the service workers at local venues. The more blues events that I attended, the more apparent it became that these racial demographics were the rule and not the exception. En masse, Black residents had decided to stay away from the town's blues scenes. Such was the case with the Black Clarksdalians I spoke with. Most of them explained that they had no interest in attending local blues venues and events. Many of them claimed to have never been to a blues event at all.

When I asked Black residents to explain their decisions to not be at Clarkdale's blues scenes, they said different things that summed to the same conclusion: Clarksdale's blues scenes were for the white folks. The music catered to white audiences. White people owned the venues. Many Black residents even saw the buildings and performances spaces, themselves, as white, places that they could not go without encountering some level of racial discomfort or unfair treatment.

For the Black Clarksdalians I spoke with, that local blues venues and events were "for the white folks" was a truth that had been verified to them in three general ways, over and over and over again. First, white folks were who Black residents typically saw at the town's blues clubs, festivals, and other events. Second, Black Clarksdalians referenced Clarksdale's historical record. In their view, the town was and had always been racist, and the businesses on the square were the spatial embodiment of that racism. Finally, Black Clarksdalians called on the wisdom of experience. They had not just seen or heard about the racial dynamics at local blues scenes. They had experienced them for themselves.

When Black Clarksdalians designated the town's blues scenes as white spaces, they were doing more than describing what they had seen, heard, or experienced at local venues and events. They were also engaging in a type of (blues) epistemology work—that is, managing their beliefs about the lived experience of race in their daily lives. Staying away from local blues scenes allowed Black residents to call out the past and enduring impact of racism in community life, while denying, or at least guarding against, the present and future prospect of racial hurt, harm, and danger in their own.

Coming and going remains elemental to Black American life. Moving is a survival mechanism, allowing Black folks to escape enslavement, Jim Crow, and gentrifying cityscapes that have been made too expensive. Moving is a manner of critique, a way to voice displeasure with the status quo. Moving is all of these things and more. So is moving on the backbeat—or, "place-unmaking." Boycotting and withdrawing from certain types of public spaces and civic services have long been ways for Black folks to challenge unequal living conditions. Black residents of Clarksdale continue in that tradition—staying away as epistemological praxis—challenging the racial status quo while minding and celebrating their own (selfhood) in the process.

4 YOU JUST GET TIRED OF IT

Like usual, I stopped by The Stoe, a service station near Clarksdale's downtown square, just before noon. When I entered, I found The Stoe manager, fifty-two-year-old Dahleen Atkinson-Knowles, behind the front counter doing many things at once. That was usual too. She passed a receipt to one customer while watching two others stumble and laugh from the back of the store to the front counter. I stood to the side, biding time.

"You come in here every day and get the same thing," Dahleen said after the store had emptied and I had stepped to the counter with my usual, a handful of cinnamon candy and cinnamon gum. I laughed because I knew she was joking. She was joking because she knew my routine: stop by The Stoe around noon to buy candy, ask a few questions about Clarksdale before I paid. "What you got for me today?" she asked.

"What you think about what they got planned for that spot on Third Street?" I had heard about the possibility of a new construction project on the downtown square. I could not remember all of the details, just that so-and-so was interested in building such-and-such new business development in place of a gutted storefront near the river.

"Ain't got nothing to do with me," she said, before rolling her eyes.

"Why you say it like that?" I said with a laugh. Then, before she could answer, I asked what she thought they would build; then, before she could answer, I asked how she felt about the assortment of new businesses and entertainment venues that had opened in town in the last several years.

"The thing, what they're doing with the blues is all right. I have no problem saying, it's got some potential. But what I always say, too, is that it can't be too particular." She waived away my attempt to pay and kept talking. "It can't be all this, 'Okay, we go'n do this over here, and this over here.'"

The more Dahleen talked, the more pointed her comments became. During the exchange, she mentioned some of Clarksdale's downtown businesses by name. One of the businesses, the New Summit Theater, had been a cultural hub for Black residents of Clarksdale and surrounding areas in the 1950s and 1960s. The space closed in 1970 after a fire damaged a neighboring building. The building was bought, renovated, and reopened in the aughts, joining a fleet of other businesses and performance spaces that had come to town on a wave of local momentum around blues tourism.

Dahleen saw as hypocritical and problematic the attention that development projects like the New Summit received while local social institutions, like the some of the local schools, continued to suffer the consequences of the town's and region's economic profile and state and local government disinvestment. "All that [blues development], but Aggie [high school] about to close down," she said. "It just don't add up." Visibly agitated, Dahleen eventually gave her comments a bookend. "I'm not really a blues person," she said. "It's just not my thing. . . . The way I see it, you got the city putting all this money into a festival or building up downtown. How can you build up a community from that? . . . This ain't just a blues place. Bring in something more, build something up for these kids to keep 'em off the streets. . . . Here, it's just the same ole, same ole. You just get tired of it after so long."

Dahleen had been living in Clarksdale for nearly forty years. Like Mac McIntosh, she had seen the town's blues development agenda go from nothing to the town's everything. During the same time span, she had seen the economic outlook of Black residents stay at nothing.

"Black folks been struggling here a long time," she told me on another one of my Stoe stops one morning in the spring. "And, when you look up, you got the mayor, you got [some of the city commissioners], you got the people here with the money and the power, they using the blues to get more of that, what they already got. . . . Clarksdale got the potential to grow, to give people work." She talked like she knew. "But we gotta be in it together. We can't keep waiting for somebody else to come in and do it for us. We can't keep waiting to see what's go'n happen. . . . We can't wait on the mayor. We can't wait on somebody to come in and build something else up. We gotta do for ourself. The blues is not helping the Blacks here. It's not helping us, and I don't think it supposed to be like that."

Dahleen's comments echo sentiments that I heard from most all of the Black Clarksdalians I spoke with. Dahleen did not like the blues. Neither did they. She doubted if Clarksdale's emphasis on blues tourism would ever reap material benefits for Black residents. So did they. She believed that Clarksdale, a place best known for the blues, should be known as more than a blues place. So did they. So, they questioned the blues. Dahleen and other local Black folks told me that in the years since the town had centered its economic development agenda on blues tourism, they had not seen it do much in the way of economic development, at least not for local Black folks. This shortfall—between what was promised and what was true—was the "it" that Dahleen was referencing when she said, "You just get tired it." It also informed Mrs. Irene's "I don't like the blues," Mac's "We have more or less pushed that old blues out," and Boyce's "That's for the white folks." This chapter is about the sensibility at the root of these and similar claims: anticipation, in particular how Black Americans anticipate and ready themselves for the (racial) future.

A number of scholars, especially in Black studies, have theorized the role of speculation–that is, the capacity to imagine both the best and worst, or as folks like Ashon Crawley and Sami Schalk might say, the "otherwise," of the racial future—for Black identity and epistemology.[1] One part of this tradition posits that, to know what Black folks want for or fear about the coming world is to start to see what they believe to be true about their place in the current one. Or, an outward prayer is a window in. Another part of this tradition reverses the course set by the first, suggesting that to understand how Black folks see themselves in the current world is to know what they might say about the coming one. Here an inward belief portends a cry out. In either case, the fundamental work of speculation is to "unsettle epistemology," or to challenge normative beliefs, in this case about the prospects of Black selfhood and Black livelihoods. Dahleen and other Black Clarksdalians show speculation on the backbeat. Their commentary about Clarksdale's future was informed by both what they wanted to see and what they did not, what they had grown exhausted by.

What Black Clarksdalians said about the preponderance of local blues venues and events typically came down to the same question: Could the blues be a real source of community and economic development for Clarksdale and all of its residents? Their verdict: it had the potential to be, but so far it had not been; and since it had been not so far, it probably would not be in the long run. Black residents said they wanted to see the livelihoods of all residents improve, especially the residents who had historically been its most vulnerable and underserved: Black folks. They wanted to see more opportunities for "good-paying," benefit-providing jobs; reliable and effective social services; and clean and safe neighborhoods. They had waited and looked for such signs of development, and such signs had never come.

Virtually all of the Black residents of Clarksdale that I talked to expressed some degree of skepticism about the town's blues development agenda. Most were like Dahleen—just tired of it. And they expressed this exhaustion in similar ways: by calling out the public officials at the helm of the local blues tourism apparatus; by wondering if blues tourism was a repeat of other, older development agendas in the region; and by laying claim to the future that they wanted to see in addition to, or instead of, more blues.

First, one of the primary ways Black Clarksdalians displayed their skepticism and frustration toward the town's blues-focused development agenda was to call out the people and institutions that they saw as the agenda's primary catalysts and benefactors. It wasn't that Black residents saw blues tourism as a burden in and of itself. Rather, they believed that the town's emphasis on blues tourism came at the expense of the needs and concerns of some residents, especially Black residents. In that way, Black folks wanted Clarksdale to be more than a blues place. And, if there were people or institutions that were preventing that vision from manifesting, Black Clarksdalians saw fit to call them out. They named the names of local elected officials. They pointed to other prominent businesspeople and public stakeholders. Like Dahleen, they singled out many of the blues-related businesses on the downtown square. No person was too big or important to be named. No place was off-limits from being called out.

Second, Black Clarksdalians showed a critical awareness of Clarksdale's racial history. History was proof, both a mirror and a looking glass. It allowed Black residents to assess and forecast the damage that could be wrought by a development agenda that did not account or care for all of the people in a place. History was also an omen, a sign of what might be to come, or, worse, what already was. Black Clarksdalians worried that the blues was helping the town's history of racial exploitation and inequality repeat itself.

Finally, Black Clarksdalians did not end their critiques with the parts of Clarksdale's blues development agenda that they did not like.[2] They did not merely call people out or claim that the blues was history repeating itself. They also articulated what they would want a different future to look like. They called for public officials and local residents to forge coalitions that included Black and white residents, spanned class lines and neighborhood boundaries, and were unimpeded by party affiliation. They claimed that there was more to Clarksdale than the blues. They wanted the town's development agenda to emphasize local civil rights history, the arts, and even expressive forms other than the blues. To them, the blues was all right, but not by itself.

"I Called His Ass": Blues Critique

"Ayo!" Peatey [pē-tē], fifty-eight, called to a slender man standing near the front counter of a popular chain restaurant on State Street. "Jabo done found out he brothers with B. B. King! We trying to see how much [money] he go'n share with us!"

It was an early summer morning and like usual, Peatey Lyles, Hosie [hōz-ē] Foster, Jabo [ja-bō] Wren, and a handful of other men, all in their fifties and sixties, had overtaken a part of the dining area of a local restaurant. Like usual, they were dressed to the nines, never mind the summer heat. One man wore a pair of dress slacks and shiny Stacy Adams. Another wore a velour jump suit and a pair of fishermen sandals that, for some reason, made it seem like he was on his way to or from a barbecue. Peatey wore a red flat cap, I think to make it seem like he was important. Hosie wore a silk shirt halfway unbuttoned, either for the weather or effect. Jabo sat back with his sunglasses propped on top of his head. I sat at a nearby table, occasionally making small talk with the men, mostly content to watch and listen.

"Shit, what good it do you to get Lucille if you can't e'en [even] play the damn guitar?" I heard Peatey say. He laughed at himself. The men quickly joined in.

"Hold on, hold on!" Jabo interjected. "Who said I wanted to play it? I'm go'n get it and sell that son-of-a-bitch!" Jabo looked from side to side, ensuring that his comrades were laughing as much at him as they had at Peatey.

I had become accustomed to these antics. On most weekday mornings, the group of men would trickle into the dining area of the restaurant, at first sitting together in silence, one of them occasionally murmuring a quick thing to the other. Eventually, as the restaurant busied and more men arrived, they would grow more animated and social. They joked with me and anyone else in earshot. They called back to the workers behind the front counter. They talked to each other, conversations that ran the gamut from half-truths about being related to famous bluesmen to phone calls about new car motors to impassioned exchanges about Clarksdale.

In one of the exchanges, Hosie recounted a conversation with the town's mayor. "I called his ass, talked to him just like you and me talking now. . . . I wanted to let his ass know that if don't nobody else know, I know what they been up there doing." Hosie told the men that he had told the official that he did not think it was fair that "certain folks" and "some neighborhoods" received "special treatments," while others "had to beg just to get a inch." Hosie drew a direct connection between this lack of infrastructural support and the prevalence of blues tourism spaces in town. "I say it like this right here. If they took just a little bit of what they put into the blues off, just take a little off the top or off one corner on the side, and put it into building up the rest of the town, Clarksdale'll be alright."

Later in the same exchange, Peatey added to what Hosie had said. Like Hosie, Peatey believed that local development was a zero-sum game, that the more time, resources, and attention that local leadership committed to the blues, the less that would be available for anything (and everybody) else. Hosie placed the blame for this "uneven development"[3] at the feet of the highest levels of the town's leadership—the mayor, city commissioners, this alderperson or that. Peatey did too, but he qualified his claim a bit more than Hosie. "[Clarksdale's elected officials] know what the hell they doing. It been this way a long time. . . . Black people around here get the leftovers . . . the scraps, you know like you give to a dog. The scraps!" The men nodded, and mhm'd, and laughed in uncomfortable agreement.

Peatey, Hosie, and Jabo echoed the sentiments of other Black residents of Clarksdale—everything from their penchant for finding humor in the unlikeliest of places, to the reticence that they reserved for the town's blues development agenda. The same impetus that informed Mrs. Irene's quiet "I don't like the blues" and Dahleen's matter-of-fact "I'm not a blues person" emerged in Peatey's joke about Jabo's apparent kinship to B. B. King. I suspect that it also informed Jabo's joke about only wanting King's famous guitar so he could sell it.

The men reserved their most direct and scathing comments, not for blues music, Lucille, or B. B. King, but for the local officials and stakeholders

You Just Get Tired of It

at the helm of Clarksdale's blues tourism development agenda—the people who, in their view, had not done enough to ensure that all of Clarksdale's residents got the support they needed. In a later, more formal conversation, Jabo added to the comments that I had overheard.

"[Clarksdale] is just a big circle! It's just a big ole' circle. Nothing new! They turned this to a blues city!" Jabo shouted, his voice cracking when he said "blues." He was mad. "They done took over the blues. They done took over the blues! They making money that way. That's what they did to a lot of the stores downtown! [The blues] was invented by a Black man! It was invented by a Black man, but the white man took over! They making money off it. . . . "

Jabo questioned who was benefiting from Clarksdale's blues development agenda, ultimately suggesting that it was "the white man." Jabo was more specific in other conversations, taking time to name the names of people and local organizations. On that note, Jabo echoed Peatey and Hosie; and the three men together echoed what I heard from other Black residents: a deep sense of exhaustion and skepticism about the impact and reach of blues tourism in the town's economic profile. Jabo, Peatey, and Hosie were tired of the blues—just like Dahleen, just like the vast majority of Black residents I spoke with.

"It's the Same Thing Over and Over": Repeating the Same Ole, Same Ole

On a different morning at the same chain restaurant where Peatey, Hosie, and the other men often met, I met thirty-one-year-old resident Steven "Steve" Harris. For a while, the morning carried on as usual. Hosie and Peatey stirred up laughter and conversation with their usual cast of characters, all crowded into and around their usual booths and tables. Cars and trucks lined up in the drive-thru. People lined up in the dining area, waiting to give their orders to the two Black women, one in her teens and the other middle-aged, at the registers.

Then, for a moment, the restaurant slowed to a stop. The cashiers and kitchen went quiet. The line of customers stood still. Steve and I stopped talking. Everyone's attention had been stolen by something that was happening in the parking lot.

"We got a bus!" The lone voice of one of the cashier's broke through the idling quiet, at once setting things back in motion. Conversation and laughter picked back up. Chatter and clangs from the kitchen seemed to grow louder. Steve and I went back to talking.

"How often do they [tour buses] come through here," I asked Steve, pointing to the bus, noting that it was the second bus I had seen in as many days.

"Shit, now it seem like every week, or every other week . . . but it just depends on the time of year. Around this time [it was early May], and then when the festivals start up." I looked through the window trying to estimate the size of the group. Steve looked skeptically at his cup of coffee. It was too sweet.

Despite Steve's public stature—he was active in local civic life—he was openly critical of the Clarksdale's approach to development; and he was especially critical of the blues tourism system. "Clarksdale is just a mechanism for the same things that's been happening in the Delta since plantation times," he said. "It's the same thing over and over. We're big on . . . the blues. Cooking, soul food, [and] blues. You got B. B. King in Indianola [Mississippi]. Here, you have Muddy Waters. . . . And people come here for that." On cue it seemed, the tour group filed into the restaurant and dispersed in different directions. Some folks walked toward the restrooms. Some took their place in line. Some closed in on vacant tables in the dining area.

"I see," I said. "A lot of people [come here for the blues], right? Is that a good thing?"

"The blues is a good thing for Clarksdale," he said with little hesitation. Then, again with little hesitation, he qualified what he said. "But right now we're not seeing the benefits. Like, where is that money [from the blues] going? Is it just going downtown? Is it going to [the mayor's] pocket? Is it going to the Chamber of Commerce? People who stay over there by where my momma stay . . . and all these Black communities ain't seeing it. They getting millions of dollars from [blues tourism]. How is the blues helping Clarksdale? I don't see it. . . . What about us? What about the kids? What about the people who make up these communities?"

What Steve said was more claim than question. He was not asking me, "Where is that money from the blues going?" He was telling me where it wasn't going: to Black residents and to the benefit of local Black communities. Other Black folks—like forty-one-year-old Rhondalyn [Rhun-da-lin] McGee—told me like Steve did.

"I can say, I have not seen where the blues has brought in something for our communities here. . . . If you a Black person here, what has the blues brought you?" Rhondalyn and I had met at a restaurant just down from the restaurant where I usually saw Peatey, Jabo, and Hosie. She had told me she was happy to "be away from work for a little while to talk." She was not so happy when what we talked about turned toward the town's blues tourism system. "I look at it like, you generating all this excess . . . revenue. Money," she said, rubbing her thumb against her middle- and index fingers. "A blues festival comes in, and what is that: money for the city. A tour bus comes through. Money for the city. A blues show over here . . ." Then, she asked me the same thing Steve had told me. "Where is the money going? You can't tell me they paying the people singing the blues. They ain't getting paid! The Blacks ain't getting paid! I asked them the price. They told me the price—say $100 or $200 for a show!"[4] What's that go'n buy you . . . $300 or $400 for a show. . . . It's slavery all over again."

My exchanges with Steve and Rhondalyn reveal a recurring pattern in how Black residents talked about Clarksdale's blues development agenda—repetition. Early in his comments, Steve claimed that Clarksdale's current development trajectory was little more than business as usual, or as he put it, "a mechanism for the same things that's been happening in the Delta since plantation times." Late in her comments, Rhondalyn said "slavery all over again." For twenty-nine-year-old Lorenzo "Zo" Hopper, Clarksdale's blues was another kind of callback.

"The infrastructure here is always go'n be the same," said Zo as we both slouched back in a booth at the Brick Oven Pizza Shoppe. We had been there for a few hours, waiting for a heavy rain shower to pass over, working through two rounds of drinks and one-too-many slices of pizza. "It's like a bus route," he continued. "The people in the positions change—don't matter we got this mayor or that mayor, this commissioner or that one." He laughed like he always did when talking about his hometown, more for effect than anything. "The bus might change. T-Bone's [blues club] used to be a cotton house [warehouse]! Stovall Plantation where Muddy Waters's cabin at, you see the same Stovall Plantation; and, downtown," he pointed toward the restaurant's main entrance, which faced one of downtown's main streets. "Well, first of all, historically speaking, before the civil rights movement, Blacks weren't even allowed downtown. . . . It was a certain time you could be out, and it was a certain time Blacks had to be off the streets."

"Nothing has changed?" I asked, faking like I didn't believe him, like it was something that must be different, that he must have missed.

"I'm telling you! Same stops, same times. . . . It's never go'n change. Might go faster, might go slower, but never go'n change, you feel me."

In another conversation, I asked Zo if he thought "things would get better," the same question I had asked other Black residents.

He sighed. "There is no hope for that here. No hope. The fate here, the reality and the fate here has been structured for centuries, for decades. If you this person, a white person, you have a good fate. If you a Black person, you have a different fate. They have the power. We don't. You can have any mayor you want. They can keep up with the blues, they can bring in new businesses . . . they can keep doing this, this, and that, and we go'n have the same fate!"

Anytime Zo and I talked about the future, whether his own or the trajectory of his hometown, his voice grew louder and more high-pitched. In a different conversation, I asked him if he was "optimistic about Clarksdale's future," and he said "not optimistic at all." In another different conversation, I used the word "hopeful," and after pausing for a moment to consider, he said, "I just don't see the hopeful in it."

Zo was not hopeful in the way that the nation's normative narrative of racial optimism would have him be.[5] He was more skeptical than anything. "For things to change here, it gotta start with the Black community here," he said in a lengthy conversation at another local restaurant. "Get the youth involved . . . you know, get everybody doing positive things for the city. People in tune with all that's going on, the corruption. People not scared to speak their voice. . . . People wanting to play a part and do something to change it. . . . I think when you have that ambition, you can change the world. . . . We have to fight back. We have to join together. We can boycott! Vote! When we come together around that common ground, the strength of the community grows!"

I had talked with Zo often, as much as anyone I met during my time in Clarksdale. I had gone with him on his work trips to Delta area high schools, and to his church, and to the gym. In all of our time together, the point that he made most often was the same point that I heard frequently from other folks: Black residents felt left out of the town's development plans, just as had been the case in the past. History was repeating itself; and the blues was helping it along.

Consider Zo's claim that "Ground Zero used to be a cotton warehouse." On the surface it is simple description. In the early 2000s, the soon-to-be mayor Bill Luckett and noted actor and Clarksdale native Morgan Freeman led the renovation of a 100-year-old cotton grading warehouse on the downtown square, making it into a blues club. Within a few years, it was one of the most popular blues institutions in the country, and one of the keystone attractions for blues travelers from around the world. A deeper reading of what Zo said reveals something more than description. Zo was making an epistemological claim—which is to say, he was outlining what to him was a truth about Clarksdale. He was drawing a direct line from the town's post-1960s blues development agenda to earlier attempts at regional development that centered on another one of the region's foremost commodities: cotton. Zo underscored his point by noting that Muddy Waters, Clarksdale's blues native son, was born on a plantation, a point that again linked the blues development agenda with earlier economic systems like slavery, tenant farming, and sharecropping.

For Zo and other Black residents, Clarksdale's development trajectory was high stakes. People were struggling. Suffering. And not for not trying but because of a development agenda that had not lived up to its promises.

"Take somebody who work at King's Chicken [a popular chain restaurant]," Zo said one day while we sat in a booth at King's Chicken. "Clarksdale got one King's, and you got some people been employed there for fifteen, maybe twenty years. That old chicken they got when they close, they gotta take home to feed some people that's living in the house—that's momma, auntie, kids, and probably a cousin or somebody else that's just living there. Then, that money she making—what's that $7.25 for forty hours, if she able to get forty hours—gotta pay every bill in the house." He laughed, again for effect. "And, paying every bill in the house, she might not have no transportation, and she don't have nothing. And, if yeen [you ain't] got nothing, yeen got nothing."

"I Really Want to See That": Anticipating the Racial Future

It was the Thursday before Clarksdale's Juke Joint Festival—the day before the night that Boyce was supposed to meet me at T-Bone's, several days before I sat with Pooh Baby in front of Dank's. Like usual, I was at Woodlawn Coffee, sitting in my usual spot at the end of a long farm table writing and people-watching. Like usual, John and Porter, two sixty-something white men, had left half-filled coffee cups and half-read newspapers at an end booth and stepped outside to smoke. Mr. Cee, who worked most every day that I stopped by, pushed a push broom delicately over the floor. Ty'wanna [tī-wən-ə] Montgomery stood behind the front register, taking people's orders.

Beyond Woodlawn's usual cast of characters (including me), there were about fifteen unfamiliar faces. Two white women stood just inside the door talking about something outside. A trio of white men moved along the sidewalk, eventually making their way inside. Then, there was Big Danny and Ms. Kathereen, respectively, a fifty-six-year-old, bald-headed Black man and a fifty-one-year-old slender Black woman with glowing skin and silver hair. They had arrived together, not long after me, placed their order with Ty'wanna, then sat beside each other and opposite me at the farm table.

"You a writer? Because you typing like you some kinda writer," Big Danny said in a low, grumbling tenor. He was a truck driver, Ms. Kathereen a retired teacher. They were both Clarksdale natives. They had come to Woodlawn that day, Danny insisted and Kathereen scoffed, on a date.

"I'm just glad our friend let us sit in his neighborhood." Big Danny said, gently nudging Ms. Kathereen. "You must be a high-class Black person. They let you just sit in over here."

Big Danny's joke, though spoken through a growing smile, rang true. I had "sat in" at Woodlawn many mornings and afternoons, finding the wide wooden tables suitable for writing and reliable stream of people suitable for people-watching. On most days, what I saw made what Big Danny said seem more fact than funny. On most days, most everyone at Woodlawn was white, except at lunch time and except for Ty'wanna, Mr. Cee, whichever few cooks and busboys were working that day, and me.

"Y'know, it's some neighborhoods around [that] they kinda don't want us in." For the first time, the tone of Big Danny's voice was serious. "You know, there was a time where we wouldn't be able to do this here what we doing now, and. . . . I can tell you when all this, here, started. This place here [and] all these [blues] festivals—when they figured out it was some money in it! . . . There was a time you couldn't cross the street over here!"

"Tell it," Ms. Kathereen added. "They don't want us over here now. They don't want us, but, what they say, money talks! They want to keep us down for as long as they can." Each word drew her closer to me. "One thing I'll tell you about Black folks," she tilted her head and looked at me through the thin frame of her glasses. "We smart. Black folk know how to make do. [We] can do what they do with our eyes closed." She nodded at John and Porter.

In a later conversation, I asked Ms. Kathereen about some of the things that had come up at Woodlawn, in particular her comments about Black folks and Big Danny's comments about the blues. She talked with the same conviction. "I have never had any desire to go to T-Bone's, not one time, blues festivals, not one time. . . . The shame in it is that [blues tourism] is making money. You know it's making money; but it's making them money. It's going in their pockets, not ours." When I asked her to clarify the "their" and "ours," she did so quickly, with two words: the first and last name of a prominent public official. Then she added, "Black people not seeing none of that from the blues."

"Do you see any of that changing?" I asked, then rephrased the question. "Or, I guess, what do you see happening here [in Clarksdale] on down the line?" She had a lot to say.

"What I would really love to see is for everybody in this town, starting from the mayor on down, everybody come together on one accord. I really want to see that. I really do; and we need to plant some companies and some organizations that will put down roots, that will actually do something that will make a difference for the people who live here, and not just put money in somebody pocket." Ms. Kathereen spoke fluently, as if she had said what she was saying many times before. There were no breaks in conversation, no double-talk, no second-guessing. "The blues seems to be making an impact, but it has shallow roots because the people who participate in the blues activities are not really here. They not from here. Some of 'em don't even live here. They come in, they blues, and they blues, and they go. And the things that they create because they're coming," she smirked and fake-laughed. "They go too. They're shallow like the blues thing. . . . We don't need more shallow."

Later in our conversation, Ms. Kathereen further explained what she wanted for Clarksdale's future. "I want to see all the school systems actually be where we can be fully funded. I want to see a group of people in charge who actually care about the people here [in Clarksdale]. I want to see us Black people come together and, what they say, be the change we want to see. You have to invest in this place. You have to put into it if you want to get out it; and I just think you have to be here, you have to be here in this place, to really understand what's going on and what it needs."

My time with Big Danny and Ms. Kathereen was telling. Big Danny's joke about where they could and could not sit at Woodlawn's, and his larger, less humorous, reminder about the specter of residential segregation in Clarksdale, echoed what I heard from folks like Boyce, Cookie, Auntie, and Thickie. Ms. Kathereen's early comments about Black folks knowing "how to make do" is a derivative of what I heard from folks like Mac, Thea, and Pastor Early.

Then there were Ms. Kathereen's comments about what she wanted for Clarksdale, her audacity to speculate about a future that was different, and in her view better, than what had come before. Ms. Kathereen rejected Clarksdale's blues development agenda, but not out of hand and not without explaining herself. In her view, blues development was not working because it had "shallow roots," which to her meant it was led by individuals with selfish motives and had been more beneficial to a select few than for Clarksdale's greater good. Ms. Kathereen's comments also took aim at the sustainability of the blues development agenda, which she believed would be limited as long as it relied on a model of community engagement carried out by individuals who, themselves, were not engaged with the community. "You have to be here," she had said.

Ms. Kathereen also said other things about what she wanted to see in Clarksdale's future. She called for more public investment in the town's social institutions, and, like Dahleen, a greater sense of urgency from and among other Black residents.

Ms. Kathereen's comments can be read as a type of Black southern speculation—not a passive or haphazard musing about what might be nice to have at some point down the unspecified line but a specific set of desires for a specific future, both hers and others'. Other Black residents speculated too. They critiqued the parts of local culture and community life that were harmful, exploitive, or otherwise counterproductive for local residents, Black residents in particular; and they supplemented those critiques with their own vision for the future.

Like Ms. Kathereen, twenty-seven-year-old Princeton "P. J." James Jr. called for sweeping changes to Clarksdale's blues development agenda; and like Ms. Kathereen, P. J. believed the problem with the current approach was a problem of perspective. I had asked him what Black residents of Clarksdale "needed" the most. He chuckled at the question, then took a second to think about it.

"Well, part of the problem is that we've been looking for the answer to that question in the wrong places. We already have what we need the most. We've been looking over our biggest asset. Like, people don't really talk about, like, the civil rights history here. They [are] all about just blues, blues, blues, blues, blues. Which, like, people created the blues, it was born here because people had the damn blues." He laughed again.

"So, wait. Do people here still have the damn blues?" I asked.

"Yeah. It just depends on who you talk to. Like, depending on who you talk to, yeah. Some people say," he said, holding the edges of his lips tightly together, talking in an exaggerated baritone voice. "'Oh, it's a great place, it's a beautiful place, and everything is fine here.'" His voice returned to normal. "But, just think how segregated it is here, and you can imagine who . . . is saying what. You can just drive through the communities and see it. Like, wow, I wonder why is it that all the, uh, people," he pointed to the backside of his hand, "are staying there and there, and other people are staying there and there. It's racial. It's economic. [It's] class. All that."

P. J. was born in Chicago and moved to Clarksdale as an adolescent. Other than his time at a state university, he had lived his entire adult life in Clarksdale and was committed to community development and outreach work, so much so that he had started his own nonprofit. In our conversation, and in other public forums, he maintained that the biggest challenge facing Clarksdale and other Delta towns was not in "finding something that is missing" but capitalizing on something that the town already had—its people.

"[Clarksdale is] not just the blues, right? Let's highlight the people who led those movements, that started those efforts, those visionaries," he clapped then held his hands together, giving his words a beat. "Those innovators, those creators, those disruptors . . . [Those] people made the blues, created the art, built the infrastructure." His voice took on the rasp of a preacher. "The civil rights history came from the people. It came from those struggles . . . and, you know what . . . it starts with the people. It starts with the people that saw something in the Delta, that saw something in this place. It started with visionaries like Aaron Henry, to step up and go into unchartered waters, to take the path least traveled. It started with the people that created the blues, that shared the blues with the world. It started with the people, and we're overlooking this asset, and we're not investing in it."

P. J. believed that Clarksdale had more than the blues to be proud of, that the town's civil rights history should hold a place in public life. P. J. had a detailed understanding of Clarksdale's racial history. He talked about the work of Vera Pigee and Aaron Henry. He mentioned local journalist Troy Catchings. In P. J.'s view, not only would memorializing and celebrating that part of Clarksdale's history lend to a more effective development agenda, but it would more fully honor the agency, voices, contributions, and spirit of Black residents.

Other Black Clarksdalians shared P. J.'s belief that there was more to local culture than the blues. Where he highlighted the town's civil rights history, folks like fifty-four-year-old Juwell Turner maintained that the town's most valuable asset was, and would remain, its culture. The blues was perhaps at the center of that culture, but she believed there could be more.

A few weeks after Juwell Turner and I sat and talked at De Casa, we sat and talked at Big Bowl, a Chinese restaurant in south Clarksdale. De Casa had been busy and loud the whole time. Big Bowl was the opposite.

The dining area was empty, save for Juwell and I; and business was slow, save for a few people coming in for pickup orders.

"What's good to eat here?" I asked Juwell as we stepped from our table to the front counter.

"Now, the chow mein is good. I'm talk'n 'bout good good," she said, barely giving me time to finish my question. "Good. It's as good as Chicago. Now, it can be a little salty, I'll go ahead and tell you that."

After ordering, we stepped back to the dining area and after Juwell prompted me to go tell the hostess to go tell the cook to "not to make it too salty," she returned to telling me about playing a blues festival the weekend after the weekend that we met at De Casa.

"I was on a roll! I did [two shows] on the Friday. Saturday, we did Moonie's! At night!" She was giddy. "We clowned. We clowned. It was wild!" She went on to tell me about a program that she had helped organize in the previous year in conjunction with three area churches. "I want to do it again this year, to bring in some cultural diversity: poets, writers, musicians, artists, bringing those people in, Black and white, people from here, people not from here, all kinds of people. . . . All the potential that's in this place, I think it can be so much more than just the blues; and [the program we organized last year] was a model for that."

"You see that here?" I asked. "You want to see more stuff like that here?"

"I want to open an art shop," Juwell responded quickly. "I want to do all kinds of stuff. I want to get some art in here. I want this to be like Oxford [Mississippi]! People can come to hear and see art, antique stores, art stores, all that. I have a vision for downtown." There was a place for the blues in Juwell's vision. In fact, she believed the blues "was one of the best things that Clarksdale has to offer," and she supported that belief by naming several Black blues singers and musicians who were either from, raised, or had played in Clarksdale: R. L. Burnside, L. C. Ulmer, Muddy Waters, Jessie Mae Hemphill, Bessie Smith, and she went on. Juwell knew Clarksdale's (and Mississippi's) blues history well, and she was happy with all—the attention, the tourists, and the revenue—that the blues had brought to Clarksdale. She just believed, like Dahleen, Ms. Kathereen, P. J., and Steve, that Clarksdale could be and do more than the blues.

"The blues is fine," she said as our conversation came to a lull and both of us began gathering ourselves and our things to leave. "We can keep doing the blues, creative economy, all that. But, right now, that's the only economy." She laughed. "Factories have closed. We've got a few, but nothing like used to be here . . . even when I first got here. . . . So, we've got to build, you know."

You Just Get Tired of It

She repeated herself—"to build"—pounding the table with her closed fist. "We need more than the blues. We need art, more art galleries. We need more antique shops. We need more food. Oh my goodness, downtown especially. [We need] different types of food. I can't go to a good Thai restaurant? You get tired of eating Mexican! There's not even a good soul food place. That bugs me. This is Mississippi, and we don't have a soul food restaurant downtown?"

Juwell was a blues-loving, blues-playing blues woman. She loved blues music, and, as she told it to me, she had lived a blues life. She believed blues tourism had brought some good to Clarksdale, just not enough of it. She believed local stakeholders should continue to position the blues as one of the town's foremost assets, just not the only asset. Like many other folks I talked to, she was tired of the blues, at least the heavy emphasis that local officials placed on blues tourism. She wanted more than the blues.

Where Ms. Kathereen had called for a development agenda of community values and public investment, and P. J. wanted official recognition of Clarksdale's civil rights history, Juwell wanted more diverse ways to highlight local art and culture. She wanted more (types of) festivals and different types of art, each of which she believed Clarksdale had the infrastructure to support and enough tourism traffic to capitalize on.

PORCH

The night made the flames of our candles seem dim and the moon seem like a streetlight, and Chester Butts's voice seem like a sermon.

"I don't know if I'm the only one that feels this way, but I'm tired," he said. He was standing on the porch of Mrs. Millie Monroe. I was standing in the front yard, among some 100 people, us all gathered for a candlelight vigil. The week before, Mrs. Millie had been sitting with her husband when they heard a knock at the door. When she answered it, a masked man shot her from from point-blank range. "It's sad," Dahleen Atkinson-Knowles had told me earlier that day at The Stoe, as we both wondered aloud why so many people seemed to "[go] too soon."

"It's sad," a woman said from some place in front of me, her voice louder than our murmurs, as the whole town seemed to wonder in quiet what it meant to remain.

"Enough is," Chester called out.

"Enough!" We responded.

"It has to stop," he called again.

"Yes!" Again, the woman was louder than everyone else.

For a while people kept coming, piling and squeezing into the yard, eventually spilling and pouring into the street. Eventually they stopped coming, and we all just stood among each other, all 150 of us, quiet but for a murmur, dark but for the dim flames of our candles, tired but for something different.

"We have to keep the fire going," Chester said, his voice weaker than earlier but still clear, still a sermon. "We cannot give up."

Chester's words were as stirring as they are illuminating: it is possible to render the Black American story as one or another metaphor about fire and burning. Olaudah Equiano, who spent a portion of his early life serving the captains of slave ships, wrote of enslavement that it worked to "depress the mind [of enslaved Black people], and extinguish all its fire." Black abolitionist and writer Frederick Douglass noted that "it is not light that [the nation] needs, but fire." And Zora Neale Hurston helped make *Fire*; and James Baldwin wrote *The Fire Next Time*, and Jesmyn Ward culled *The Fire This Time*; and the arc of Richard Wright's life, as documented in the opening line of *Black Boy*, began in fire: "One winter morning in the long-ago, four-year-old days of my life I found myself standing before a fireplace, warming my hands over a mound of glowing coals, listening to the wind whistle past the house outside."[6]

In the popular imagination, fire and burning equate to persistence and hopeful expectation. To "light a fire underneath" something is to compel it to action. A "burning" desire is an infinite and insatiable one. They say there is no smoke without fire, which, I suppose could mean there is no "struggle without progress"; and Black Americans must always have fire, and smoke, and more progress—or so the story goes. When Equiano wrote that enslavement was about extinguishing the fire in the minds of Black people, he was claiming that slavery was, above all else, an apparatus meant to manage, curtail, and repress possibility. Douglass's fire meant action. Hurston's meant life. Other Black people's fire meant other things—Baldwin's was urgent, Ward's ambitious, Wright's ravishing. Clarksdale native and former Mississippi NAACP president Aaron Henry talked about fire too;[7] his was an emblem of hope and optimism, an explanation for the bravery it must have taken for about 700 Mississippians, most of them Black, to occupy an Air Force Base in Greenville in protest of the state's arrested development.

Black life is fire, but as we heard from Mrs. Irene Sandiford in this book's opening pages and Dahleen, P. J., Jabo, Zo, and others in this chapter, fire can mean different things. It can give voice and meaning to the persistent hope and hopeful expectations of Black life. It can be about lighting the way to forward movement, cultivating an active mind, or owning a steely determination. It can also be about exhaustion, a sign that folks have grown tired. Sometimes the fire burns out.

This chapter started at The Stoe. I had stopped by to buy some candy and talk to native resident Dahleen Atkinson-Knowles. For a stretch during my time in Clarksdale, I followed this routine nearly every day: stop by The Stoe, buy candy, ask Dahleen about Clarksdale.

And our conversations ran the gamut, from her amused reflections about growing up on what she called "the outskirts of Clarksdale" to her defiant appraisal of the town's blues development agenda. While Dahleen allowed that Clarksdale's recent emphasis on blues tourism had the potential to improve the town's socioeconomic profile, she was doubtful of its capacity to provide material benefits to Black residents and Black neighborhoods in particular. She was openly critical of the town's elected officials and other public stakeholders, and she insisted that there were other, more effective pathways to development. Dahleen wanted Clarksdale to do and be more than the blues.

So did other Black residents. They wanted the town to emphasize other parts of its history, like its key role during the Delta's Black Freedom Struggle. They wanted other entertainment options—not just old-style blues but also jazz, southern soul blues, and more contemporary genres like hip-hop. They wanted elected officials who "actually cared" about all residents, with no exceptions for class, race, neighborhood, and so on.

Though I talked with Black Clarksdalians about the blues in different contexts, and for different lengths of time, and with different points of emphasis, they all seemed to arrive at the same conclusion: Clarksdale's blues development agenda had development potential, but as far as they could see, it had not delivered meaningful development; and since it had not in the past, it likely would not in the future.

Not only did their conclusion say the same thing, but they often arrived at it in the same way. First, they openly called out local elected officials, business owners, and other public stakeholders. Second, Black residents charged that the town's ongoing blues development agenda was little more than the "same ole, same ole" repeating itself: local elected officials and public stakeholders, most of them white,[8] making the decisions about the town's development agenda and reaping its benefits, and local residents, especially Black folks, doing neither. Finally, Black Clarksdalians said what changes they wanted and needed to see in Clarksdale's development future. From more diverse entertainment options to more dynamic programming for the town's young people to more public investment, what Black residents wanted seemed to always sum to the same thing: an opportunity to build a meaningful life, with meaningful work, adequate educational opportunities for their children, and reliable social and civic services for themselves.

To start, Black Clarksdalians' critiques of the town's blues development agenda were rooted in firsthand experience. They were describing what they had seen and experienced, and what they had seen others experience, in the years since the town made itself into a blues tourism place. Yet their critiques were about more than description. They were also about epistemology.

Black Americans have always been engaged in what some scholars have called "speculation" about the future—hypothesizing what might be possible, making claims about what should be possible, or, as was often the case in my conversations with folks in Clarksdale, bracing themselves for what would likely play out. Indeed, at the root of Black residents' critiques about Clarksdale's blues development agenda was speculation on the backbeat— here, a sense of exhausted anticipation that the future would portend more of the same for the region, more of the same for local social and economic relations, and more of the same for them. They were tired of more of the same.

Burning is a recurring theme of Black American life, whether the "burning desire" and determination of Black folks to resist and overcome racial domination or the actual fires that have terrorized and arrested Black life at every turn. Burning can happen in different ways. "Burnout" is the sense of exhaustion that comes from prolonged or repeated exposure to stress; and even as Black Americans have long shown a desire to "keep the fire burning," they have also sometimes been burned out. In some ways, Black residents of Clarksdale are burned out, exhausted by centuries and decades of uneven community and economic development approaches. Sometimes, some of them anticipate more of the same, and that makes them tired. Sometimes others of them anticipate calling and fighting for something different, and that makes them tired too—not for better or for worse, just for rest.

CONCLUSION

"What you going out there fuh [for]?" Teryeia [terē-ā] asked me, her voice like it always was, blunt but with a comforting rasp. I had told her I was going to the Juke Joint Festival the following day. She was not impressed. "I went [to the Juke Joint Festival] back when it was first getting started," she said. "I would say a lot of the Blacks here did. . . . go out there, you know . . . more of a just to see what it was about." Teryeia Pigees [pē-gēz], thirty-four, and I were sitting in a restaurant on State Street. It had been three years since I moved to Clarksdale in 2014, two years since I had last been in town for the April festival, a little more than a year since I had moved away. As I had tried to do with many of the folks I had met, I had kept in touch with Teryeia.

"You go'n go out there with me?" I asked her again, smiling. Knowing. She did not answer me again, until she did, with a look. It was the same look Pooh Baby had given me after the tourist couple had called him a "real blues player," and almost the same look Mac made after I told him how much time I had spent on the downtown square, and exactly the same look Boyce Shumpert had half-given me on that drive to the casino after the blues show that he did not come to. Dahleen Atkinson-Knowles had given me her version of the look too, two times that morning at The Stoe, first, when the two young men stumbled there way from the back, and then when I asked her about a possible new blues development project around the corner.

As the look had been with Dahleen, Boyce, Mac, and Pooh Baby, it had been with other Black residents; and as it had been with them, it was that day with Teryeia. It started with her fully relaxing the muscles in her forehead, forcing her eyelids down slightly, her jawline still for a moment, her glare almost like Mrs. Irene's, just less unflinching, more performance. She completed the look by pressing her lips together firmly and outward slightly, drawing two sharp creases in her cheeks. In some ways, the look spoke for itself. It was the answer: she wasn't going.

"Why you look at me like that," I loud laughed.

"You know why I looked at you like that . . . " She didn't pay my laughter much attention.

"You go'n go? It's the blues!"

She sucked her teeth. "Who blues? They wouldn't know blues if it sat in they lap." Her face stood still. She looked how she always did, then got more serious than she usually was. "That blues is different from what we grew up on, you know, Johnnie Taylor, you know, Marvin Sease, you know, you know," she searched for names. "Jackie Neal, Tyrone Davis. . . . I like the blues, but I don't like the blues like they like the blues."

The first part of this last thing that Teryeia said summarizes what *I Don't Like the Blues* is about: Black residents of Clarksdale, Mississippi, don't like the blues. With the exception of contemporary styles like southern soul (e.g., the group of singers that Teryeia named), they don't listen to much blues music or go to the town's blues scenes. They see the local obsession with the blues as shallow, as one-dimensional, a disappointment. While Black Clarksdalians freely acknowledge the (economic) potential of the town's blues development agenda, they question when, or if, it will tangibly benefit the livelihoods of local Black folks. The folks I spoke with had yet to see the proof.

"When I said I was done with the blues here," Teryeia continued, "was when I saw how they push so many festivals and so many this and that, but then to not see that money being used to help the Blacks here. Help them people! Use the blues to help, not to just put more money in your own pocket."

As we stood from the table, Teryeia made one last comment about Juke Joint. This one was not about the festival's history or economic impact. It was practical, and it came with that same look from earlier.

"Get out there early if you wan'a find a park."

In some ways, you could read this as a blues development and tourism story. That Black Clarksdalians doubt the long-term viability of the town's blues development agenda echoes a voluminous body of scholarship on the ways place natives respond to the inclusion of tourism in a place's economic development plan, entertainment scenes, and commercial landscape. The recurring story is that they respond with resentment and skepticism. This story echoes that one, except with more details (i.e., by considering how race, power, and history mediate local perceptions).

It's also possible to read this as a blues music story. That Black residents of Clarksdale don't like the blues and don't attend the town's blues entertainment and performance scenes underscores what blues scholars and cultural critics have been saying for a while—that is, blues music has been declining in popularity among Black audiences at least since World War II. What Black Clarksdalians told me show that that is still the case.

Beyond blues music and blues development, though, this is a blues epistemology story. It is a story about what the post–civil rights rural South looks like, and what Black life there sounds like. It is a story that plays a backbeat, or emphasizes that which usually is not: the *nonaffirming, or negative, sensibilities that constitute Black identity and lived experience.* What does it mean to *not like* something, to *not go* to certain places, to *not want* certain things, or certain futures? From 2014 to 2019, Black folks in Clarksdale told and showed me.

Mac's "We ain't [the blues] no mo'" was about racial identity and group belonging, about Black folks laying claim to an agentive and self-determined "I," marking space between themselves and "they," and celebrating a collective "we" along the way. It was about Hessie Trice knowing what had made him who he was, about Juwell Turner knowing what she had been made to do, and about Pastor Early Anderson knowing that he, his congregation, and his city were both "on their way" and far from gone. It was about a parade, both the one in 1962 to which some Black residents were denied access and the one I watched go through in 2014 that had Black folks and rhythm and Black folks and blues.

"We ain't that no mo'" is desire on the backbeat, what I call "negation," an affective disposition characterized by liking and not liking the same thing at the same time. Black folks in Clarksdale used negation to mark identity and make claims about group belonging.

Boyce's "[the blues is] for the white folks" was about remapping racial geographies, about Black folks making determinations about if, when, and for how long they want to be in a place. It was about Shaunice going to Juke Joint but not for herself. It was about Thickie and Deuce going to the Brickhouse, but not for long. It was Cookie Echols seeing and believing, Bugg and Big Lap knowing and telling, and Auntie and Mrs. Rube just knowing. It was about church and local churches like Haven and First Baptist and King's Temple and Boyce's momma's that had been, and still were, indispensable institutions in local Black life.

"That's for the white folks" is placemaking on the backbeat—place-unmaking. It is about Black people being vigilant about race, and staying away from the places that they deem uncomfortable or unsafe.

Dahleen's "You just get tired of [the blues]" was (about) speculation. It was about Black folks anticipating different futures, even as they knew at least one of those futures might end being the same ole, same ole. It was about how the blues reminded Steve of "plantation times" and Zo of cotton and Rhondalyn of slavery. It was P. J. saying "blues" all them times back to back, tired with Clarksdale's blues development. It was about Ms. Kathereen saying words like "stay" and "roots," tired of the blues and wanting a different type of development. It was about Chester Butts standing on the front porch of the late Mrs. Millie Monroe, 150 people standing around holding candles like streetlights, balloons in the sky beside them, Chester holding forth and talking about fire.

"You just get tired of it" is speculation on the backbeat—exhaustion. It is about Black people anticipating what they do not want, while saying and claiming what they do.

For Black residents of Clarksdale, the blues was not just a style of music. It was not just about singing or playing an instrument, about B. B. King or Muddy Waters or whoever else. It was not a festival or T-Bone's, mere entertainment, or a powerful economic development tool. For folks like Mrs. Irene, Pooh Baby, Mac, Boyce, Dahleen, Teryeia, and all the Black residents of Clarksdale that they talk like and speak for, and all the Black Delta communities that they live near and know about, and all the Black Americans "here, there, and wherever they may be"[1] that they all represent, the blues was and is a method. It was an epistemology, a way of doing, seeing, and being in the world, responsive to the conditions of Black life in the post-civil rights U.S. South, attentive to the dangers and uncertainties of the day.

When the Black folks in Clarksdale talked about "blues," they were moving back and forth between music and methods, between Mrs. Irene's "I don't like the blues" and Teryeia's "I don't like the blues . . . like they like the blues." They were talking about the blues as if it were its own thing (e.g., a music genre, aesthetic, or style of instrumentation) and drawing on the blues to say and do other things (e.g., claim truths, critique power inequality). These are all distinctions with a difference. Is the blues the end or a means to an end? In Clarksdale, Black folks talked about it as if it could be neither one or both at the same time, and in *Development Arrested* Clyde Woods lays the foundation for making that make sense. He calls the blues a social epistemology, and suggests that the epistemology has three parts—like a tree with roots, trunk, and branches.

According to Woods, the blues epistemology is "rooted" in Black southerners' desire for humanistic autonomy, in Black folks wanting to live, live long, and live well, and to (be allowed to) make space to work through their beliefs about life as they do the living. The "trunk" of the blues epistemology includes the methods that Black southerners have deployed in pursuit of humanistic autonomy: anticipation, boycotts, church, dance, desire, food, Hamer, King, language, literacy, love, guns, movement, organizing, place-making, Randolph, singing, speculation, subversion, voting, waiting, watching, and so on. The "branches" of the blues epistemology are multiple, and one of them is the blues expressive tradition, a loose-fitting reference to the sound of the backbeat, call-and-response, hollers, I-IV-I-V, improvisation, moans, and "squals" that have long defined Black life and sensibility.

Blues music is but one part, or "branch," of the blues epistemology, not the whole of it. That is how Mac could want to remember the blues and not remember the blues at the same time, how Pooh Baby could "not have to play blues" but see the blues every day still, how Black folks in Clarksdale could hold hope and doubt in the same hand, say yes and no at the same time.

That is how Mrs. Irene could looove the guy that sings "Mom's Apple Pie" and still not like the blues.

CODA

When I finally got to Clarksdale's downtown square for the Juke Joint Festival, I remembered Teryeia's advice: "Get out there early if you wan'a find a park." I had not gotten out there early, at least not early enough; and I had not found a park, at least not one as close as I would have liked. Instead, I made a place on the shoulder of Sunflower Avenue several blocks south of the square. After I parked, I made my way back north, stopping where Sunflower crosses the railroad tracks to look. I didn't remember the square being so busy and full the last time.

When I made it to the festival crowds, I did. I remembered. I remembered how happy and excited the white folks seemed to be to hear "real blues players" play "real blues." That's how it was again, except more white folks and more blues. The Juke Joint Festival had seen consistent growth since its inaugural year in 2004. I was standing amid the growth—people everywhere. I remembered the tents, vendors, and carnival games. They were there again, except more of them.

I spent an hour on Delta Avenue, walking and looking and listening; two hours near the Delta Blues Museum Stage watching blues act after blues act after blues act; an hour on Third Street talking, another hour on Second just listening.

I spent the most time on Yazoo Avenue in front of Woodlawn, doing what I always did at Woodlawn: people-watching. I watched people walk and stumble by, and make space to sit down on the concrete sidewalk. I watched people try to sing on key and dance on beat. Most of them could do neither, but one elderly couple did both. The man wore a loose-fitting pair of khaki shorts and a button-up shirt that was the same color but a different shade. The woman wore a brightly colored shirt and pants rolled to just above her ankles. A two-man blues band played under a white tent a few paces away from them.

The couple danced, and danced, and danced. They rocked and stepped, and locked hands. The woman spun the man, then he spun her, then she twisted underneath then through the arc that their arms made as they held them above their heads. For a moment, the man and woman faced away from each and leaned outward, their hands still interlocked, feet still tapping, bodies moving in a circle. It is hard to name the thing that they were doing, but "do-si-do" comes close.

The do-si-do was enough.

I left. I retraced my steps from Yazoo Avenue onto Third Street, from east to west to Sunflower Avenue, back down Sunflower, south. When I got to the railroad tracks, I stopped. From where I stood, I saw a group of adolescent boys in front of me, the square behind me. Some of the boys were on bikes, some running, some with their shirts off, all of them in various states of contentment—laughter, shouting, talking. The boys on bikes rode in circles in the parking lot of the Church of God in Christ (COGIC) national headquarters to my left. They cursed as they went around. Two boys ran from the parking lot of the Bishop T. T. Scott Fellowship Center on my right. When their feet hit Sunflower, they turned south and laughed away, their Black backs eventually just Black, silhouettes; their laughter a passing car, the evening a Black night, the boys on bikes chasing. I listened at them go, and I remembered.

I remembered where I was standing—the railroad tracks, the boundary between where Black folks used to couldn't go and where they had to make their own New World, the "Great Divide" as Eddie Kane Jr. had called it, the color line. It had remained. Everything had remained.

All the adolescent boys were Black—all six of them. Most everything in front of me (south of the racks) was Black—the road, the fellowship center, the COGIC headquarters, Saint James, Red's, Martin Luther King Jr. Avenue. The night. It was all Black.

Most everything behind me, to echo Cookie and Auntie and other Black folks, was white—most of the people standing in the small parking lot on the side of Ground Zero, talking, laughing, and carrying on; most of the folks filing along the sidewalk in front of the old boarded warehouse of Delta Whole Hardware Co., every single one of the people crossing Sunflower Avenue, some coming from the festival, others going, all of them white. The old couple dancing the do-si-do, white. The people rocking and clapping on the "one" and "three" around them, white. The two men playing the blues under the white tent as they went, the exception.

I listened at the street and the people and the railroad tracks, and I remembered. I remembered what had brought me to Clarksdale, in the heat of a too-hot summer day three years before, boxes and naive ambition in hand; a small desk, a bed, and some books in the third bedroom; a house near the dead-end of a dead-end street by the river. I remembered what I wrote in my journal that night, what I had wondered about doing, what I had said about "saying," what had made me be wrong for thinking, from the beginning.

I remembered when I first met Thea, when she rolled her eyes at the "research" I had come to "[her] city" to do. I remembered Toya Johnson and Bugg, how every time we talked, they had their work uniforms on, and how Shundrick usually had his in his hand or the backseat. I remembered Cookie's "grandbabies" and Auntie's one and half cans of Coca-Cola, and Deuce drinking that damn Budweiser, and Pooh Baby's "motherfucka." I remembered Hessie, Hosie, and Jabo, Mrs. Classi'Mae, Juwell, and Dahleen, how their voices went when they talked, how the time felt when they didn't. I remembered Boyce and his momma's church, and the choir singing "Come and Go to That Land," and coming from church to go to the casino, and Pastor Early Anderson kicking off his shoes two nights before the Third Day. I remembered riding with Eddie Kane Jr. and crying in the streets with a candle up for Mrs. Millie.

I looked at my phone—a text from Teryeia—and I remembered. *"You was right."*

Rural South places like Clarksdale have changed since the civil rights movement. They are new. The labor market more strained, jobs harder to find, a living wage more impossible to earn, public infrastructure just impossible, people moving away. All of that is new. A different kind of new, but new still.

But not everything.

There is still something that remains in the rural South, a continuity: racial domination, Old South power relations, history being heavy, Jim Crow, the railroad tracks separating the haves from those who had theirs taken.

Now, the blues. State stakeholders call it a promise. Black folks call it the same ole, same ole; said they tired of it. Hope be damned.

But not all the way.

Continuity is a backbeat too. Black folks finding ways to survive and say who they are and work toward what they want—and insist on what they don't like—is continuity too. It's the blues still. Just different.

I looked at the railroad tracks, and I remembered 1962. Clarksdale Mayor W. S. Kincade had forbidden the all-Black marching bands from Higgins High School and Coahoma County Junior College from marching in Clarksdale's holiday parade.[1] After meetings and debate among local civic and civil rights organizations, Black residents had decided to boycott the downtown square. The fire of the civil rights movement had been burning in Clarksdale since 1951, when a white man named Roach skirted conviction for two separate accusations of rape, both made by Black women. The fires had burned into the 1960s. Black residents were calling for change everywhere—a call to desegregate the city schools and local social institutions, a call to extend voting rights to all residents, a call to address the violent tactics of local law enforcement and white vigilantes. The downtown boycott was continuity.

As the boycott carried on, the local white power establishment started to agitate and carry on too. Local police arrested prominent Black residents and movement leaders, five of whom were charged and sentenced to six months in jail and $500 in fines, and whom a local investigator called "five of the most vicious agitators in Mississippi." In the summer of that year, under the guise of "beautification," the city banned leafletting on the downtown square, another avenue to harass and arrest civil rights workers and protestors. In response, Black residents met in groups at strategic intersections just beyond the downtown square. The boycott had to go on. One of the intersections was at Issaquena and South Edwards, one at Desoto and Third Street, one at the Second Street Bridge, one at the First Street Bridge, one on Cutrer Hill, and one where the old tracks of the Illinois Central Railroad cross Sunflower Avenue, where I stood.

I looked at the tracks, and I remembered. Fifty and some odd years earlier some number of Black folks had stood where I stood, not liking things as they were, tired but committed to making things different, fighting the good fight and keeping the faith even if they didn't expect to finish the course. Among them was a man, one of the leaders who had been arrested earlier in the year, one of the five "most vicious agitators in Mississippi," Robert L. Drew. Drew was one of the formative figures of the Black Freedom Struggle in Clarksdale. By 1962, he had served as a secretary for the Southern

Christian Leadership Conference (SCLC) and as chairman of the state's NAACP Executive Board.

Drew was also the operator of the United Order of Friendship, a credit union that among other things enlisted agents to sell encyclopedias both as a fundraising effort and as a way to help Black residents establish credit, at a time when local economic institutions had become a tool of intimidation and racial control. In addition to the credit union, Drew was the pastor of a local church and the owner and director of a funeral home, the same funeral home where he and others had met with Dr. Martin Luther King Jr. in 1958, the formative years of the SCLC; the same funeral home that had housed his church, the same church that Pastor Early Anderson's father had pastored until he died, and that Pastor Early had pastored ever since; the same funeral home that I had sat in on that too-hot-to-be-outside morning two and a half years earlier with Mrs. Irene Sandiford.

R. L. Drew was Mrs. Irene's uncle.

"Growing up, my uncle Drew would have all these sets of encyclopedias," Mrs. Irene had told me. "He had red ones. He had white ones." She turned to one of two bookshelves behind her, tracing her hand toward a short stack of books near the top. "And he would keep all of them up on bookshelves. He would have all these encyclopedias." She laughed to herself. "And, he kept his records by his books—Bibles, Sunday church programs—just all of these books by his blues records."

I looked up, and I remembered growing up in a small town on the other side of the state. "I remember my grandmamma used to read the newspaper every day, every morning with her breakfast," I said smiling. "And she had two sets of encyclopedias!"

Mrs. Irene smiled too, two creases in her cheeks, maybe at me, maybe at my grandmamma; maybe she was still thinking about "Mom's Apple Pie" or the guy who sings it. Or her uncle. "Oh, my uncle loved his encyclopedias! He would give them as gifts!"

"And the blues," I started.

"And his blues records," she finished. "He would, he would play the blues all of the time. I never understood it." Her face went between smiling and remembering, between desire and "we ain't that no mo,'" between being there and "I've never even been," between loving and not liking. Like she wanted to do them all at once.

"That was his thing," she said.

"And you kept these all that time," I said, or thought.

"All that time . . . they belong to us. They were his. They will remind me of him."

I remembered. It was time to go. The morning had already, replaced by an unflinching afternoon sun, its rays falling across Mrs. Irene's desk heavy, stopping at the bottom of the bookshelf in the corner, light, like it knew not to go too far. I looked up at the encyclopedias, stacked on top of papers and what looked like booklets, the binding torn but remaining.

Like the blues.

"I don't like the blues," I remembered.

Then wondered.

Then I asked Mrs. Irene what I had asked just about everybody before and after her. "What do you want for this place . . . moving forward?" Her glare let up. My voice stayed down, quiet, like it knew. Like Black folks (in Clarksdale and in the Delta and in Mississippi and in the rural South) do. Like the blues do.

"For us to have something . . . that can be ours."

ACKNOWLEDGMENTS

Daddy used to tell my brother and me all the time, "Use three hands if you ain't got nothing but two!" He was a carpenter and country, wanted me and my brother to be too. Made us nail nails and saw on stuff. Paint. Strip, wax, and buff floors. Lay fences. Buy, raise, and sell cows. And, goats. Whenever we moved too slow, whether "we" was me or my brother, or both of us, or the nailing, sawing, or any of the other stuff, daddy would lean into his truth. "Use three hands if you ain't got nothing but two!"

There was no love, only the day, and only doing with two that which required three—or, with three that which required the day.

"Use three hands," when he was mad, and when he was frustrated, and if he was trying to be funny. That was where things stood up to now.

Now, I tell myself a different story about daddy and his "three hands." It is a lie, but sometimes lies sound like a poem. I tell myself that "use three hands" was not frustration but belief. "Use three hands," because I know you can. Because you have always done three-hand work. Because humans have two hands, and you are something else. "Use three hands," or do what is impossible. Thank you.

I wrote this book with three hands, except not how daddy was talking about. My three hands have been many—so, so many people who poured into this work by pouring into me. Thank you is not enough, but it is what I have here.

To momma. You are the first and the last, the why and the how. The most important thing. Thank you.

To *all them people and all that time* in Clarksdale—for trusting me with your story, for not liking the blues. Thank you.

To the late Clyde Woods. *Development Arrested* is the big joker. I hope *I Don't Like the Blues* can be a small spade. Your work has become the root that you wrote so defiantly and precisely about. We are growing from it. Thank you.

To Zandria. However far I get and whichever way I get there, if there is any good in it, it will be because of you. I know you came from the future. When you go back, know that you showed us more of it than we would have otherwise seen. Thank you.

To Marcus. For modeling the world that you want to make, for giving us tools to model the worlds that Black folks have made; for being kind. Thank you.

To Karolyn Tyson, Andy Andrews, and Mosi Ifatunji. I will say the same thing now that I said back then, but differently. Thank you for having the faith that I would one day catch up with myself, and for giving me the map to cover the ground.

To some folks who write how I want to live—Regina Bradley (for writing how we talk, country), Tressie McMillan Cottom (for *Thick*, and do-si-do), Jamie Hatley (for "Hating the Blues"), Kiese Laymon (for *Long Division* and *How to Slowly Kill Yourself and Others in America* and *Heavy* and how you talk about "*revision,*" and so on), Kevin Quashie (for "quiet"). Y'all are the "makers of aesthetics" that Achebe talked about; and y'all are helping me make mine, such as it is. A footnote was not enough. This isn't either. Thank you.

To Blake. Brother. I don't know if we'll ever get them three hands daddy was talking about, but I like to think that we can be each other's. We are each other's. Thank you.

To Zo (Dr. Hopper) and Steve (Dr. Harris). Brothers. Y'all do that thing that family does—like magic—lift me up and hold me down at the same damn time. We going white label for this one. Thank you.

To Felicia (Dr. Arriaga). Friend. You give so much of yourself to your dreams, and every day you fight to make what you dream be how you live.

You fight so that other folks can dream and live too. We can learn from you. Thank you.

To Ty, Dom (Dr. Scott), and Lil' Bro (Gary). For helping keep me, for trusting me, for all them nights with words and laughter. Thank you.

To the institutions and people that helped facilitate both where this project started and where it has come after all this time—the Association of Black Sociologists; the National Science Foundation (Grant No. DGE-1144081); the American Sociological Association (Minority Fellowship Program, Cohort 42); the University of North Carolina at Chapel Hill (the Department of Sociology, the Graduate School, Kathy Wood and the Initiative for Minority Excellence, and "Team Tyson"—Atiya, Courtney, and Kari); the University of Mississippi (the Department of Sociology and Anthropology; the Center for the Study of Southern Culture; and Drs. Katrina Caldwell, Kirsten Dellinger, Shennette Garrett-Scott, Jeff Jackson, Katie McKee, Ted Ownby, Kirk Johnson, Willa Johnson, and J. T.); and some select people and institutions in Clarksdale (Amanda, Brad, BT, Cortez, Edward and Keisa Thomas, the late Mrs. Fair, Mr. Johnny, Randy, Ray, Rosalind, Sanford, Tieryaa, Tim A., Tim L., King's Temple, and Spring Initiative Inc.). Thank you.

To Ms. Demetria. I had to give you your own line. You helped me walk mine. I didn't know what a PhD was before McNair. Thank you.

To my tribe, my ancestors living. Tip (Dr. Mayfield), since day one, the streetlights, the pasture, the series, "You try'n'a get on these bones," the backroads and the back way, since day one. Woods, for always making me remember where I came from. Bernard, DB, Enos, Grud, Princeton, and Travis for brotherhood, for still standing after all this time, for laughter, for balance. Carlin, for reminding me how good it is to be happy, for showing me. Allison (Dr. Mathews), E. (Dr. Claude), Kimber (Dr. Thomas), and Rufi (Dr. Ibrahim), for making North Carolina feel familiar. Piko (Dr. Edwoozie) for your brilliant mind, for making this project better, for always having a hip-hop metaphor handy. Thank you.

To my village and the land—Shannon, Baldwyn, Booneville, Trice Street, Lee County, the Path, the Bottom, Johnson Chapel (the church) and Johnson Chapel (the community). For being what a village is, shelter and home. Thank you.

To the late Jesse Scott. I have kept all those papers from your senior capstone course. All of them. I still revisit your comments. Still. Sometimes for my day's seven laughs, sometimes for your pointed critique, sometimes to remember. And, I will—your affirmations, the Popeye's, what you said about being blue-chip and "decorum" and respectability and Tommie Shelbie. And, you, *The Black Fantastic.* Thank you.

To momma. You are the first and the last, the why and the how. The most important thing. Daddy said "Use three hands" 'til he died. You let me do what life called for with the two I already had. Showed me two are enough. You are more than that. Thank you.

A SPIRIT
IN THE DIRT(Y):
A METHODOLOGICAL
NOTE

I think I had the story all along, even back a long time ago, when I knew better, when I thought all you needed to build and make things was dirt. Back then, when I was eight or maybe ten, I thought everything started from dirt. My pastor had said that somebody in the Bible had said that God made Adam from the "dust" but that since we lived in Mississippi, dust just was dirt. And if God made stuff from dirt, I believed people could too. I believed I could too.

I believed stuff lived in the dirt, stuff to help you build. Not worms or crawdads but spirits. Like the ones in the movies: the magic genie always came out of a magic lamp that had been buried under ground.

So I took to burying stuff. A coffee cup from the back of momma's cabinet. A half-cracked vase from that room in grandma's house that didn't nobody go in. One of daddy's empty Budweiser cans. Anything. Time would tell if the vessel was good enough, and you would know if you heard. A caught spirit hollers.

Sometime after I was eight, or maybe ten, folks started telling me you built and made things with other things. My granddaddy said you needed a blueprint. My daddy said you needed to clear the land and pour the foundation first. My brother said you needed tools; or, rather, he liked tools like you needed them. Momma said I needed to make up my bed.

There were other folks who said other things too. People at school said you built and made things with ambition. You believe, and you work, and you go to college; and when you get to college, they tell you need a degree; and when you get the degree, they tell you need two more. So when I graduated from the University of Mississippi in 2011, I went to get my two more. I entered the sociology doctoral program at the University of North Carolina at Chapel Hill. When I got there, I still wanted to build and make things from dirt; but I couldn't say it like that, or so I thought. Building and making was okay, but I had to do it as a "sociologist" and under the guise of "research," and I didn't need no dirt. I needed other things.

In "Justifying Knowledge, Justifying Methods, Taking Action" (2007), Stacy Carter and Miles Little outline what some of the "other things" are. First, they say to do effective research, you must first identify and acknowledge your epistemology. Questions of epistemology are questions of truth and inquiry. What do we know, how do we know we know it, how do we go about proving it, and how do we count what is proof? Is knowledge an absolute and finite thing that one can go look for and find; or is knowledge situated, meaning that what and where it is is contingent on who is looking and where they go look?

Second, Carter and Little say we need to choose a methodology, which "provides justification for the methods of a research project."[1] If epistemology tells the researcher how to think about what they ought to do—like a blueprint—then methodology is the guidebook and approach that the researcher relies on to do it with, like "pouring the foundation first."

Third, what methodology calls for, methods help accomplish. To pour a foundation and build up from there, you need materials and matter, tools: a mixer and a transport truck, footing, concrete, hammers, nails, lumber, and so on. Similarly, to conduct an effective research study, you need data collection and analysis techniques, methods: interviewing, participant observation, coding, regression, life histories, and so on.

The final step of the research process is communicating what you found, or making what you built look good. Just like, according to momma, there is an acceptable and an unacceptable way to make a bed, there are best practices for reporting on what you did and what you found in a research study: hypotheses can only be supported or "not supported," never disproven; if you want to say "the ways in which," just say "how"; "use" is better than "utilizes"; "show, then tell." And so on.

The "epistemology modifies methodology dictates methods provide data for knowledge production" framework is right. It made sense and meshed with everything else I was reading and hearing at UNC, and the more I read and heard, the more I wanted to read and see how the framework worked in practice. If that was how you built and made things, what were some of the things that some of the folks (other sociologists) who were interested in what I was interested in (racial disparities in education) had built and made.

That was a lie.

I was not interested in what they had built or made. I only wanted to build and make my own, but I faked it. I fake-read Jonathan Kozol's *Savage Inequality*, about the trials and travails of schooling for poor and Black young people in some of the nation's cities: Chicago, New York, Washington, D.C., and elsewhere. Three or four times, I faked my way through *Ain't No Makin' It*, an exhaustive and exhausting account of inequality among two groups of boys-turned-young-men in Boston. Along the way, I fake-read a slew of other books about people in other places—books about men "on the corner" in South Side Chicago, books about "street" and "decent" men in Philadelphia, books about "bad boys" and "women without class" in California.

I fake-read a lot of books. They were good, just not me. I did not doubt that what the books said was happening to them people in them places was both true and knowable. It just was not true to me. I just did not know it. Their blueprint was different from mine, or mine apparently not legible to them. The reason was clear to me. They were writing about places with concrete and dust. The place that I knew—the rural South—had dirt.

If epistemology is the blueprint for what we believe is true and knowable, my epistemology was dirt. That was true, and I had known it the whole time, since I was eight, or maybe ten. I believed that people became who they were because of where they were, that growing up in Chicago meant one thing and that being in Mississippi, even if it might've been the same, was different. That is "constructivism,"[2] the belief that truth and knowledge, and all that those two slippery terms connote and require, are at once situated and situational, or put differently, a function of where one is in the world and what one encounters while there.

The more I considered the dirt, the more I felt compelled to return to it. If Carter and Little and the folks at UNC were right, then a dirt epistemology meant I needed a dirt methodology. That dirt methodology was "grounded theory."[3] It sounds like what it is, a general approach to theory-building and systematic inquiry that moves from individual cases—whether a group, a community, an institution, or a place—to conceptual categories, or from the dirt up (i.e., induction). If constructivism says that truth and knowledge are situated and situational, grounded theory says the way to get to truth and knowledge about a thing is to go where the thing is situated and observe as many situations as possible. If you are interested in students or schooling practices, go to school. If you are interested in God or religion or maybe other things, go to church. If you want to know the dirt, go to the dirt(y). That is "ethnography"—immersing oneself in a social setting to understand something about the social setting or to use something that is happening in the social setting to understand something else.

By my fourth year at UNC—2014—I had stopped lying, or I guess I kept lying to other folks but decided to keep it real with myself. I let people call me a sociologist, but I told myself I was just building stuff, stories. I started framing what I did with words like "constructivism," "grounded theory," and "ethnography," but I was thinking, the whole time, of dirt. What was the use of a blueprint or a foundation, if there was no ground? The ground, my truth, was dirt. My epistemology needed to be too. So did my methodology. My research questions already were. They were not about Black students in schools. They were about Black folks in the country (South), folks like my granddaddy and them. Dirty questions made dirty methods, and dirty methods meant going back to where the dirt was—the rural South; so I went, to Clarksdale. I have already told you what I saw and heard while I was there. This note is about what I did.

BEING IN CLARKSDALE

I Don't Like the Blues is based on five years and twenty-six days of ethnographic data collection in Clarksdale, Mississippi. The study spans July 23, 2014, when I first moved to Clarksdale and August 16, 2019, when I had to stop going to finish this story. While the five-year timeline represents one continuous research engagement, the nature of fieldwork changed in significant ways at two different time points, making for three somewhat unique phases.

Phase One: July 23, 2014–August 31, 2015

I first moved to Clarksdale on July 23, 2014. I lived in a house with two Teach For America (TFA) Corps Members, one who had already fulfilled his two-year service term in another Delta town and was working as an assistant principal at a local secondary school. The other was entering his first year in TFA, arriving to the Delta, like me, for the first time. I was two degrees of separation from the first one. We were both University of Mississippi alumni, and I had been referred by a friend to a friend of his, who then referred him to me. I was three degrees of separation from the other. He was a University of Mississippi alumnus too, and I met him through the first one.

After settling in, I set some parameters for the first month of the study. At the time, I planned to live in Clarksdale for one year, which initially made me want to move fast, to talk to as many people and go to as many places as possible, as fast as possible. The dirt—my research epistemology—told me to be slow.

I tried to be slow.

I told myself that, for the first month or so, I would live in Clarksdale as a "normal person." No interviews. No observations. Instead, just find a barber, a gym, a church, a place to buy groceries. Subscribe to the newspaper.

I was not slow.

After about two weeks, I had already met a dozen people, most through unprompted introductions facilitated by my roommates. For instance, on my first weekend in town, one of my roommates agreed to give me a tour of Clarksdale. We drove along some of the town's main streets, and made two stops, one at a convenience store and the other at Woodlawn Coffee on the square. By the time we were back home, I had met six people, two of whom insisted that they would love to "talk more about what [I] would be working on in Clarksdale."

After about three weeks, I had met another dozen people and gone to something like a dozen places. I had spent time at the Sunflower River Blues and Gospel Festival, the town's second-largest and longest-running blues festival of the year. I had gone to something called a "Night Out against Crime." I had gone to Ground Zero, the town's most popular blues club. I never really figured out how to introduce myself to people. In those early weeks, I usually went with some derivative of "I'm a student working on a project about inequality in the Delta," or "I'm studying race in the Delta."

It was also during this early period of fieldwork that I joined Eddie Kane Jr. on a riding tour of Clarksdale (see chapter 1). Eddie was one of two people—the other Teryeia Pigees from the conclusion—whom I knew personally (both through shared connections at the University of Mississippi) before moving to Clarksdale. On the riding tour, Eddie told me as much as he could remember about how Clarksdale was when he last lived there. He named and showed me the town's neighborhoods, warned me about gang activity and local gang turf lines, and introduced me to a bunch of folks: his parents, several old classmates, and former church members.

One of the folks Eddie introduced me to was Dorothea [dohr-thē-a] "Thea" Goolsby, fifty-one (mentioned in chapter 2). Eddie and I had saw Thea, one of Eddie's high school classmates, by chance. She was checking her mailbox at the same time we were driving by.

Eddie had introduced me after blowing his horn too loud and too many times as he slowed his sedan to a stop, still on the street but at the end of her driveway.

"This Brian Foster. He go'n' be in Clarksdale for a few months . . ."

"Mhm, I'm here working on a research project," I said clumsily.

Thea frowned up at me before I had finished. "What kind'a *research*?" She asked. Her response caught me off guard.

"You frowned up like you, like you feel some type of way, like you're skeptical." I said, trying to laugh away the nervous.

"What kind'a research?" Thea asked again.

"Well, I'm interested in education, um, yeah, um, particularly, um, interested in Black young men. I'm a graduate student."

"You doing your doctoral thesis?" she said, again before I could finish.

"Exactly." I smiled.

Most of my interactions in the first several weeks were clumsy, like the one with Thea. I forgot people's names. I mixed up places and times, knocked on the wrong doors, conducted whole interviews without remembering to start my audio recorder. I turned down the wrong street 101 times. One of those times, a group of young men of varying ages, holding varying things in their hands, blocked me from passing through. One time, one person said to another person, after I had explained what I was in Clarksdale to do, "That's Clarksdale for you. People always coming here doing the strangest things." Another person told me to not "get too much into the race stuff" because "that's not a good thing for people to do around here."

Most of the relationships that I developed in Clarksdale between 2014 and 2019 evolved like mine and Thea's too. Thea and I did not talk for a little while after the conversation at the mailbox; but when we finally did we laughed about how "green" I was at first. Then we talked for a long time about a lot of things. Then we hugged, said nice things to each other, and parted ways.

Beyond meeting people and learning my way around Clarksdale, I spent the first few months (August–October 2014) developing a system for collecting and curating archival and demographic data. I wanted to see Clarksdale's bigger picture. Who lived in Clarksdale? Where did they work? What was the town like in the 1990s? In the 1970s? Talking to local folks helped with these questions, but I relied on other resources too: the Minnesota Population Center's National Historic Geographic Information System and Integrated Public-Use Microdata Series, a number of archival collections (discussed later), local and state newspapers and radio stations, social media content, and handbills and fliers from around town. I referenced these resources early during my time in Clarksdale and continued referencing them over the next several years.

By October 2014, I had picked up the pace in identifying local folks to talk to. I leveraged preexisting contacts both in Clarksdale (my two roommates, Eddie, and Teryeia) and in other parts of the state. I followed up with folks I had already met and initiated conversations with. I took advantage of happenstance encounters, typically with local residents and tourists who saw me around town—usually writing or reading—and asked what I was working on (similar to Big Danny's "You a writer?" from chapter 4). Finally, as my roster of acquaintances grew, I started asking folks if they knew folks I might want to talk to or who might want to talk to me.

In my fourth month in Clarksdale, I took on a more active role in some parts of community life. I began volunteering—twice weekly—with two nonprofit organizations broadly focused on "youth enrichment." I also began working at an area elementary school, an opportunity presented to me by my roommate who was working as a principal in the city school district. With some reluctance—I was unsure of the time demands and, honestly, of my capacity to teach students—I agreed, and for the next ten weeks (October–December), I taught two groups of third-grade students (thirty-nine students in total). I wrote lesson plans, attended faculty meetings and birthday parties, and met with parents about student report cards and progress reports.

While I ultimately decided not to include any scenes or people from my time at the school in the foregoing account, I did inform my colleagues and students of my status as researcher. For my students, it became easier to explain to them that I was "in college." For parents and my colleagues at the school, I either explained that I was a "graduate student" or that I was "in Clarksdale working on a project about the Delta."

At what I had initially thought was the halfway point of my time in Clarksdale (December 2014), I refined some of the questions that I was asking folks. For instance, broad questions about the structure of the school system in Clarksdale became more pointed questions about specific schools. What had been just a handful of questions about some of the town's blues scenes grew into an extended set of talking points about blues music, the growth of blues tourism in the town's development plan, and how folks defined and thought about the blues in their own lives.

In January 2015, drawing inspiration (and instruction) from W. E. B. DuBois's work in *The Philadelphia Negro* (1899) and Elijah Anderson's work in *The Cosmopolitan Canopy* (2011) I set out to document as much of Clarksdale's geography as possible. After finding Google Street View to be outdated and incomplete, I commenced with daily "street ride" neighborhood observations—organized by pairing community-defined neighborhood boundaries with Census Tract–Block Group designations (which I discuss later).

I spent the spring and summer months talking with as many local folks and going to as many local places as possible. I found comfort and angst in knowing that I would almost certainly see at least one or two pervious acquaintances pretty much anywhere I went whenever I went. I spent time at virtually every public venue in town, from the string of blues places on the downtown square to the stores and restaurants on State Street to local parks and green spaces. I stopped in barbershops and sat in churches. I went to sporting events, community meetings, and meetings of local government. I attended two candlelight vigils, both honoring homicide victims (I describe one such gathering in the "Porch" section that concludes chapter 4). I ran a local 5k and made my rounds on the town's blues festival circuit.

Phase Two: September 1, 2015–January 6, 2016

Before entering the field, I planned on living in Clarksdale for about a year. August 2014 was the start of my final year on a Graduate Research Fellowship from the National Science Foundation, and I would need to return to UNC by the following August (2015) to teach. However, in the spring of 2015, I was awarded two additional fellowships—an Off-Campus Dissertation Fellowship from the Graduate School at UNC and a Minority Fellowship from the American Sociological Association. The awards meant that I could extend fieldwork at least through December 2015. That fall I also joined the Department of Sociology and Anthropology at the University of Mississippi as a visiting scholar, and decided to move to Oxford, Mississippi, where in addition to continuing what I had started in the previous year, I committed more time to interview transcription.

The increased attention to interview transcription constitutes one of the two defining features of Phase Two. The second was the inclusion of participant observations of almost three dozen local folks with whom I had built rapport—folks like Boyce, Dahleen, Big Lap, Pooh Baby, Banner, Teryeia, and Zo. I call these "observations" what they were—"kickin' it with folks."

Kickin' it with folks including joining residents on weekend outings, for example at local entertainment venues or the casinos in Tunica County (see opening scene with Boyce Shumpert in chapter 3). I sat through busking sessions, guitar lessons, and midnight performances with blues musicians (see opening scene with Pooh Baby in chapter 1). I met folks at church (see concluding scene with Boyce in chapter 3) and for Sunday dinner afterward. Where possible, I joined them at work (see conversation with Dahleen in chapter 4) and spent time in their homes (see conversation with Cookie in chapter 3). I went to PTA meetings with parents, basketball tournaments for students, and barbecues with people's aunties and cousins.

Phase Three: July 11, 2016–August 2016, 2019

In January 2016, I moved back to North Carolina, where, beyond monthly "check-in" (i.e., off-the-record) phone conversations with some residents, I turned my attention fully to interview transcription and data analysis. At this point, I had about eighteen months of journal logs, field notes, and memos; and 161 on-the-record interviews (132 from Phase One and 29 from Phase Two) with 127 people (102 from Phase One and 25 from Phase Two). I had already spent Phase Two (August 2015–December 2015) working through daily interview transcriptions. I continued that through the summer of 2016.

In April 2016, I accepted an offer to join the University of Mississippi as an assistant professor of sociology and southern studies. That meant that I would again be moving to Oxford and would again be able to engage in fieldwork, as I had during Phases One and Two.

Between the summers of 2016 and 2019, I made more than forty site visits to Clarksdale and conducted an additional 87 interviews.

THE DATA

I Don't Like the Blues relies on (1) what I heard during 185 on-the-record conversations with 131 Black residents of Clarksdale (and hundreds more less-formal conversations with them and other local Black folks); (2) what I saw while working, living, and visiting in Clarksdale between July 2014 and July 2019; (3) what I gleaned from demographic data on Clarksdale and Coahoma County dating to 1940; and (4) and what I collected from archival sources in Clarksdale, Atlanta, and Chapel Hill.

Interviews

Between 2014 and 2019, I collected the names and contact information for more than 400 residents of Clarksdale. I talked with 183 folks from this roster, conducting a total of 248 interviews (inclusive of follow-up interviews). I am defining "interview" as any conversation of twenty minutes or more in which I gained consent (i.e., a signed Institutional Review Board consent form) and used an audio recorder. I use two sets of descriptors to further differentiate interviews: formal and informal, and structured and unstructured.

Formal interviews were scheduled, and *informal* ones were not. For instance, the scene that opens chapter 4 constitutes one of several informal interviews with Dahleen Atkinson-Knowles. While our conversations happened somewhat regularly over the course of Phases One and Two, they were never scheduled ahead of time. My conversation with Pooh Baby (chapter 1), while it took place as he played his guitar on the sidewalk of the downtown square, counts as a formal interview because he had agreed to sit for the interview ahead of time. Of the 248 total interviews, 190 were formal and 58 were informal.

Structured interviews included the use of an interview schedule (i.e., list of interview questions, subdivided by themes). Early in the study, I brought a digital or paper copy of the questions I intended to ask. In time, I started working from memory. I updated and revised the interview schedule at two different times during fieldwork—the first was December 2015, when it started to become evident that the blues would be at least one of the study's prevailing themes, and the second in the summer of 2016, when the story arc for the book had begun to take shape. The scenes with Mrs. Irene Sandiford (introduction and chapter 3) and Mac (chapter 2) are examples of structured interviews.

During *unstructured interviews*, I did not rely on a predetermined set of questions but rather entered the conversation with a general theme in mind or with the plan to let the conversation develop organically. The riding tour with Eddie Kane Jr. (chapter 1) and the conversation with Boyce Shumpert on the way to the casino after the blues show at T-Bone's (chapter 3) are examples of unstructured interviews. Of the 248 total interviews, 156 were structured and 92 were unstructured.

Finally, I include in this account several direct quotations from exchanges that did not take place in the context of an interview. Recall the conversation between Thickie, Deuce, and me after playing basketball (chapter 3) and the banter between Peatey, Hosie, and Jabo (chapter 4) at the chain restaurant. I documented both exchanges in my ledger notes within ten minutes of their taking place—with Thickie and Deuce as soon as I got in my car after the exchange, and with Peatey, Hosie, and Jabo in real time (I was seated two tables away from the main table with a journal and my laptop). While I do not count such exchanges or conversations as "interviews," I use them as such (i.e., direct quotations), with consent.

Analytic Sample

Of the 183 residents I interviewed, 152 were Black—81 women and 71 men; twenty-eight were white—15 women and 13 men; and 3 identified as multiracial, all women. Most were born and raised in Clarksdale (n = 130), what I call "native" residents, or were not born in Clarksdale but had been living in Clarksdale for ten-plus years (n = 27), "long-term" residents. Seventeen folks (n = 17) had been living in Clarksdale for less than ten years, "short-term" residents. The remaining nine people (n = 9) were either tourists (n = Shelbie and Himmens White from chapter 1, and five other people) or were otherwise only visiting for a short time (n = 2). Interviewees ranged from eight to seventy-one years of age, though most of the people I spoke with were between twenty-five and fifty-eight (forty-two years of age on average).

As I have mentioned, my analytic focus centers the perspectives of Black residents who had lived in Clarksdale long enough to have witnessed, experienced, or have close secondhand knowledge of the ways the town changed in the years following the civil rights movement. I operationalize "years following the civil rights movement" as the twenty-five-year period from 1964, when Black residents took legal action to integrate the city schools, to 1989, about fifteen years after their efforts had translated to a court-mandate desegregation order (in 1972). According to many residents, the 1980s were also the years when many of Clarksdale's neighborhoods "started turning," a reference to the precipitous racial turnover that played out both at the neighborhood level (see discussion of the "Oakhurst" neighborhood in chapter 1 and tables 5–11) and in Clarksdale, Coahoma County, and the Mississippi Delta more broadly (see tables 2–4).

My interest in Black residents who either came of age during, bore witness to, or had close secondhand knowledge of the twenty-five-year period

Table 1. Selected descriptive statistics for samples and interviews

Respondent Characteristics	Full*	Analytic**	Book***
Total Number of People	183	131	43
Average Age (in years)	40	43	43
Race			
Black	152	131	43
White	28	—	—
Other	3	—	—
Gender			
Women	99	70	23
Men	84	61	20
Nativity			
Native (i.e., born in Clarksdale)	130	110	40
Long-term (i.e., lived in Clarksdale for 10+ years)	27	21	3
Short-term (i.e., lived in Clarksdale for <10 years)	17	—	—
Other (e.g., tourists)	9	—	—
Residency			
Resident (i.e., lived in Clarksdale at the time of study)	172	129	42
Nonresident (i.e., did not live in Clarksdale at the time of study)	11	2	1
Interview Details			
Total number of interviews	248	185	74
Average length (in minutes)	47	58	82

*The total number of folks whom I interviewed on the record.
**The subset of folks whose perspectives and insight informed this story the most.
***The subset of folks who are mentioned in book.

A Methodological Note

between 1964 and 1989 meant talking the most to Black residents who were at least twenty-seven years of age, and who had lived in Clarksdale for at least ten years (i.e., were "long-term" residents). These specifications meant focusing most closely on what I heard from 131 residents (70 Black women; 61 Black men) in a total of 185 interviews (average length of 58 minutes). Of the 131, 110 were native residents and 21 were long-term residents. Eddie Kane Jr. (chapter 1) was one of two people in the analytic sample who did not live in Clarksdale when I was there. I feature 43 of the 131 Black residents as "book characters."[5] As I show in table 1, the demographics of the book characters match those of the full analytic sample 131.

Interview Transcription

I listened to all 248 audio-recorded interviews twice and have partial or full transcriptions for 197 of them. I transcribed 176 of these interviews manually, relying on a combination of voice-to-text transcription applications (e.g., Dragon Dictate) and more standard, manual techniques (i.e., I used audio applications like GarageBand to slow the tempo of audio playback such that I could transcribe while limiting the number of times that I needed to pause the audio). I used online transcription services (e.g., rev.com) for the remaining 21.

I transcribed all of the 185 interviews (with the 131 Black residents) that constitute my analytic sample manually. Note that I began interview transcription within the first six months of fieldwork and dedicated a substantial share of Phases Two and Three (September 1, 2015, and July 10, 2016) to interview transcription only.

Observations

I spent time in virtually every public space in Clarksdale at least once between 2014 and 2019, including most of the city and county schools and dozens of local events. I categorize my time in these spaces in four ways: general observations, focused observations, "kickin' it with folks," and "street rides." *General observations* include what I saw and heard during my daily rounds. I often refer to my approach to ethnography as "living in a place and taking notes as I go." To this end, a general observation might include what I saw when driving from my house to somebody else's house for an interview, or while writing at Woodlawn Coffee, or while "making groceries" at Kroger or Walmart. For example, my interactions with Peatey Lyles, Hosie

Carpenter, and Jabo Wren (chapter 4) came about while I was conducting general observations at the chain restaurant where they met every morning. After seeing me there on back-to-back mornings, Alfa told me to tell him who I was, which led to several subsequent conversations with the men over the course of two months of daily observations, and on-the-record interviews with each of them (including my exchange with Jabo from chapter 4).

Focused observations were more discrete and selective than general observations. Put differently, they were a general observations that "focused" on something in particular—for instance, not just what I saw when driving from my house to somebody else's house for an interview but a detailed account of the types of cars (and who was driving them) that I passed along the way, or whether there were people outside, where they were, and what they were doing.

Focused observations also included the time I spent at local events, whether a blues festival, an awards ceremony, a town hall meeting, a parade, and so on. Much of what I discuss in chapter 3 (i.e., the racial demographics of Clarksdale's blues scenes) began with general observations at various blues venues in town, and were complimented by extensive follow-up, focused observations. Between the summers of 2014 and 2019, I did focused observations at every blues venue in Clarksdale and at every blues event (e.g., festivals, concerts, live music showcases) on the town's annual calendar.

If general and focused observations focused on "what was happening" in this place or at that moment, *kickin' it with folks* focused on what was happening with a given person, or group of people, at this place or in that moment. In total, I kicked it at least once with thirty-two of the folks I spoke with while living and spending time in Clarksdale. This included joining folks at work and on work trips, accompanying them as they ran errands, going to church with them, or spending an evening at their home as they cooked, watched TV, or just relaxed. The scene with Thickie and Deuce (chapter 3) is an example of "kickin' it."

I spent a considerable amount of time between January and December 2015 documenting Clarksdale's geographic terrain. This included riding along every public road in town, what I call *street rides*, with a camera mounted to my dashboard recording video footage. After each street observation, I watched the recorded footage, taking image stills, or "screenshots," every thirty seconds (after I which deleted the footage but kept the images). I organized these observations by Census-defined "neighborhood blocks," which I had mapped onto resident-defined neighborhood boundaries. The photo gallery generated from the street rides (more than 10,000 photos) was intended to compile a comprehensive "portrait" of Clarksdale during the time of the study, and to aid in later descriptions of the town's spatial landscape.

I logged observations in a number of ways. For general, focused observations, and when I was just "kickin' it with folks," I took *ledger notes*, or a running commentary of what I heard and saw over the course of a given day. I took ledger notes in three ways: I wrote notes in a small notebook that I carried with me most of the time; I used talk-to-text, note-taking, and messaging apps on my phone; and I typed them on my laptop. The choice of method depended on the timing and practical mechanics of the observation.

First, regarding timing; while I preferred taking ledger notes in real time (.e.g., documenting Pastor Early's Good Friday sermon, from chapter 2, *during* the sermon), it was sometimes necessary or just made more sense to wait until after an event or observation had taken place (e.g., the chapter 3 conversation with Thickie and Deuce after the basketball game). In these instances, I documented ledger notes immediately afterward (in most all cases within an hour or so of when the observation had ended).

Second, regarding practical mechanics: taking notes on my phone worked well for focused observations in which I was a spectator (again, Pastor Early's sermon, or the holiday parade that I recount at the end of chapter 2). Typing notes on my laptop worked well for general observations in which I was passively present (e.g., while writing at Woodlawn Coffee). Talk-to-text worked better for focused observations and after I had kicked it with folks (again, which I did after the observation was over, e.g., with Thickie and Deuce). At the end of each day (or sometimes after a given event) I compiled all of my ledger notes into a single *field note.*

While I did not take ledger notes for streets rides (or include commentary from them in my field notes), I did compile short *place descriptions* of each round of observations. In these descriptions, I identified the order of the streets that I had ridden along (e.g., west to east on Riverside Avenue to three-way intersection at State Street. Turn south onto State Street. North to south on State Street to Washington Avenue, etc.). I also made special note of the streets (or, where more useful, landmarks) that bounded the observation area in each direction.

Beyond ledger notes, field notes, and observation descriptions, I logged the study in five other ways: journals, reflection memos, reading notes, analysis memos, and "retrospectives."

Journals were what they sound like—a log of how I was feeling from day to day, regardless of what was happening in the context of my work in Clarksdale.

Reflection memos were journals but with a more direct tie to the work itself. Put differently, if journals were about how I was feeling at a given time, reflection memos were about how I was feeling about some part of the work that I was doing at a given time. This might include my feelings about a recent conversation or observation, or my emotional response to something that happened during my time in Clarksdale (e.g., the murder of and memorial for Mrs. Millie Monroe that I describe in the concluding scene of chapter 4).

Reading notes included my notes on a selected list of books and peer-reviewed journal articles that I read while living in or visiting Clarksdale. In addition to a general summary of the reading, I also took time to flesh out how an idea, framework, or claim from the reading might inflect, challenge, or reinforce either something I had seen or heard in the field or an idea about something that I had seen or heard in the field. Here is an example of how I used reading notes, this note about the "mother text" of *I Don't Like the Blues*, Clyde Woods's *Development Arrested*:

> Woods (1998) seems to be writing, at best, *in conversation with*, or, more aptly, in *opposition to*, the idea that Black folks are always, mostly, and indeed *only* engaging in expressive *counterculture*. Hip-hop is counterculture. The Black Arts movement was counterculture. Black Power, counterculture. Of course, the blues . . . counterculture. Woods talks back. He is saying, yes, Black expressive culture is not just about acting *against* inequality but also about explaining it . . . and about creating spaces of sustainment and agency not despite it, but out of, or at least veiled from, its view. It's funny to think about what happens at places like [Clarksdale Blues Club] and [Clarksdale Blues Festival] as that . . . but that is what it is. . . . Black folks are critiquing what has happened to the blues, yes, but are they also doing something else?

I used *analysis memos* to flesh out the study's theoretical framing and possible broader theoretical contributions. Analysis memos were less about documenting what I had seen (that's what ledger notes and field notes were for), heard (interviews), or how I felt about it all (journals and reflection memos), and more about what I thought all of it might mean. It was in an analysis memo titled "Blues Place, Post-Blues People" that I hashed out some of the ideas that shaped the foregoing account, and how I wanted to talk about it.

Finally, I used *retrospectives* to "look back" over a period of time in the field, reflect on all that I had seen and heard (interviews, ledger notes, field notes) and all that I had felt and wondered (journals, reflection memos). I also used them to formulate early thoughts about what it all meant and how to make sense of it (reading notes, analysis memos) as well as to speculate about what to do next to make it all make sense a little more. While I wrote thousands of ledger notes, field notes, observation descriptions, journal logs, and memos, I wrote retrospectives only occasionally, typically in five- to eight-month increments.

Demographic Data

In addition to interviews and observations, I collected, compiled, and, where necessary, calculated demographic data for the eleven-county[6] Mississippi Delta region (table 2), Coahoma County (table 3), Clarksdale (table 4), and each of Clarksdale's seven major neighborhood enclaves (tables 5–11) as defined by local residents.

First, table 2 shows six panels of demographic indicators for the "central" Mississippi Delta Region, which includes the following counties: Bolivar, Coahoma, Humphreys, Issaquena, Leflore, Quitman, Sharkey, Sunflower, Tallahatchie, Tunica, and Washington. I calculated the data in table 2 as follows: I compiled information for the eleven indicated counties individually and aggregated (summed or averaged, where appropriate) up. For instance, the "Population (Total)" of the central Delta region represents the aggregated total of the "Population (Total)" for the eleven included counties. All percentages are averages for the eleven included counties. I curated data spanning 1970–90 from the Minnesota Population Center's National Historical Geographic Information System, data for 2000 and 2010 from the U.S. Decennial Census (collected through the American Fact Finder), and data for 2013 from the American Community Survey (also through the American Fact Finder).

In general, the data in tables 3 and 4, for Coahoma County and Clarksdale, respectively, were curated following the conventions used in table 2, save the need to aggregate or average up.

Finally, beginning with the riding tour with Eddie Kane Jr. (chapter 1), one of my earliest "findings" about Clarksdale was that residents had a distinct, almost universally shared, nomenclature for identifying local neighborhoods. The five most commonly repeated ones were the "Brickyard," "Oakhurst," "Riverton," the "Roundyard," and "Snob Hill." There were two others that, while used less frequently, were repeated often enough and mapped onto historical and archival accounts consistently enough that I have included them with the above: the "New World" district, which some Black residents called "Black Downtown," and the "Tennessee Williams" district, named for the playwright who was born there.

The more I learned about Clarksdale's history of residential segregation, heard folks talk about past and present community life, and thought about what I saw from day to day, I wondered if Clarksdale's demographic story—of labor market polarization; persistent, extreme poverty; infrastructural decline; and population turnover—might play out in different ways (or at different magnitudes) in different neighborhoods. How was Snob Hill different from Riverton, Oakhurst from the Roundyard? The more I wondered, the more I searched for a method to capture and test what I wondered.

I found what I was looking for in one of those books that I had fake-read when I was pretending to be a good sociologist during my first three years at UNC: David Harding's *Living the Drama* (2010). Harding used data from the Census Tract and Block Group level to parse the demographic characteristics of discrete neighborhood blocks. Harding had done the kind of thing that I was envisioning, with one important difference.[7] Harding had focused on differences between geographic areas as defined by the U.S. Census (e.g., a particular grouping of Census Tracts or Block Groups), and I was interested in the demographic profile of geographic areas as defined by the people who lived there.

Harding's method provided the scaffolding for mine: beginning with a wealth of commentary from local folks and archival accounts of Clarksdale, I sketched the socially defined neighborhood boundaries onto a map of Clarksdale with Census Tracts and Block Groups notated. With exceptions along the outer bounds of Clarksdale, every Census Block was implicated in the seven neighborhood enclaves, and the boundaries of the former aligned neatly and discretely with the boundaries of the latter. The consistency and accuracy were striking. It was as if residents had used the Census when determining which neighborhoods were which, or vice versa. For instance, for the 2000 and 2010 Decennial Censuses, Oakhurst corresponded to the following six Census block groups—Census Tract (CT) 9504–Block Group (BG) 3;

CT 9504–BG 4; CT 9505–BG 1, CT9505–BG2, CT9505–BG3. The Round-yard was CT 9506–BG 2. The Brickyard included CT 9504–BG1, CT 9507–BG1, CT 9507–BG2, CT 9507–BG3, CT 9507–BG4, and CT 9507–BG5.

After mapping the resident-defined neighborhood designations onto the Census map, I populated a table with demographic data corresponding to each CT-BG dyad. (Note that Block Groups are the smallest geographic designations for which the Census keeps publicly available data.) For neighborhoods comprising only one such dyad (e.g., the Roundyard), I treated the demographic profile of the CT-BG dyad as the demographic profile of the neighborhood. For neighborhoods that comprised multiple CT-BG dyads, I compiled demographic profiles for each implicated CT-BG dyad and aggregated and averaged up (similar to what I had done of the eleven-county Delta region). This process, though tedious, was surprisingly straightforward, with one important consideration: between 1990 and 2013, the Census added, combined, and eliminated some CT-BG dyads. Two such reclassifications are notable here. First, while Oakhurst corresponded to the same five CT-BG configurations at panels 2013, 2010, and 2000, it included six CT-BG dyads in 1990. Second, between 2000 and 2010, the New World district came to include the full span of the "historic" downtown square, which had been grouped in the CT-BG dyad with the Tennessee Williams district in years prior (I discuss how this second reclassification came about, as well as some of its implications, in note 22 of chapter 1).

Archival Data

During my time in Clarksdale, I collected print or digital copies of every article, including letters to the editor, from the *Clarksdale Press Register*, the town's primary newspaper, dating to 2005. I filed paper copies by year, month, week, and day of publication, and I downloaded and indexed digital copies by year, month, and week of first release. I supplemented local newspapers with more than 200 newspaper and magazine articles, profiles, and feature stories from larger publications, including the *Jackson (MS) Clarion Ledger*, the *New York Times*, the *Washington Post*, and *The Economist*. During analysis, I read every article of the local newspaper that overlapped with my time in the field, pulling and coding articles that were especially pertinent (e.g., articles about the opening of a new blues venue or publicizing a coming blues festival).

In addition to the 248 interviews that I conducted personally, I also relied on interviews and interview excerpts from archival sources. First, I identified and downloaded source material from two digital archives: the Civil Rights Movement in Mississippi collection at the University of Southern Mississippi (23 audio files and transcripts) and the Project South collection at Stanford University (2 interview transcripts). Second, I visited Emory University to pull items from the Southern Regional Council: Will the Circle Be Unbroken oral history collection (13 transcripts) and to UNC to pull items from the Allard K. Lowenstein Archives (2 interviews transcripts only). These forty interviews spanned from 1972 to 1996 and include residents and civil rights organizers who were either native residents of Clarksdale or Coahoma County, or had organized or otherwise worked in the area. I also relied on the work of other scholars, namely Françoise Hamlin in *Crossroads at Clarksdale* (see chapter 3 and the conclusion) and Clyde Woods in *Development Arrested* (see chapter 1).

Data Management

In total, my work in Clarksdale produced 197 interview transcripts; more than 1,500 field notes; more than 800 journal logs, memos (reflection, analysis), and retrospectives; and dozens of interview transcripts and other documents from the archives (e.g., I took 112 photos to capture the transcript of a single interview in the Southern Regional Council: Will the Circle Be Unbroken oral history collection at Emory). I stored and organized all of these materials in a database.

I built the database as follows: I generated and attached a unique *item identifier* to every item that I collected (interview transcripts; ledger notes; field notes; journals; reflection and analysis memos; reading notes; retrospectives; digital and paper copies of the *Press Register*; physical items from the field; transcripts and other documents from the archives; and audio, photo, and video files). Item identifiers paired the type of item with the date on which the item was collected or curated, and the sequential number in which it was collected and curated on that day. For instance, April 10, 2015, was the day of Clarksdale's Juke Joint Festival. On that day, I compiled dozens of ledger notes that I consolidated into a single field note, titled "150410 Field Note (Juke Joint Festival)." This field note included dozens of photos, each labeled as "150410 Photo," "150410.02 Photo," "150410.03 Photo," and so on. I recorded audio and video files and named them using the same conventions. I conducted two official interviews that day, which I labeled "150410 Interview" and "150410.02 Interview."

For items that featured or involved local folks in some way, I also appended *person identifiers* that I had generated using the last two numerals of the academic year in which the person became involved in the project and the place that the person occupied on my roster. So, for the sixtieth person recruited during the 2014–15 academic term, I used the person identifier, "1415060." Thus the full labels for the two aforementioned interviews were "150410 Interview (Participant 1415026)" and "150410.02 Interview (Participant 1415039)." While I generally avoided capturing photos and video of local folks, in cases where I did (and did not delete them), I included person identifiers in the labels for those files as well, for example "150410.2 Photo (Participant 141539)."

Using person identifiers served two purposes. It allowed me to scrub all documents of folks' real names, which I stored separately from all files and records related to the study; and it made it easier to batch and search for fieldwork items that involved the same person. For instance, the same person might be featured in seven field notes, six memos, one retrospective, and three interview transcripts over a three-year period.

I also used "place identifiers," which paired the pseudonyms for the name of a venue, event, or neighborhood with the Census Tract–Block Group dyad in which the venue, event, or neighborhood was located. While including both pieces of information is in some ways a fool's errand (Why anonymize place names if I am also going to specify the Census coordinates of its attendant neighborhood?), it at least makes identifying specific locations in the city something less than straightforward, while also allowing me to batch fieldwork items by Census Tract and Block Group. While I established and built the foregoing system of data management manually at first, I eventually integrated my system with a computer-based, qualitative data analysis program (Atlas.TI for Mac). This made searching and batching documents more seamless and efficient, and allowed for more sophisticated analytic procedures.

Analysis

My dirt epistemology, grounded theory approach translated to three decisions about data analysis: (1) I began analysis *during* data collection and allowed early findings and suppositions to inform the project as it was developing (e.g., altering the interview schedule); (2) I often relied on language that I heard and saw in the field to make sense of what I heard and saw in the field (note chapter titles and section headings throughout the book); and (3) I coded everything—photos, field notes, reflection memos, and retrospectives.

In general, I used five types of codes in data analysis: descriptor, in vivo, meaning unit, thematic, and analysis. Each code corresponds to a "higher level" of analysis:[8] beginning with descriptor and in vivo codes, moving to meaning units, and ultimately working up to thematic categories and analysis codes. Here's an example: in the transcript for the informal interview with Boyce Shumpert after the show at T-Bone's (chapter 3), I coded his "That's for the white folks" claim with the in vivo code "for white folks" and several descriptor codes, including "race." Then I appended the same passage with the meaning unit codes "blues dislike" and "racial boundary," which I had also appended to several field notes and photos from general observations. Next I grouped Boyce's "That's for the white folks" comment, and the attendant codes, under the thematic category "Space/Place Designation" and the analysis code "racial boundary work as racial attitude as racial performance."

I also used Atlas.TI to assess other types of relationships between codes. This included generating code frequency tables (to assess how many times certain words or codes were used), code matrices (to see which words and codes co-occurred the most), and word clouds (to assess more complex relationships between words and codes), among other tools. To continue with the previous example, the foundation of the analysis in chapter 3 began with the fieldwork items at the intersection of "blues dislike" and "space and place in Clarksdale."

As my intentions shifted from "making sense of the data" to "finding the best way to tell the story" of what sense the data made, I relied on narrative analytic techniques. First, I compiled "life history profiles"[9] for forty-seven of the people I spoke to. This included a very basic, if extensive, profile of a person's life, as told by them, from their earliest memories to the present. I compiled life histories for a majority of the folks featured as book characters. I also used a version of an "evidence board" (think *Law and Order: SVU*, *American Gangster*, or *Homeland*) to identify narrative overlap and interesting narrative throughlines. The most powerful example of the usefulness of this "boarding" method is the coda, where the intersection of Sunflower Avenue and the railroad tracks becomes a fulcrum for many of the stories key figures, findings, and context.

THE DIRT REMEMBERS, THE SPIRIT HOLLERS

What I did in Mississippi between 2014 and 2019 is questionable. There are questions of power and privilege. As I have mentioned, I received funding

A Methodological Note

from three different sources in the first two "phases" of my work in Clarksdale (the National Science Foundation, the Graduate School at UNC, and the American Sociological Association) and was working as a college professor for a significant part of the third one. That raises questions of power and privilege. Who I am and present myself as (a cisgender, able-bodied, apparently heterosexual man/masculine person) raises questions of power and privilege. That I am a "scholar," presumed to be one who "generates knowledge," and in this case, one who interprets and "makes sense of" other people's lives is a question of power and privilege.

There are other questions.

How can the empowered and privileged answer questions of power and privilege? How does the emperor know whether or not he has clothes on? I do not profess to actually have the answer, but one possibility is that he looks—again, and again—in the mirror, or he lays himself and his things bare. That is what I try and have tried to do in my work; and I welcome questions about process and inquiries about data.

Yet there are other questions, questions about the work itself, some of which, no matter how inappropriate for qualitative approaches,[10] will likely rear their heads at some point. Can one do what I did and find what I found (i.e., a question of replicability)? Do the data really say and show what I say they do (i.e., validity)? Do the data say and show what I say they do in a way that, no matter how many times I or someone else listens and looks, I or they will hear and see the same thing (i.e., reliability)? How did my presence or perspective jumble the collection, analysis, or presentation of the data (i.e., reactivity)? What is the broader import of my questions, methodology, methods, and findings; or does what I say and show really say and show anything beyond Clarksdale (i.e., generalizability)?

There are other questions.

How does the well-meaning ethnographer find his way to the "big kids' table," where the blue chips do their work? I do not profess to actually know the answer, but one possibility is that he leaves enough breadcrumbs as he walks his own route as quickly and as far away from the table as possible. That is what I try and have tried to do in my work, knowing well that for some that will be—tricky.

Yet there are, I'm sure, other questions too. How did he remember what all them people said? How did he do all of that in that time? Why is the writing like it is? How did he remember?

How does one remember? There I think know the answer, and I have known it the whole time, since I was eight or maybe ten. There are spirits in the dirt, and to catch them we just need a vessel and time; and to know we have caught them, we just need to listen.

Somebody told me one time that to be an ethnographer is to "become the research instrument," which I think is a fancy way of saying "vessel" (or maybe "vessel" is a fancy way of saying what he said). If I have been the vessel the whole time, then I just needed time. It took five years and twenty-six days, 131 Black people in Clarksdale, way more stories than that, way more writing and revising than that, way more being wrong than that, but I have the story.

I think.

I Don't Like the Blues is the holler.

APPENDIX: DEMOGRAPHIC TABLES

Table 2. Selected demographic characteristics for the eleven counties of the central Mississippi Delta, 1970–2013

	2013	2010	2000	1990	1980	1970
Population (total)	220,664	223,276	260,855	266,656	295,449	312,950
Change (since previous panel)	-1.17%	-14.41%	-2.18%	-9.75%	-5.59%	N/A
Change (since 1970)	-29.49%	-28.65%	-16.65%	-14.79%	-5.59%	N/A
Children (<18 yrs.)	58,334	59,636	79,942	89,631	108,820	135,833
Elderly (>65 yrs.)	26,918	26,507	29,869	34,671	36,425	32,038
Family households	50,890	53,782	62,660	63,127	67,990	91,850
Race/ethnicity						
Non-Hispanic white (total)	59,653	60,569	81,696	99,704	114,607	122,770
Change (since previous panel)	-1.51%	-25.86%	-18.06%	-13.00%	-6.65%	N/A
Change (since 1970)	-51.41%	-50.66%	-33.46%	-18.79%	-6.65%	N/A
Non-Hispanic Black (total)	153,767	156,059	173,361	164,167	175,783	188,754
Change (since previous panel)	-1.47%	-9.98%	5.60%	-6.61%	-6.87%	N/A
Change (since 1970)	-18.54%	-17.32%	-8.16%	-13.03%	-6.87%	N/A
Non-Hispanic Asian (total)	1,124	1,080	1,203	831	1,157	UA
Non-Hispanic other (total)	1,371	1,545	1,454	226	263	UA
Hispanic/Latino (total)	4,749	4,023	3,141	1,728	3,639	UA
Sex						
Male (total)	106,568	107,831	124,767	124,910	140,124	150,068
Female (total)	114,096	115,445	136,088	141,746	155,325	162,882
Socioeconomic status						
Aggregate poverty	36.78%	35.37%	32.69%	40.79%	38.70%	46.87%
Child poverty	52.53%	50.69%	43.41%	53.08%	49.83%	61.71%
White aggregate poverty	12.80%	12.52%	11.05%	11.51%	12.67%	14.57%
Black aggregate poverty	45.95%	44.82%	43.03%	58.09%	55.78%	68.06%
Median household income	$27,441	$25,546	$22,448	$13,840	$8,713	UA
Median household income (white)	$45,895	$42,298	$36,163	$23,797	$14,533	UA
Median household income (Black)	$21,703	$19,442	$16,956	$8,694	$5,968	UA
Education (population 25 years and older)						
4-year degree or higher	16.78%	15.53%	14.89%	13.40%	11.85%	7.45%
2-year degree or equivalent	6.46%	6.37%	4.45%	4.01%	7.15%	7.21%
Some college, no degree	21.30%	18.96%	17.02%	14.10%	4.12%	6.94%
High school graduate (or GED)	28.29%	29.40%	25.72%	22.04%	20.87%	16.46%
No high school diploma	27.17%	29.74%	37.92%	46.45%	56.02%	68.88%
Employment (16 years and over)						
In labor force	52.88%	54.68%	53.20%	54.88%	51.77%	50.55%
Employed	42.71%	44.74%	46.43%	47.96%	46.78%	46.65%
Unemployed	19.14%	18.18%	12.62%	12.34%	4.99%	3.91%
Housing						
Housing units	89,908	91,482	96,015	94,123	97,017	93,286
Occupied (owner)	42,773	45,127	52,859	51,070	52,038	41,203
Occupied (renter)	33,559	33,287	34,961	35,468	38,187	42,557
Vacancy rate	15.10%	14.28%	8.54%	8.06%	6.43%	9.77%
Median home value (owner-occupied)	$66,127	$62,627	$51,300	$36,900	$24,909	UA
Median "gross rent" (renter-occupied)	$536	$501	$337	$239	$143	UA

U.S. Census | UA = Unavailable

Table 3. Selected demographic characteristics for Coahoma County, 1970–2013

	2013	2010	2000	1990	1980	1970
Population (total)	25,815	26,151	30,622	31,665	36,918	40,447
Change (since previous panel)	-1.28%	-14.60%	-3.29%	-14.23%	-8.72%	N/A
Change (since 1970)	-36.18%	-35.35%	-24.29%	-21.71%	-8.72%	N/A
Children (<18 yrs.)	7,457	7,664	10,098	10,814	13,671	17,703
Elderly (>65 yrs.)	3,198	3,184	3,778	4,496	4,825	4,462
Family households	6,470	6,393	7,479	7,538	8,484	8,846
Race/ethnicity						
Non-Hispanic white (total)	5,854	5,918	8,898	10,933	13,016	14,232
Change (since previous panel)	-1.08%	-33.49%	-18.61%	-16.00%	-8.54%	N/A
Change (since 1970)	-58.87%	-58.42%	-37.48%	-23.18%	-8.54%	N/A
Non-Hispanic Black (total)	19,614	19,698	21,099	20,335	23,306	26,013
Change (since previous panel)	-0.43%	-6.64%	3.76%	-12.75%	-10.41%	N/A
Change (since 1970)	-24.60%	-24.28%	-18.89%	-21.83%	-10.41%	N/A
Non-Hispanic Asian (total)	40	114	143	105	151	N/A
Non-Hispanic other (total)	171	128	206	21	18	202
Hispanic/Latino (total)	136	293	276	271	427	UA
Sex						
Male (total)	11,873	12,003	14,065	14,412	17,292	19,096
Female (total)	13,942	14,148	16,557	17,253	19,626	21,351
Socioeconomic status						
Aggregate poverty	38.20%	35.50%	35.80%	44.20%	39.82%	49.38%
Child poverty	53.45%	54.10%	45.88%	56.93%	51.80%	63.38%
White aggregate poverty	9.72%	12.10%	11.50%	11.68%	9.17%	9.66%
Black aggregate poverty	46.51%	43.10%	46.05%	62.34%	57.75%	71.36%
Median household income	$27,735	$24,726	$22,338	$13,780	$8,591	UA
Median household income (white)	$48,768	$48,352	$39,438	$26,476	$16,142	UA
Median household income (Black)	$21,871	$20,144	$16,374	$7,318	$5,520	UA
Education (population 25 years and older)						
4-year degree or higher	17.50%	14.30%	16.20%	14.15%	12.09%	8.92%
2-year degree or equivalent	8.50%	10.30%	6.10%	5.85%	12.23%	7.06%
Some college, no degree	23.80%	20.60%	18.50%	15.18%		
High school graduate (or GED)	26.80%	29.00%	21.50%	18.24%	19.47%	15.21%
No high school diploma	23.50%	25.80%	37.80%	46.01%	56.20%	68.81%
Employment (16 years and over)						
In labor force	54.30%	55.70%	52.13%	52.16%	50.95%	48.35%
Employed	43.80%	46.80%	46.75%	44.84%	44.99%	44.62%
Unemployed	19.40%	16.00%	10.11%	13.74%	12.48%	7.72%
Housing						
Housing units	10,780	10,792	11,490	11,495	12,937	12,736
Occupied (owner)	5,046	5,331	6,045	5,966	6,306	5,068
Occupied (renter)	4,418	4,020	4,508	4,564	5,386	6,117
Vacancy rate	12.21%	14.45%	8.15%	8.39%	8.23%	UA
Median home value (owner-occupied)	$55,600	$53,400	$51,200	$36,700	$27,900	UA
Median "gross rent" (renter-occupied)	$574	$545	$360	$247	$140	UA

U.S. Census | UA = Unavailable

Table 4. Selected demographic characteristics for Clarksdale, Mississippi, 1970–2013

	2013	2010	2000	1990	1980	1970
Population (total)*	17,964	18,091	20,345	21,050	21,137	21,673
Change (since previous panel)	-1.32%	-13.00%	4.71%	-6.72%	-2.47%	N/A
Change (since 1970)	-18.22%	-17.12%	-4.74%	-9.03%	-2.47%	N/A
Children (<18 yrs.)	5,471	5,493	6,795	6,565	7,466	8,776
Elderly (>65 yrs.)	2,239	2,202	2,671	3,029	2,966	2,465
Family households	4,454	4,346	5,071	4,728	5,017	4,978
Race/ethnicity						
Non-Hispanic white (total)	3,332	3,460	6,135	7,360	7,960	9,840
Change (since previous panel)	-3.70%	-43.60%	-16.64%	-7.54%	-19.11%	N/A
Change (since 1970)	-66.14%	-64.84%	-37.65%	-25.20%	-19.11%	N/A
Non-Hispanic Black (total)	14,135	14,140	14,105	12,117	12,872	11,703
Change (since previous panel)	-0.04%	0.25%	16.41%	-5.87%	9.99%	N/A
Change (since 1970)	20.78%	20.82%	20.52%	3.54%	9.99%	N/A
Non-Hispanic Asian (total)	35	98	120	81	116	N/A
Non-Hispanic other (total)	164	96	151	14	11	130
Hispanic/Latino (total)	59	168	134	145	178	UA
Sex						
Male (total)	7,962	8,065	9,286	8,835	9,706	10,000
Female (total)	9,763	9,897	11,359	10,882	11,431	11,673
Socioeconomic status						
Aggregate poverty	40.86%	35.83%	36.25%	41.51%	35.27%	35.41%
Child poverty	56.11%	56.36%	46.34%	52.84%	46.20%	49.51%
White aggregate poverty	9.87%	10.48%	12.27%	10.96%	8.09%	7.27%
Black aggregate poverty	47.86%	42.40%	46.29%	60.36%	52.54%	59.16%
Median household income	$25,707	$24,740	$26,592	$14,860	$10,769	UA
Median household income (white)	$46,659	$48,159	$47,149	UA	UA	UA
Median household income (Black)	$19,029	$21,353	$18,600	UA	UA	UA
Education (population 25 years and older)						
4-year degree or higher	17.90%	14.80%	18.20%	16.03%	13.58%	11.03%
2-year degree or equivalent	7.90%	11.30%	5.90%	5.85%	13.92%	9.44%
Some college, no degree	24.1%	20.00%	19.00%	17.10%		
High school graduate (or GED)	28.80%	30.40%	20.90%	19.98%	21.34%	19.31%
No high school diploma	21.20%	23.50%	35.90%	41.04%	51.15%	60.22%
Employment (16 years and over)						
In labor force	52.10%	54.00%	52.55%	53.14%	53.91%	54.59%
Employed	42.50%	45.80%	46.89%	46.27%	48.26%	51.16%
Unemployed	18.40%	15.20%	10.72%	12.94%	10.49%	3.43%
Housing						
Housing units	7,218	7,494	7,757	7,210	7,513	6,987
Occupied (owner)	3,113	3,413	3,868	3,812	4,015	3,513
Occupied (renter)	3,229	2,893	3,365	2,947	3,154	3,046
Vacancy rate	12.14%	15.85%	6.76%	6.26%	4.51%	6.11%
Median home value (owner-occupied)	$56,500	$57,100	$53,000	$37,300	$28,300	UA
Median "gross rent" (renter-occupied)	$586	$537	$362	$253	$141	UA

U.S. Census | UA = Unavailable | * Population totals for panels 1990, 2000, 2010, and 2013 are derived from the Census Tract–Census Block Group figures used in Tables 4–11. Population totals for panels 1980 and 1970 are taken directly from the U.S. Census.

Table 5. Selected demographic characteristics for the New World district, 1990–2013

	2013	2010	2000	1990
Population (total)	694	697	1,183	1,725
Change (since previous panel)	-0.43%	-41.08%	-31.42%	N/A
Change (since 1970)	-59.77%	-59.59%	-31.42%	N/A
Children (<18 yrs.)	179	191	418	713
Elderly (>65 yrs.)	50	87	112	219
Family households	141	167	252	360
Race/ethnicity				
Non-Hispanic white (total)	22	13	6	8
Change (since previous panel)	69.23%	116.67%	-25.00%	N/A
Change (since 1990)	175.00%	62.50%	-25.00%	–
Non-Hispanic Black (total)	649	660	1,163	1,707
Change (since previous panel)	-1.67%	-43.25%	-31.87%	N/A
Change (since 1990)	-61.98%	-61.34%	-31.87%	–
Non-Hispanic Asian (total)	0	0	0	0
Non-Hispanic other (total)	23	0	7	0
Hispanic/Latino (total)	0	24	7	10
Sex				
Male (total)	349	348	556	829
Female (total)	345	349	627	896
Socioeconomic status				
Aggregate poverty	60.95%	45.92%	67.17%	63.87%
Child poverty	UA	UA	74.48%	72.94%
White aggregate poverty	UA	UA	N/A	0.00%
Black aggregate poverty	UA	UA	67.17%	63.87%
Median household income	$14,550	$17,012	$14,575	$9,364
Median household income (white)	$26,346	N/A	N/A	UA
Median household income (Black)	$13,550	$16,768	$14,575	UA
Education (population 25 years and older)				
4-year degree or higher	7.14%	3.42%	8.71%	11.84%
2-year degree or equivalent	2.90%	10.08%	1.39%	7.05%
Some college, no degree	11.38%	6.65%	11.85%	13.60%
High school graduate (or GED)	38.62%	30.80%	13.76%	10.71%
No high school diploma	47.99%	49.05%	64.29%	56.80%
Employment (16 years and over)				
In labor force	69.54%	UA	48.49%	56.86%
Employed	58.24%	66.92%	38.79%	42.86%
Unemployed	16.25%	UA	20.41%	24.63%
Housing				
Housing units	378	335	462	640
Occupied (owner)	112	125	165	195
Occupied (renter)	201	141	213	365
Vacancy rate	17.20%	20.60%	17.75%	12.50%
Median home value (owner-occupied)	$38,300	$28,000	$32,100	$30,467
Median "gross rent" (renter-occupied)	$570	$588	$383	$235

U.S. Census | UA = Unavailable

Table 6. Selected demographic characteristics for the Brickyard neighborhood, 1990–2013

	2013	2010	2000	1990
Population (total)	6,158	6,151	7,495	8,090
Change (since previous panel)	0.11%	-17.93%	-7.35%	N/A
Change (since 1990)	-23.88%	-23.97%	-7.35%	N/A
Children (<18 yrs.)	1,992	1,954	2,691	3,095
Elderly (>65 yrs.)	910	821	958	1,193
Family households	1,575	1,458	1,765	1,770
Race/ethnicity				
Non-Hispanic white (total)	127	116	151	234
Change (since previous panel)	9.48%	-23.18%	-35.47%	N/A
Change (since 1990)	-45.73%	-50.43%	-35.47%	N/A
Non-Hispanic Black (total)	5,937	5946	7,221	7,786
Change (since previous panel)	-0.15%	-17.66%	-7.26%	N/A
Change (since 1990)	-23.75%	-23.63%	-7.26%	N/A
Non-Hispanic Asian (total)	0	5	20	16
Non-Hispanic other (total)	40	35	75	3
Hispanic/Latino (total)	54	49	28	51
Sex				
Male (total)	2569	2668	3189	3,384
Female (total)	3589	3483	4306	4,706
Socioeconomic status				
Aggregate poverty	50.26%	43.38%	46.21%	59.26%
Child poverty	UA	UA	57.60%	65.52%
White aggregate poverty	UA	UA	56.49%	68.66%
Black aggregate poverty	UA	UA	46.11%	59.10%
Median household income	$21,290	$18,937	$16,877	$7,350
Median household income (white)	N/A	N/A	$16,037	UA
Median household income (Black)	$20,018	$18,940	$14,279	UA
Education (population 25 years and older)				
4-year degree or higher	15.89%	10.74%	10.98%	12.01%
2-year degree or equivalent	10.03%	9.71%	7.63%	8.02%
Some college, no degree	25.91%	20.30%	18.95%	12.22%
High school graduate (or GED)	26.45%	29.49%	17.75%	13.64%
No high school diploma	28.72%	29.77%	44.68%	54.11%
Employment (16 years and over)				
In labor force	41.88%	UA	44.96%	44.59%
Employed	34.35%	33.67%	38.69%	36.78%
Unemployed	17.98%	UA	13.95%	17.52%
Housing				
Housing units	2,558	2,475	2,727	2,696
Occupied (owner)	935	801	995	1,106
Occupied (renter)	1,350	1,461	1,567	1,471
Vacancy rate	10.67%	8.61%	6.78%	4.41%
Median home value (owner-occupied)	$43,950	$48,250	$47,383	$34,014
Median "gross rent" (renter-occupied)	$490	$459	$295	$236

U.S. Census | UA = Unavailable

Table 7. Selected demographic characteristics for the Oakhurst neighborhood, 1990–2013

	2013	2010	2000	1990
Population (total)	6,095	6,551	6,477	6,100
Change (since previous panel)	-6.96%	1.14%	6.18%	N/A
Change (since 1990)	-0.08%	7.39%	6.18%	N/A
Children (<18 yrs.)	1,910	1,969	1,823	1,467
Elderly (>65 yrs.)	698	766	1,031	1,112
Family households	1,527	1,624	1,784	1,762
Race/ethnicity				
Non-Hispanic white (total)	1,847	2,181	4,567	5,993
Change (since previous panel)	-15.31%	-52.24%	-23.79%	N/A
Change (since 1990)	-69.18%	-63.61%	-23.79%	N/A
Non-Hispanic Black (total)	4,179	4,227	1,761	11
Change (since previous panel)	-1.14%	140.03%	176000.00%	N/A
Change (since 1990)	37890.91%	38327.27%	15909.09%	N/A
Non-Hispanic Asian (total)	7	50	54	42
Non-Hispanic other (total)	62	29	38	7
Hispanic/Latino (total)	0	64	57	47
Sex				
Male (total)	2,718	3,002	2,997	2,832
Female (total)	3,377	3,549	3,480	3,268
Socioeconomic status				
Aggregate poverty	30.25%	28.63%	18.86%	8.33%
Child poverty	UA	UA	24.80%	13.01%
White aggregate poverty	UA	UA	11.34%	8.38%
Black aggregate poverty	UA	UA	30.24%	0.00%
Median household income	$35,996	$33,347	$35,689	$27,102
Median household income (white)	$50,495	$46,094	$40,774	UA
Median household income (Black)	$29,792	$27,744	$26,702	UA
Education (population 25 years and older)				
4-year degree or higher	20.30%	16.70%	25.22%	23.46%
2-year degree or equivalent	7.12%	9.85%	5.11%	5.17%
Some college, no degree	25.13%	22.46%	20.70%	22.55%
High school graduate (or GED)	27.50%	33.79%	26.25%	27.00%
No high school diploma	24.91%	17.21%	22.72%	27.51%
Employment (16 years and over)				
In labor force	58.55%	UA	63.65%	55.49%
Employed	50.43%	57.22%	59.01%	53.31%
Unemployed	13.88%	UA	7.18%	4.75%
Housing				
Housing units	2,560	2,636	2,723	2,633
Occupied (owner)	1,258	1,529	1,807	1,879
Occupied (renter)	865	817	684	579
Vacancy rate	17.07%	11.00%	5.77%	6.65%
Median home value (owner-occupied)	$66,780	$63,780	$58,880	$40,850
Median "gross rent" (renter-occupied)	$683	$666	$452	$382

U.S. Census | UA = Unavailable

Table 8. Selected demographic characteristics for the Riverton neighborhood, 1990–2013

	2013	2010	2000	1990
Population (total)	1,853	1,707	2,189	2,340
Change (since previous panel)	8.55%	-22.02%	-6.45%	N/A
Change (since 1990)	-20.81%	-27.05%	-6.45%	N/A
Children (<18 yrs.)	613	533	790	904
Elderly (>65 yrs.)	217	172	201	257
Family households	462	378	477	499
Race/ethnicity				
Non-Hispanic white (total)	249	218	442	528
Change (since previous panel)	14.22%	-50.68%	-16.29%	N/A
Change (since 1990)	-52.84%	-58.71%	-16.29%	N/A
Non-Hispanic Black (total)	1,556	1,453	1,694	1,761
Change (since previous panel)	7.09%	-14.23%	-3.80%	N/A
Change (since 1990)	-11.64%	-17.49%	-3.80%	N/A
Non-Hispanic Asian (total)	28	0	27	10
Non-Hispanic other (total)	20	16	12	3
Hispanic/Latino (total)	0	20	15	38
Sex				
Male (total)	847	776	1,006	1,063
Female (total)	1,006	931	1,183	1,277
Socioeconomic status				
Aggregate poverty	43.87%	43.02%	50.67%	53.27%
Child poverty	UA	UA	67.78%	57.19%
White aggregate poverty	UA	UA	8.04%	30.85%
Black aggregate poverty	UA	UA	56.32%	59.26%
Median household income	$12,122	$16,825	$13,452	$10,371
Median household income (white)	$8,125	$38,661	$21,762	UA
Median household income (Black)	$12,889	$16,475	$10,717	UA
Education (population 25 years and older)				
4-year degree or higher	7.09%	6.40%	12.70%	3.92%
2-year degree or equivalent	4.48%	22.58%	2.55%	1.92%
Some college, no degree	23.51%	23.55%	25.14%	13.34%
High school graduate (or GED)	41.60%	22.00%	20.83%	21.02%
No high school diploma	29.20%	25.48%	38.79%	59.80%
Employment (16 years and over)				
In labor force	56.91%	UA	43.05%	42.92%
Employed	38.46%	37.62%	37.62%	32.21%
Unemployed	32.41%	UA	12.50%	24.96%
Housing				
Housing units	691	690	661	709
Occupied (owner)	248	257	266	269
Occupied (renter)	379	353	395	394
Vacancy rate	9.26%	11.59%	6.51%	6.49%
Median home value (owner-occupied)	$50,000	$43,200	$38,950	$29,400
Median "gross rent" (renter-occupied)	$794	$516	$316	$234

U.S. Census | UA = Unavailable

Table 9. Selected demographic characteristics for the Roundyard neighborhood, 1990–2013

	2013	2010	2000	1990
Population (total)	575	504	734	735
Change (since previous panel)	14.09%	-31.34%	-0.14%	N/A
Change (since 1990)	-21.77%	-31.43%	-0.14%	N/A
Children (<18 yrs.)	173	157	258	287
Elderly (>65 yrs.)	68	68	100	119
Family households	121	120	170	170
Race/ethnicity				
Non-Hispanic white (total)	0	13	4	4
Change (since previous panel)	-100.00%	225.00%	0.00%	N/A
Change (since 1990)	-100.00%	225.00%	0.00%	N/A
Non-Hispanic Black (total)	575	484	727	728
Change (since previous panel)	18.80%	-33.43%	-0.14%	N/A
Change (since 1990)	-21.02%	-33.52%	-0.14%	N/A
Non-Hispanic Asian (total)	0	0	0	1
Non-Hispanic other (total)	0	7	3	0
Hispanic/Latino (total)	0	0	0	2
Sex				
Male (total)	289	208	319	318
Female (total)	286	296	415	417
Socioeconomic status				
Aggregate poverty	28.35%	21.45%	49.59%	60.40%
Child poverty	UA	UA	56.44%	76.40%
White aggregate poverty	UA	UA	N/A	N/A
Black aggregate poverty	UA	UA --	49.59%	60.40%
Median household income	$26,429	$27,857	$13,719	$8,042
Median household income (white)	N/A	N/A	N/A	UA
Median household income (Black)	$26,429	$27,857	$13,719	UA
Education (population 25 years and older)				
4-year degree or higher	5.47%	17.31%	13.01%	12.50%
2-year degree or equivalent	10.64%	30.45%	4.34%	7.93%
Some college, no degree	14.89%	20.30%	11.08%	15.85%
High school graduate (or GED)	36.47%	12.84%	13.01%	5.79%
No high school diploma	42.86%	19.10%	58.55%	57.93%
Employment (16 years and over)				
In labor force	56.97%	UA	40.87%	41.71%
Employed	41.54%	42.15%	32.77%	37.79%
Unemployed	27.07%	UA	19.82%	9.39%
Housing				
Housing units	213	228	256	251
Occupied (owner)	78	95	127	150
Occupied (renter)	98	100	119	83
Vacancy rate	17.37%	14.47%	1.95%	7.17%
Median home value (owner-occupied)	$34,200	$67,900	$28,100	$23,100
Median "gross rent" (renter-occupied)	$589	$914	$509	$273

U.S. Census | UA = Unavailable

Table 10. Selected demographic characteristics for the Snob Hill neighborhood, 1990–2013

	2013	2010	2000	1990
Population (total)	1,795	1,963	1,341	1,270
Change (since previous panel)	-8.56%	46.38%	5.59%	N/A
Change (since 1990)	41.34%	54.57%	5.59%	N/A
Children (<18 yrs.)	387	390	278	318
Elderly (>65 yrs.)	281	240	175	122
Family households	465	446	332	306
Race/ethnicity				
Non-Hispanic white (total)	1,212	1,105	846	721
Change (since previous panel)	9.68%	30.61%	17.34%	N/A
Change (since 1990)	68.10%	53.26%	17.34%	N/A
Non-Hispanic Black (total)	536	784	464	534
Change (since previous panel)	-31.63%	68.97%	-13.11%	N/A
Change (since 1990)	0.37%	46.82%	-13.11%	N/A
Non-Hispanic Asian (total)	0	38	21	8
Non-Hispanic other (total)	14	7	1	1
Hispanic/Latino (total)	33	29	9	6
Sex				
Male (total)	827	1,006	682	645
Female (total)	968	957	659	625
Socioeconomic status				
Aggregate poverty	12.92%	18.24%	7.98%	12.43%
Child poverty	UA	UA	6.88%	24.00%
White aggregate poverty	UA	UA	1.90%	1.05%
Black aggregate poverty	UA	UA	26.44%	45.79%
Median household income	$59,844	$65,086	$44,706	$36,429
Median household income (white)	$63,125	$73,333	$54,417	UA
Median household income (Black)	$80,625	$38,092	$25,455	UA
Education (population 25 years and older)				
4-year degree or higher	35.83%	30.71%	36.76%	41.90%
2-year degree or equivalent	8.12%	5.36%	7.62%	3.30%
Some college, no degree	15.88%	13.67%	19.23%	22.53%
High school graduate (or GED)	25.36%	33.56%	20.80%	21.70%
No high school diploma	18.05%	16.70%	15.60%	10.58%
Employment (16 years and over)				
In labor force	61.34%	UA	52.47%	60.12%
Employed	56.07%	54.41%	49.18%	54.96%
Unemployed	8.60%	UA	6.27%	8.58%
Housing				
Housing units	665	668	491	418
Occupied (owner)	489	467	317	233
Occupied (renter)	160	152	147	152
Vacancy rate	2.41%	7.34%	5.50%	7.89%
Median home value (owner-occupied)	$150,500	$118,200	$176,100	$91,800
Median "gross rent" (renter-occupied)	$660	$626	$441	$391

U.S. Census | UA = Unavailable

Table 11. Selected demographic characteristics for the Tennessee Williams district, 1990–2013

	2013	2010	2000	1990
Population (total)	794	518	926	790
Change (since previous panel)	53.28%	-44.06%	17.22%	N/A
Change (since 1990)	0.51%	-34.43%	17.22%	N/A
Children (<18 yrs.)	175	133	264	173
Elderly (>65 yrs.)	92	52	94	117
Family households	180	143	191	180
Race/ethnicity				
Non-Hispanic white (total)	370	176	308	564
Change (since previous panel)	110.23%	-42.86%	-45.39%	N/A
Change (since 1990)	-34.40%	-68.79%	-45.39%	N/A
Non-Hispanic Black (total)	419	331	601	206
Change (since previous panel)	26.59%	-44.93%	191.75%	N/A
Change (since 1990)	103.40%	60.68%	191.75%	N/A
Non-Hispanic Asian (total)	0	5	3	9
Non-Hispanic other (total)	0	4	4	1
Hispanic/Latino (total)	5	2	10	10
Sex				
Male (total)	451	229	461	412
Female (total)	343	289	465	378
Socioeconomic status				
Aggregate poverty	28.21%	29.21%	22.09%	19.19%
Child poverty	UA	UA	16.15%	26.53%
White aggregate poverty	UA	UA	19.42%	9.57%
Black aggregate poverty	UA	UA	25.14%	88.89%
Median household income	$47,986	$32,012	$30,945	$22,500
Median household income (white)	$49,643	$44,500	$24,837	UA
Median household income (Black)	$41,607	$30,061	$33,000	UA
Education (population 25 years and older)				
4-year degree or higher	32.53%	22.91%	25.59%	19.07%
2-year degree or equivalent	6.26%	8.17%	6.13%	1.06%
Some college, no degree	36.16%	19.12%	19.82%	23.52%
High school graduate (or GED)	12.12%	32.87%	16.76%	30.51%
No high school diploma	20.20%	16.93%	31.71%	25.85%
Employment (16 years and over)				
In labor force	40.88%	UA	60.25%	52.22%
Employed	38.15%	52.58%	58.70%	49.37%
Unemployed	6.69%	UA	2.58%	5.47%
Housing				
Housing units	251	219	337	292
Occupied (owner)	164	131	159	147
Occupied (renter)	87	81	153	133
Vacancy rate	0.00%	3.20%	8.61%	4.11%
Median home value (owner-occupied)	$65,600	$52,600	$54,600	$44,100
Median "gross rent" (renter-occupied)	$572	$597	$424	$323

U.S. Census | UA = Unavailable

NOTES

PRELUDE

1. In *Chocolate Cities*, Marcus Hunter and Zandria Robinson (2018) write that "black life in modernity is a boomerang rather than a straight line of progress" (3). I am using "boomerang" here as they did there—to suggest that a thing has taken a roundabout and turbulent route to get to where it is. The "thing" that they were referencing was Black American lived experience and social outcomes—for instance, movement from racial progress to backlash, from enslavement to emancipation to Jim Crow, from civil rights to poverty, from Barack Obama to Donald Trump.

The "thing" that I am referencing is the blues. In the beginning, Black southerners crafted the blues to survive the Peculiar Institution. Now they (say they) don't like the blues as a way to describe, critique, and imagine anew what life has been (and might be) in the wake. "Blues" has covered a lot of ground in the time in between, the route roundabout and turbulent, like a boomerang.

INTRODUCTION

1. I am using "backside" here in a *Chocolate Cities* (Hunter and Robinson 2018) kind of way—that is, as a reference to the spatial manifestation of both the enduring reach of structural racism and the steadfast ingenuity of Black Americans in light of said racism. Why might a place have a "backside" (i.e., a place where lots of Black folks live)? One answer begins with federal policies, institutional practices, and local customs. Think

about the role that the New Deal, redlining, and local anxieties about racially integrated neighborhoods played in the rise of residential segregation in the twentieth century (Sugrue 2005).

Another answer to the backside question begins with the beliefs, behaviors, and episodes of collective action that have helped Black folks—and Black communities—survive the violence of structural racism. Think about the Contract Buyer's League, an organization established by Black residents of the Lawndale neighborhood in Chicago to counter practices like redlining and contract selling that were systematically defrauding and displacing Black folks from their homes (Coates 2014).

In the first answer, racism made the backside. In the second answer, Black folks maintained it and gave it life. That's how it is in Clarksdale.

Mrs. Irene's funeral home is located south of the old tracks of the Illinois Central Railroad, in the "New World" district, which some Black residents call "Black Downtown." Neither the location nor the names are happenstance. As is the case in many southern towns, the railroad tracks mark Clarksdale's "color line," a sociospatial boundary, created and maintained by policy and custom, separating white and Black commercial, residential, and civic life. As I discuss in chapters 1 and 3, as recently as the 1970s, Black Clarksdalians faced both formal and informal sanctions for being north of the railroad tracks (in the "white part of town") depending on the day and time.

For most of the twentieth century, Black residents stayed south of the tracks, in the New World. They started businesses there. They built communities there. They sang and played the blues at the New Roxy Theater on Issaquena and Red's on Sunflower. They preached, sang, and got baptized at a half dozen churches—Haven United Methodist, Friendship AME, First Baptist, St. James Temple COGIC, and Centennial. They started financial institutions, barbershops and beauty shops, and funeral homes. Racism had made the backside. Black folks gave it life.

As Hunter and Robinson note, every place has a backside.

Zora Neale Hurston writes in her autobiography *Dust Tracks on a Road* (1942) that she "was born in a Negro town. I do not mean by that the Black *backside* [emphasis mine] of an average town" (3). Soul-stirring soul singer Lou Rawls talked about the Black backside too, just with different names. "In Detroit we call it Black Bottom," he said during a set at a stop along the Chitlin' Circuit. "In Cleveland they call it Euclid Ave., 55th Street, 105th, Central Avenue; in Philadelphia they call it South Street. In New York City, they call it Harlem.... I speak about this place because I'm quite familiar with it. Everyone is in some sense or other" (see Hunter and Robinson 2018, 45). What Black Bottom is to Detroit; Euclid, 55th, 105th, and Central are to Cleveland; and South Street is to Philadelphia; and Harlem is to New York; and the New World, where Mrs. Irene's funeral home is, is to Clarksdale. The backside.

2. With some variation on the finer points, the "Crossroads myth" holds that Robert Johnson sold his soul to the devil for mastery playing the blues. Legend aside, Johnson was a real person. He was born in the Mississippi Delta in 1911 and took interest in the guitar at a young age. At some point in his teens, Johnson left Mississippi's Delta for Arkansas's. When he returned, he brought back with him an uncanny deft and feel on guitar. That is where the legend comes in. Word is, that somewhere between somewhere in Mississippi and somewhere in Arkansas, Johnson and the devil crossed paths. The devil left with Johnson's soul. Johnson left with the blues (see Gussow 2017).

Robert Johnson went on to record one of the most captivating, if limited and idiosyncratic, blues catalogs in the Delta blues tradition (Wald 2004). Today, while several places purport to be the "real" location of the Crossroads where Johnson did his dealing, Clarksdale carries the mantle. There is a monument—marked by three interlocking blue blues guitars—at the intersection of Mississippi Highway 61 (often referred to as the "Blues Highway") and Mississippi Highway 49 on State Street in Clarksdale.

3. Henshall 2018.

4. *I Don't Like the Blues* is a work of nonfiction. It is based on hundreds of conversations with Black residents of Clarksdale, Mississippi, between 2014 and 2019, a five-year span in which I either lived in, lived near, or regularly visited the town. I use a mix of real names and pseudonyms to represent the people and places in this book. For the people: I use the real names of historical figures like Aaron Henry, Vera Pigee, and Frank Ratcliff; and I use pseudonyms for all of the local folks I spoke with. For the places: I use the real names of all businesses and social institutions, except when they are referenced in a harsh or unflattering way.

What Mrs. Irene said about the local blues club is not especially harsh. It is perhaps unflattering, though. "Moonies" is a pseudonym.

5. The Mississippi Delta is one of the most "developed" regions in the industrialized world—development, here, meaning the policies and initiatives implemented by elected officials, public stakeholders, and power elites to dictate the economic systems, land-use practices, residential patterns, and social and organizational infrastructure of a regional bloc (Pike et al. 2006). Historically, development in the Delta has been "uneven" (Ashman 2012; Woods 1998), meaning among other things that it impacts different constituents and social groups in different ways. For the Delta's white planters and their descendants, development has meant the accumulation and hoarding of wealth and social dominance, for Native people displacement and genocide, and for Black folks enslavement, disenfranchisement, and cumulative disadvantage.

In *Development Arrested*, geographer Clyde Woods chronicles the Delta's development history, highlighting the many factors that set the stage for contemporary patterns of inequality in the region. Some of these factors include the forced removal of Native people by English colonialists during the region's settlement years, the rise of chattel slavery in the nineteenth century, the hoarding of federal relief funds by white planters in the years after the Mississippi River Flood of 1927 and again with the New Deal programs of the 1930s and 1940s, local responses to food stamp and minimum-wage policies in the 1960s, and the establishment of the Lower Mississippi Development Commission in 1988.

6. "More than 200 Black residents of Clarksdale" refers to the total number of local Black folks that I spoke to both on and off the record between 2014 and 2019. The findings and commentary in this book are based on exchanges with the 131 Black native and long-term residents (all but two lived in Clarksdale at some point during the five-year span of this project) that constitute this work's "analytic sample." I talk at length about my approach to the work that I did in Clarksdale—and explain who I talked to and why—in the methodological note.

7. For a review, see Harrill 2004 or Thomas 2014.

8. See Neal 2002; or Hall 1993.

9. Historian (and genius) Saidiya Hartman defines the "afterlife of slavery" as the enduring reach and impact of American slavery in and on contemporary public thought, social life, and patterns of racial domination and inequality in the United States (and beyond). "If slavery persists as an issue in the political life of black America," she writes

in *Lose Your Mother: A Journey along the Atlantic Slave Route* (2008), "it is not because of an antiquarian obsession with bygone times or the burden of a too-long memory, but because black lives are still imperiled and devalued by a racial calculus and a political arithmetic that were entrenched centuries ago. This is the afterlife of slavery—skewed life chances, limited access to health and education, premature death, incarceration, and impoverishment" (6).

10. Beginning after World War II, Black consumer audiences began shifting away from turn-of-the-century expressive forms like old-style blues toward more modern forms like soul and rhythm and blues. Cultural critic Nelson George profiles the social and political currents that came both before and with this shift in the aptly titled *Death of Rhythm and Blues* (1988). See also Jones 2007; and Wald 2004.

11. Cultural critic Mark Anthony Neal (2002) calls "Soul Babies" those Black Americans who came of age between the 1963 March on Washington and the 1978 *Regents of the University of California v. Bakke* Supreme Court decision (which weakened affirmative action). Neal suggests that Soul Babies adopted a new expressive and political frame— what he calls a "post-soul aesthetic"—to help them explain and resist the structural challenges of the day. The frame needed to be new because the challenges were.

Soul Babies came of age at the fault lines of the civil rights movement and Ronald Reagan. Their reality was a riddle: deindustrialization and extreme poverty alongside unprecedented economic opportunity for a small segment of Black Americans and a growing Black middle class; the early years of the largely failed project of desegregation alongside increased rates of educational opportunity and attainment; new and inventive avenues of disenfranchisement alongside growth in Black political representation. Soul Babies answered the riddle with soul and other more postmodern interpolations of the blues sound (i.e., rhythm and blues). Neal's work in *Soul Babies* is both an homage and update to the earlier work of Nelson George in the 1992 *Village Voice* feature "Buppies, B-Boys, BAPS, and Bohos" (see George 2001); Leroi Jones in *Blues People* (1963); and William Van Deburg in *New Day in Babylon* (1993).

12. Jones 1963; Palmer 1982; and Wald 2004 give effective descriptions of the key components of the early blues sound.

13. One of the smallest units of music is a "beat." Multiple beats together (i.e., a pattern of the smallest units) make a measure. Many measures together (a series of patterns of the smallest units) make a song. A similar, if not perfectly parallel, relationship might be that of word-sentence(s)-paragraph. In music, there are many types of beats; and those beats, by definition, are played in different ways within the bounds of a measure; in the same way that in language there are many types of words (e.g., adjective, noun, verb, etc.), and those words, by definition, are arranged in different ways within the bounds of a sentence. What the words are and how the words are rendered help give a sentence unique meaning, and how sentences are arranged dictates the structure, function, and meaning of a paragraph (or some other larger unit, like a chapter, book, etc.). The same for beats, measures, and songs. How beats are arranged and, thus, played gives measures a unique sound and structure, and as the measures go, so goes the song.

Imagine a four-beat measure: [one-two-three-four]. The "one" is referred to as the "downbeat." It comes first, is typically stressed, and helps sets the tone and rhythm of the measure. The "four" is referred to as the "upbeat." It comes last, is not stressed, and anticipates the transition from one measure to the next. Take that as [Downbeat-two-three-upbeat]. The "one" and "three" are "on-beats," the stressed beats in the measure; and the "two" and "four" are "off-beats," which are not stressed (note: the downbeat is a type of on-beat, and the up- a type of off-). Assuming a standard composition, that would play as [Downbeat/onbeat—off beat—on beat—off beat/upbeat] or for illustrative purposes [*CLAP-stomp-CLAP-stomp*]. There are other ways to play the measure too. One could emphasize each beat the same way, as with four claps (or stomps) of equal velocity and volume: [*stomp-stomp-stomp-stomp*], or [*CLAP-CLAP-CLAP-CLAP*]. That is a "flat four" or "four-to-the-floor" beat. One could also emphasize the "two" and "four," as with [*stomp-CLAP-stomp-CLAP*]. That is playing a backbeat.

14. See Tsuruta 1981, 72.

15. Hurston 1990, 24.

16. Wright 1997, 145.

17. Robinson 2018.

18. Quashie 2012, 6.

19. Here I am echoing Quashie (2012, 4): "This is the politics of representation, where black subjectivity exists for its social and political meaningfulness rather than as a mark of the human individuality of the person who is black. As an identity, blackness is always supposed to tell us something about race or racism, or about America, or violence and struggle and triumph or poverty and hopefulness. The determination to see blackness only through a social public lens, as if there were no inner life, is racist—it comes from the language of racial superiority and is a practice intended to dehumanize black people."

20. Quashie 2012, 9.

21. This is a potentially thorny claim. I'll take each point in turn.

First, to be clear, "ethnographic work on the rural Black South" is a reference to a particular type of inquiry—ethnography—rather than a general topical area or disciplinary subfield. For instance, there is quite a bit of work on the rural South in rural sociology, but even there, contemporary ethnographies are hard to find. Which is the point.

Second, to my point about recency (which I discuss more in text): as Larry Griffin (2001) and Zandria Robinson (2014), among others, note, ethnographic studies of the rural South were once quite common in the social sciences. This was especially the case in the years after Emancipation, when the places and people who had enslaved millions of Black people for more than two centuries were forced to face their humanity, Black folks' and their own. However, between then and 1940, as Black southerners left rural places in the South for urban places everywhere, it became less common to see ethnographic studies set in rural, southern communities.

Third, there is an impressive collection of work on Black life in the rural South in literature. I am thinking here of recent work by Regina Bradley (2017), Kiese Laymon (2013, 2018), and Jesmyn Ward (2011, 2016). Cultural studies also has a strong tradition of work on the rural Black South. There is Riché Richardson's *Black Masculinity and the U.S. South: From Uncle Tom to Gangsta* (2007), E. Patrick Johnson's *Sweet Tea* (2011) and *Honeypot* (2019). I would also cite a few well-done New Media projects, for instance Alysia Burton Steele's *Delta Jewels: In Search of My Grandmother's Wisdom* (2015) and Vann R. Newkirk II's "The Great Land Robbery" (2019). This work is compelling and includes some of the best writing on Black life in the rural South to date. It is just of a different kind than *I Don't Like the Blues*. In fact, I would say that the presence of deft and illuminating writing about the rural Black South in literature, cultural studies, and elsewhere is actually a call for sociologists to at least attempt to do the same. *I Don't Like the Blues* is my attempt at that attempt.

To be sure, a few somewhat recent monographs on Black life in the rural South are worth noting. Carol Stack (1996) chronicles the experiences of southern families returning to their pre–Great Migration homes in the Carolinas. William Falk (2004) profiles the experiences of a Black family living in a coastal Georgia community with the goal of better understanding the social aftermath of the Great Migration. And Angela Howell (2015) explores how family, religion, and ideas about community shape social life for Black folks in a rural Alabama town.

To my ear, neither Stack, Falk, nor Howell tell the story that I try to tell here. Stack's work is about Black folks returning to the rural South after the Great Migration, useful but both dated and limiting. Following the work of Robinson (2014), I want to imagine Black life as a thing that can both be and be of value beyond the shadow of the "Great Migration." Falk's work is about Black folks living in a particular place in the rural South— coastal Georgia—but is both dated and, advisedly, does not seem to care much for interrogating or theorizing Black life, just documenting it. That is not to say that the work or the place it documents is unimportant or not useful—just that it is not useful in the way that I hope *I Don't Like the Blues* can be. Finally, Howell's work is compelling, but I think it falls where Falk's fell. It is more descriptive than anything, useful but lacking in theoretical novelty.

Finally, there are some recent (and forthcoming) ethnographic accounts of Black life in the rural South, and in rural contexts more broadly, that are good, aspirational: Danielle Purifoy's work in rural North Carolina, including "In Conditions of Fresh Water" (2017), her multiplatform, multimedia exhibit with Torkwase Dyson; Karla Slocum's *Black Towns, Black Futures: The Enduring Allure of a Black Place in the American West* (2019); Karida Brown's *Gone Home: Race and Roots through Appalachia* (2018). I'd also cite Ashanté Reese's *Black Food Geographies: Race, Self-Reliance, and Food Access in Washington D.C.* and forthcoming work by Joseph C. "Piko" Edwoozie Jr. (in Jackson, Miss.) for prescient insight about Black life in the post–civil rights South.

22. Lloyd 2012.

23. Gayarré 1877.

24. Du Bois 1898.

25. Earl Wright II writes about W. E. B. Du Bois's work with the Atlanta Sociological Laboratory in *The First American School of Sociology: W. E. B. Du Bois and the Atlanta Sociological Laboratory* (2016). In *The Scholar Denied* (2015), Aldon Morris also chronicles Du Bois's work in Atlanta, ultimately arguing that Du Bois and the Atlanta School pioneered American sociology. Reflecting the broader empirical focus of the discipline at the turn of the century, Du Bois's series of monographs on Black life in the rural South are among the first studies in the Black community study tradition.

26. Writing in 1903, Harvard archaeologist Charles Peabody describes hearing Black field hollers and work songs during an excavation in Coahoma County. "During May and June of 1901 and 1902 I was engaged in excavating for the Peabody Museum of Harvard University a mound in Coahoma County, northern Mississippi. At these times we had some opportunity of observing the Negroes and their ways at close range. . . . Busy archaeologically, we had not very much time left for folk-lore, in itself of not easy excavation, but willy-nilly our ears were beset with an abundance of ethnological material in song—words and music. . . . The music of the Negroes which we listened to may be put

under three heads: the songs sung by our men when at work digging or wheeling on the mound, unaccompanied; the songs of the same men at quarters or on the march, with guitar accompaniment; and the songs, unaccompanied, of the indigenous Negroes."

In the decades following Peabody's observation, Alan Lomax did quite a bit of work documenting and archiving blues singers and musicians in the Delta region. See, for example, Lomax (2002).

27. There is lots of work on the migration of Black Americans from the rural South to places all over the United States—west to California and Kansas (Painter 1977), within the South to cities like Louisville and Atlanta (Adams 2006; Hobson 2017), and north to places like Chicago and Harlem (Lemann 1992; Wilkerson 2011).

28. In 1938, the Carnegie Corporation commissioned Swedish economist Gunnar Myrdal (1944, ix) to produce a "comprehensive study of the Negro in the United States, to be undertaken in a wholly objective and dispassionate way as a social phenomenon." Six years later, Myrdal completed *An American Dilemma*, a two-volume, 1,500-plus-page report he compiled with the help of almost 100 special staff members, assistants, and consultants. While Myrdal's work was certainly not the first report on the condition of Black Americans (see, for example, *The Philadelphia Negro* [1899] by W. E. B. Du Bois), it has come to be one of the best-known and most widely cited.

29. Frey (2004) and Hunt, Hunt, and Falk (2004) write about Black "return migration"; and Frey (2014), Lloyd (2012), Reed (2003), and Ribas (2015) address various questions about the "New South." See Lacy (2007) for a depiction of a "New Urban South" center— Washington, D.C. Finally, Zandria Robinson (2014), Wanda Rushing (2009), and Patricia Yaeger (2000) have done important work in and on the historic urban South—Robinson and Rushing in Memphis, Yaeger in New Orleans.

30. By "monographs profiling a person or period from the region's history," I am thinking especially of the expansive catalog of work on the civil rights movement (e.g., Andrews 2004; Crosby 2005; Dittmer 1995; Etheridge, Wilkins, and McWhorter 2008; Hamlin 2012; Lackey 2014; Moye 2004; or Sokol 2008). By "humanistic accounts of the region's culture," I am thinking especially of work on southern dance, fashion, food, music, and so on (e.g., Edge 2017; Richardson 2007; and Twitty 2017).

31. Reed 2003.

32. *Henry v. Clarksdale Municipal Separate School District*, 433 F.2d 387 (Fifth Circuit, 1970), https://www.clearinghouse.net/detail.php?id=13733.

33. As I explain in full in the methodological note, in addition to compiling demographic profiles for the eleven-county "central" Delta region, Coahoma County, and Clarksdale, I also compiled profiles for Clarksdale's seven major neighborhood enclaves. This approach revises a similar method used by David Harding (2010). First, I subdivided Clarksdale into the seven neighborhood enclaves that I heard mentioned the most during exchanges with Clarksdale residents and that I read the most about in historical accounts of the town: the New World/Black Downtown, the Brickyard, Oakhurst, Riverton, the Roundyard, Snob Hill, and the Tennessee Williams district. Second, I overlaid the neighborhood map with a map showing Census tracts (CT) and block groups (BG), the smallest spatial designations for which there are publicly available data. This method of defining neighborhood boundaries the same way that residents do, then pairing the resulting entities with CT-BG designations, provides a unique opportunity to sketch and track the demographic characteristics of one of the smallest configurations of social life: the community, or, more germane to this work,

the "black village" (Hunter and Robinson 2018). Where there are pros, there are cons. While there are scores of available data for Coahoma County and Clarksdale—county-level data date back to the nineteenth century—CT-BG data are more limited. For BGs in Clarksdale, I found data for just three Census panels (1990, 2000, and 2010).

Thus, I begin this comparison with the year 1990 because that is the earliest panel for which BG-level data are available.

34. Johnson and Lichter (2019) examine rates of population loss across the nation's 3,141 counties (or county equivalents). They find that 746 counties (or 24 percent of all counties in the country) are experiencing some degree of "depopulation," which they define as "an absolute population decline of significant size over an extended period rather than an episodic or occasional decline" (9). In their study, a county was depopulating if it "reached its maximum population by 1950 and had a population at least 25 percent below its peak population in 2010" (10).

35. In 1924, Coahoma County Agricultural High School (CCAHS) was established as an agricultural high school for Black students. At the time, it was the first such high school in the state of Mississippi, and until recently was one of only three. In the 1940s, the administration added a junior college curriculum and changed the name to Coahoma Junior College and Agricultural High School. By 1990, the two institutions had split. The high school reverted to its previous name, and the junior college became Coahoma Community College.

In the late 1990s, CCAHS, or "Aggie" as most local residents call it, began to amass considerable debt, $100,000 by 1998, when it was placed on probation by the state. Between 2012 and 2015, local and state officials considered closing the high school. The remaining students would be absorbed by the city school district (Clarksdale High School). In 2016, instead of closing it, lawmakers converted CCAHS to an early college high school, under the umbrella of Coahoma Community College.

Just as public officials in Clarksdale settled the dilemma with the high school, they faced a new one, with the Northwest Mississippi Regional Medical Center (NMRMC). In 2018, Curae Health, a nonprofit healthcare company that owned several healthcare facilities in Mississippi (including Clarksdale's NMRMC), filed for Chapter 11 bankruptcy. This immediately put the medical center at risk of closure. I discuss the NMRMC more fully in chapter 1.

36. This excerpt is taken from Woods (1998, 16). See also the following discussion of the blues epistemology from Woods (1998, 29): "The intellectual traditions and social organizations through which working class African Americans lived, understood, and changed their reality have typically emerged in spite of, and in opposition to, plantation powers. This conflict is one of the defining features of African American social thought. From the unique experience and position of the enslaved Black Southern working class there emerged a self-referential classificatory grid. This distinct and evolving complex of social explanation and social action, this praxis, provided support for the myriad traditions of resistance, affirmation, and confirmation that were to follow. This pillar of African American identity is referred to in this work as the blues epistemology."

37. A number of scholars have examined the interrelations between race and economic development in the Mississippi Delta (e.g., Brandfon 1967; Cobb 1994; Jong 2016; Willis 2000; and Woodruff 2012). In general, while the region's "development agendas" (Woods 1998) have played out in different ways, arising at different time points and in response to different sociopolitical conditions, they have almost always given way to

the same dance: a "do-si-do" (see Cottom 2018), as it were. In the beginning, there is a disruption to the social or economic status quo. Emancipation was that. The Mississippi River Flood of 1927 was that. The civil rights movement was that. In the aftermath of said disruption, the region's power elites (i.e., white planters and their descendants) work to reestablish some semblance of the status quo that was ruptured. After Emancipation, that was the Black Codes. After the Great Flood, that was exploiting federal relief aid. In the midst of the civil rights movement, that was the "final solution" (Woods 1998). Finally, as the power elite work to double down on their power and influence, marginalized groups (Native people, Black people, working-class communities) organize and resist. Do-si-do.

38. In the first two decades of the twentieth century, the sounds that Black southern life had been making for a generation came to be called the "blues." For the next fifty years, "blues music," as it were, took on a life of its own, developing along two trajectories, as Elijah Wald (2004) ably chronicles in *Escaping the Delta*: music played "off the record" for personal entertainment and satisfaction, and music played "on the record" for label executives, archivists, and folklorists.

The on-the-record sound, which has come to define most conventional thinking about the blues genre, derived largely from the expectations of industry gatekeepers. Black musicians were pegged as blues artists despite having diverse sound and style repertoires, and white musicians were recognized for playing a range of styles, from "hillbilly" to classical, even if they also played blues.

Off the record, blues did not involve such rigid boundaries: Black musicians lumped under the "blues" category played a variety of instruments other than the guitar, including the banjo and the fiddle, and they were well-versed in styles other than the blues, for example Tin Pan Alley pop. Further, white musicians enjoyed widespread popularity and success on the blues circuit, even if they were not routinely producing blues cuts.

By the middle of the twentieth century, blues music was its own thing. Black audiences had already started to not like it (George 1988; Wald 2004). To them, it was an artifact of the past, not as resonant as emergent expressive forms like R&B (after World War II) and soul (by the 1960s). In turn, white audiences had come to love the blues more and more, infatuated by what they believed it represented—something exotic and primitive, something nostalgic. That was the sentiment that fueled the blues and folk revivals of the 1960s, and that stirred the blues revival of the 1980s, which ultimately stirred the tides of blues tourism that have overtaken parts of the United States, nowhere more fully than in the "land where the blues began" (Lomax 2002)—Clarksdale and the Mississippi Delta.

To say that "blues music" is merely the label assigned to what Black southerners were already doing is not a challenge to the foregoing history (or maybe it is, kind of). In fact, to say that the blues comes out of Black life is not a historical claim at all (or maybe it is, kind of). It is an ontological one. Trace the lineage of an apple back far enough, and you will eventually get to a seed. No matter what happened after the seed germinated—how long the tree took to grow the apple, whether it grew in someone's yard or in an orchard or in the wild, or how many applies it yielded—the apple came from an apple seed. Trace the lineage of what people have come to call "blues music" back far enough, and you will eventually get to Black folks. No matter what happened after Black folks made and did what people have come to call blues—how gatekeepers used the "blues" genre label, who has come to take the most interest in the genre recently—it started with Black folks.

For more on blues methods and the blues epistemology, see Jones 1963; Neal 1972; Powell 1989; Robinson 2014; Ruffin 2009; Salaam 1995; or Woods 2005.

CHAPTER 1

1. Mississippi Blues Trail, "WROX," http://msbluestrail.org/blues-trail-markers/wrox, retrieved January 12, 2020.

2. One of the prevailing questions about poverty in the Delta has been "how many." How many people in the region live below the poverty line? How many children? How many Black folks? Since 1970, the answer to that question has been something like "a lot, but fewer than in years past." Since 1970, poverty rates in the eleven core counties of the Mississippi Delta have declined—from about 47 percent in 1970 to about 37 percent in 2013. The same is true for poverty rates for the region's children (from 62 percent to 53 percent) and the region's Black residents (from 68 percent to 46 percent). While improved, these figures beg more questions, the answers to which point to more problems.

For instance, what if the question is not "how many" but "how far," as in, How far do the region's poverty rates exceed the threshold associated with the most significant, systemic problems? Many studies suggest that this threshold is 20 percent. Where aggregate poverty rates exceed it, educational outcomes plummet and residents have a more difficult time rising above the poverty line (see Galster 2012 for discussion). Every county in the "central Delta region" (i.e., Bolivar, Coahoma, Humphreys, Issaquena, Leflore, Quitman, Sharkey, Sunflower, Tallahatchie, Tunica, and Washington Counties) has an aggregate poverty rate that far surpasses this 20 percent threshold.

And, what if the question is not just "how far" but "how long," as in, How long have people faced the challenges that come with a lack of economic resources? How long have a place's poverty rates been high? "Persistent poverty"—a designation for counties that have had poverty rates of 20 percent or more for at least thirty years—accounts for this question of duration (see Dalaker 2019). Each of the eleven core Delta counties is a persistent poverty county, and in most cases, they have been for far longer than the thirty-year benchmark.

Finally, what if the question is not just "how many," "how far," or "how long" but "at what cost" and "with what prospects of mobility"? In each instance, the answer is a problem; and as Clyde Woods (1998), James Cobb (1994), Greta de Jong (2016), and others have noted, in each instance the answer has been a problem most of all for Black folks in the region.

3. Hardwell 2004.

4. MDAH 2003.

5. For a full account of the growth and expansion of the Mississippi Delta's blues (tourism) development agenda, see Henshall 2018; King 2011; or Motley 2018.

6. Foster 1991.

7. Bessman 1993.

8. Hamilton 1992.

9. *Jazz News* 2006.

10. King 2011, 63.

11. Oliver 1980.

12. Hamilton 1992.

13. Palmer 1988.

14. Hamilton 1992.

15. Hamilton 1992.

16. Murray 2001.

17. Shack Up Inn, "The Ritz We Ain't," https://www.shackupinn.com/ourstory, accessed March 16, 2017.

18. Johnson 1998.

19. Stewart 2001.

20. Henshall 2018 offers an impressive, and comprehensive, overview of the economic impact of blues tourism in the Delta, Coahoma County, and Clarksdale.

21. Clarksdale Revitalization's Facebook page, https://www.facebook.com /RevitalizeClarksdale/, accessed August 22, 2019.

22. John Henshall, one of the founders of Economic Essentials, has been tracking blues development in Clarksdale since the firm was hired in 2008. In a 2018 book, Henshall sheds light, perhaps unintentionally, on how the town's blues tourism apparatus has brought uneven economic development, noting that "one of [Clarksdale Revitalization's] first initiatives . . . was to have the downtown Census tracts re-defined by the U.S. Census" (153). Indeed, in 2000 the downtown square was a part of the first Census Block Group (BG) of Census Tract (CT) 9504. By 2010, the square had been added to the first BG of CT 9506 (see the methodological note for a discussion of how I use CT and BG designations to track demographic change at the neighborhood level in Clarksdale). The boundary change drastically reshaped the socioeconomic profile of the downtown square.

In 2000, before Clarksdale Revitalization proposed the CT redefinition, the downtown square shared a CT and BG with the all-white Tennessee Williams district (CT 9504, BG 1), which was above both the Clarksdale and Delta averages for various measures of economic well-being. That year, the Tennessee Williams District/Downtown Square CT, BG had a median household income of $30,945 (see table 11 in the appendix), compared to $26,592 for Clarksdale and $22,448 for the Delta region. Similarly, the poverty rate for this area was 22 percent, compared to 36 and 37 percent, respectively.

In 2010, because of the redefinition, the downtown square shared a CT, BG with the all-Black New World district, an area with the most depressed socioeconomic profile in Clarksdale. That year, the New World's poverty rate was 46 percent (compared with 29 percent in the Tennessee Williams district and 36 percent in Clarksdale); and the New World's median household income was $17,012 (compared with $32,012 and $24,740, respectively).

Before the redefinition, the downtown square presented as a stable, economically able mixed-use enclave. After the redefinition, according to the Census, it was one of the poorest places in the United States. Nothing had changed but where the lines were drawn. And to what end? Henshall (2018, 153) writes, "as a result of the initiative to re-draw the Census boundaries, *Clarksdale Revitalization* could apply for the 'new markets program' which provides opportunities for tax credits as investment incentives in low-income areas."

Businesses on the downtown square, the epicenter of Clarksdale's blues tourism apparatus, immediately had access to loans and financing options with low interest rates, low origination fees, lower debt coverage ratios, longer maturities, and other benefits (U.S. Department of the Treasury). According to the U.S. Treasury, the New Markets program is meant to attract new business to "distressed communities." The redefinition made the downtown square appear as such, even—as my discussion in chapter 3 shows—as the people living in the distressed community (i.e., Black folks living in the

New World), who enabled the square to qualify for the New Markets program, did not frequently patronize the businesses that the program helped underwrite.

23. Henshall 2018.

24. Henshall 2018.

25. See Austin et al. 2009; Delta Regional Authority 2015; Henshall 2018; Woods 1998; and the U.S. Census.

26. See Autor, Katz, and Kearney 2006; and Autor and Dorn 2013.

27. See Austin et al. 2009; and Delta Regional Authority 2015.

28. Woods (1998, 203) notes that "the increasing outbreaks of violence after 1964, combined with the campaigns of [the Congress of Racial Equality] and the NAACP to boycott firms that continued to locate in states that maintained segregation, led various industrial promoters and business leaders to moderate official extremism. According to one industrial recruiter, one 'lynching and we've wasted two hundred thousand dollars in magazine advertising.'" James Cobb (1982, 144) notes that "developers generally assumed that incoming plants would hire no blacks unless all or parts of their operations required labor so arduous, distasteful, and low-paying as to be unappealing to most whites.... A Yazoo City development leader admitted in 1966 that he and his colleagues were not seeking employment opportunities for blacks.... white leaders feared a black political takeover if a chance for industrial employment should stem the tide of black outmigration." See also Cosby et al. 1992; and de Jong 2016.

29. Voth, Sizer, and Farmer 1996.

30. Data USA, "Clarksdale, Mississippi," https://datausa.io/profile/geo/coahoma -county-ms, retrieved August 22, 2019.

31. Each of the figures related to Toya's income and public assistance benefits (Toya's pay rate, weekly earnings, child support payments, and SNAP benefits) are based on what she told me in several on-the-record interviews, all conducted between 2014 and 2018. The figures that I report are the figures that she shared, and the figures that she shared are consistent with state policies and protocols related to minimum wage, child support, and SNAP benefits.

32. "Living wage" is an alternative measure of economic well-being. Unlike standard indicators like "poverty," it accounts for the cost of living in a place beyond a basic food budget. The $11.04 figure quoted here was derived using a formula created in 2004 by Amy K. Glasmeier, a development scholar at the Massachusetts Institute of Technology. Glasmeier's (2019) formula "draws upon geographically specific expenditure data related to a family's likely minimum food, childcare, health insurance, housing, transportation, and other basic necessities (e.g., clothing, personal care items, etc.) costs." The formula also accounts for income and payroll taxes. Though the living wage is an improvement on the most commonly used indicators of economic well-being, it likely does not fully capture the full scope of a person's or family's financial necessities and responsibilities. For instance, Glasmeier's formula "does not allow for what many consider the basic necessities enjoyed by many Americans. It does not budget funds for pre-prepared meals or those eaten in restaurants. It does not include money for entertainment nor does [sic] allocate leisure time for unpaid vacations or holidays. Lastly, it does not account for planning for the future through savings and investment or for the purchase of capital assets (e.g., provisions for retirement or home purchases)" (Glasmeier 2019).

33. According to the official record of the Mississippi Department of Archives of

History, "The Bobo Senior High School served the Clarksdale community from 1930 to 1999, first as a white school and . . . fully integrated after 1970."

34. Françoise Hamlin (2012) chronicles the Roach case in *Crossroads at Clarksdale: The Black Freedom Struggle in the Mississippi Delta after World War II*. She positions the case as one of several catalysts that pushed Clarksdale fully into the fray of the Black freedom struggle.

35. The Citizen's Council was established in July 1954 with the expressed mission of opposing school integration. By October, several chapters had formed across Mississippi and had joined under the umbrella of the Association of Citizen's Councils of Mississippi (ACCM). Clarksdale's chapter was established in 1955 amid a nationwide surge in Citizen's Council activity. By some estimates, there were more than 60,000 members across the country (see Rolph 2018 for a comprehensive account).

Often comprised of high-ranking community officials and public stakeholders, Citizen's Councils deployed several tactics to carry out their mission. "We won't gin their [Black folks'] cotton," said one Yazoo County planter. "We won't allow them credit; and we'll move them out of their rented houses if necessary to keep them alive" (Hamlin 2012, 33). On the matter of schooling, Citizen's Council members often conspired to establish private academies, which were the de facto all-white alternatives to the newly integrating public schools (Andrews 2004; Munford 1973; Walder and Cleveland 1971). In many cases, they were founded and opened in a matter of days, with little planning and infrastructure. Schools opened in churches and vacant, or sparsely used, civic buildings and typically pilfered teachers, furniture, and supplies from the local public school. That was the case with Clarksdale's Lee Academy, established in 1968.

36. Prior to the implementation of a court-mandated school integration order in 1972, white students attended Bobo Senior High School (see note 33), and Black students attended Higgins and Coahoma County Agricultural High School.

37. I explain my methodology for compiling demographic profiles of Clarksdale's neighborhoods at length in the methodological note.

38. See Cobb (1994).

39. As historians like James Cobb (1994) and Greta de Jong (2016) have noted, Black residents of the Delta were doing one of two things: leaving the region altogether or relocating from small towns to medium-sized ones.

40. See Cobb 1994.

41. Amy 2015.

42. Alan Lomax (2002, 28–30), an ethnomusicologist who did extensive work in Clarksdale and the Mississippi Delta during the first half of the twentieth century, described the differences between the downtown square and the New World:

The business district [the downtown square] might have been that of any prosperous Midwestern American city. I had to remind myself that it was the cotton capital of the nation, locus of the biggest cotton plantations in the South. . . . These quiet streets of uptown Clarksdale in no way prepared me for what I encountered when I crossed the railroad tracks and walked into Clarksdale's black business district [the New World], the social and amusement center for all the plantation workers for thirty miles around. . . . Peanut vendors and Mexican hot-tamale salesmen peddled their wares. Fried catfish was proclaimed available in every restaurant window. Wagons bulging with huge green watermelons stood at every corner. Inside the bars . . . jukeboxes moaned and blasted. Blues, hot spirituals, jazz sweet and jivey—everything that Chicago had recorded to please Mississippi—washed across this pleasant, country crowd while they milled and gossiped on the sidewalk in the evening light.

CHAPTER 2

1. Black identity is not just about how (Black) people see themselves or what they do from day to day. It is also about what Black people feel, especially what they feel with respect to the lived realities of race in the United States. Eduardo Bonilla-Silva (2019) and others call these feelings "racialized emotions," arguing that racialized societies produce racialized subjects who develop, express, and transact feelings consistent with their position in the social and power hierarchy (as a way to preserve, reinforce, and reproduce the hierarchy). Fear and disgust make enslaving and lynching people seem right and necessary. There is pleasure, contentment, and perhaps relief in protecting one's property, especially when that property is power and domination, and even if that protection means pillaging and plundering people from their homes and their lives. Indeed, "domination," Bonilla-Silva notes, "produces the entire emotional gamut: hate and love, disgust and pleasure, aversion and empathy." So does Blackness.

Black people hate and love. They find disgust and take pleasure in things. They feel aversion and practice empathy. The Black person approaching the apprehensive pedestrian might, themselves, feel apprehensive. They might be afraid. They might be afraid of making the pedestrian afraid because they know that the consequences of other people's fears of Blackness can be dire for Black folks. Being called a "superpredator" or "nappy-headed ho" might stir anger or frustration, or collective action. Black freedom movements have been, among other things, movements of feelings. "I felt more annoyed than frightened" (Tracy 2009, 29) remembered Rosa Parks of her decision to stay in her seat at the front of a Montgomery city bus. Angela Davis talked about feeling fear. Nina Simone sang about "feeling good." James Baldwin wrote about feeling rage, and pain, and alive. And so on.

It is easy, and perhaps tempting, to frame what Black people feel as always and only a response to something. When Rosa Parks felt annoyed, she must have been responding to something that was annoying. Fear must be a response to something frightening. Happiness must come from pleasure or entertainment. Or must it? Emotions are not just responses. They can also be reasons, which is to say emotions can be "constitutive forces," which is to say emotions can "do" things. Why did the apprehensive pedestrian cross the road? Why did the disgusted white woman move to a different seat (see Lorde and Clarke 2007)? The answers are in the questions: emotions, in particular the emotions evoked by Blackness. The stories herein—before and after this chapter—echo the work of other scholars in showing the constitutive power of emotions, in this case the backbeat of desire, except I do not focus as much on whether emotions can do things as I do on how people use emotions to do things.

2. Hunter and Robinson (2018, 123) write, "A melodic steel drum echoes. Black women chant down Babylon. The funk is infected with the skank of Lee Scratch Perry. 'If you are a big, big tree,' Bob Marley announces in rhythm, 'then we are a small axe.' In a four-part harmonious refrain, Marley coos 'Ready to cut you down, to cut you down.' In a modest studio under a Jamaican sun, 'Small Axe,' recorded in 1973, would appear that same year on Marley's album Burnin.'" Hunter and Robinson position the small axe as a metaphor

for the many modes and manners of Black resistance. I am using the metaphor in a similar way here.

3. "Linked fate" is a concept used most widely in political science. In general, it refers to the belief that the success or failure of one Black person, or Black place, is linked in a causal or symbolic way to the successes and failures of a larger Black collective (i.e., a group of people or a collection of places). For a more thorough discussion, see Hunter 2013; or Dawson 2011.

4. In *Real Black* (2005), John Jackson Jr. considers the role that sincerity plays in how race is imagined and transacted in daily life and the public imagination. Jackson suggests that, like its discursive cousin authenticity, sincerity colors how people see and think race; but whereas authenticity is typically a label ascribed to objects (i.e., an assessment of how close a thing comes to some imagined racial essence), Jackson notes that "sincerity is an attempt to talk about racial subjects [emphasis his] and subjectivities" (17). If authenticity is a quality that things have, sincerity is a way that people are and do (things). To draw on an example that is more germane to my work in Clarksdale, if authenticity cares about how well a person plays the blues, sincerity cares about why they are playing in the first place. If authenticity is the property of audiences and consumers, sincerity is transacted by the performer.

5. Henshall 2018.

6. In the lexicon of several Black religious traditions—Pentecostalism chief among them—to "tarry" is to wait with expectation (for a blessing or answer from God). It is not specific to any one action. It could manifest as a clap, a prayer, a song, a "hallelujah," or in some other way. Crawley (2006) defines tarrying as "stilled intensity and waiting, as well as raucous praise noise" (4), and he offers the following example: "What the congregants at Butts Miracle Temple COGIC in Daytona Beach, FL . . . enunciate through voice, through flesh—screams and yelps, orations of 'Jesus!' and 'Hallelujah,' the handclapping and murmuring—is anything but easy to recount through writing. This joyful noise, this tarrying praise is not fully representable through writing; it avoids its own representation" (166).

7. Hamlin 2012, 85.

CHAPTER 3

1. According to Robinson (2014), Black southerners don't "fret" over race. She writes, "In conversations about their perceptions of race and racism, the overarching narrative was surprisingly consistent across age and class groups: 'You can't fret about it.' 'White folks are racist.' 'That's just how it is.' . . . [Residents of Memphis] refused the notion of paranoia, taking comfort in what they saw as a known quantity—white racism" (99).

2. Hunter et al. (2016) define "black placemaking" as "the ways that urban black Americans create sites of endurance, belonging, and resistance through social interaction"(2).

3. There are racial lessons to be learned from the places that Black people go. Places have power and can influence and help reproduce a society's power order (see Gieryn 2000 for a review). Places are social. They can facilitate group interaction or bring about patterns of isolation and estrangement. Places shape individual behavior and collective action. Places are gendered (i.e., "women belong in the kitchen") and classed (i.e., "a house on the hill").

Places are also racialized (see Browne 2015; McKittrick 2006, 2011; McKittrick and Woods 2007; Shabazz 2015; Summers 2019). There are white places, what sociologist

Wendy Moore (2007) defines as institutions that have historically and contemporarily catered to white sensibilities, and continue to reproduce notions of white supremacy and patterns of racial inequality (see also Anderson 2014).

There are Black places too. In a sociological adventure to and through America's "Chocolate Cities," Marcus Hunter and Zandria Robinson (2018) unpack the racial meaning inherent in place designations like "the hood" and "the bad part of town."

Robinson and Hunter also remind us that not all racialized places are made equal. Some are made by and in the image of structural racism—the plantation in antebellum America, tent cities in the 1930s, the urban ghetto in the 1950s. Where these Black places continue to tower in the historical and contemporary terrain of the United States, other Black places creep in the shadows beneath and beside them. These other Black places are made for and by Black folks. Black patrons at a gay nightclub meet to dance, celebrate, and expand their support networks. Black friends meet for "family reunions" in the vacated lots where their homes once stood. Blocks of Black folks flock to Washington Park on Saturdays for Little League games. Hunter et al. (2016) refer to these practices and interactions as "black placemaking."

Yet placemaking is not merely about where people go and what they do when they get there. Equally important are the concurrent decisions that individuals and groups make about where to stay away from. While geographers and development scholars have given some attention to these processes of place disengagement, what some have called "place unmaking" (e.g., Akinwumi 2005; Aoki and Yoshimizu 2015; Bacchi and Goodwin 2016) and "placelessness" (e.g., Birkeland 2008); they typically opt for top-down approaches that position people and communities as the hapless victims of macro processes like gentrification or deindustrialization—chess pieces in a larger game of invisible hands and "market forces."

I Don't Like the Blues removes the guard from such assumptions, clearing space for a new way to see and understand how Black people move in the world. It is certainly the case that people sometimes leave or relocate from a place because they have to. The building is demolished. The apartment becomes too expensive. But sometimes people avoid or withdraw from, or "unmake," places because they want to, because there is something about the place that they believe to be harmful, toxic, or otherwise off-putting. In these cases, absence is not happenstance or overdetermined from without. It is an act of political agency, indeed an epistemological strategy, honed and crafted from within.

4. Touré chronicles this racial uncertainty in the chapter "The Most Racist Thing That Ever Happened . . ." from his book *Who's Afraid of Post-blackness? What It Means to Be Black Now* (2012). In the book, he queries several celebrities about personal experiences with racism. His most common response was some version of "I'll probably never know." What Touré demonstrates journalistically, John Jackson Jr. fleshes out theoretically in *Racial Paranoia: the Unintended Consequences of Political Correctness* (2010), in which he situates the pervasive and enduring anxieties that Black Americans have about unfair treatment as a product of apparent declines in blatant forms of racism and the normalization of "colorblindness" in American rhetoric and imagination.

5. Henshall (2018) chronicles the decline of commercial activity on Clarksdale's downtown square.

6. Hamlin (2012, 105) documents these tactics at length. For instance, she notes that many of the Black folks who participated in voter registration drives "or other civil rights activity were told that they no longer qualified for government commodity winter relief.

In the Delta, under the economic heel of sharecropping, many families relied on aid to stretch their meager crop payments through the winter." See also note 35 from chapter 1.

7. Stolle 2013.

8. Henry 2000, 144.

9. See Hamlin 2012; and Pigee 1975.

10. Hunter and Robinson 2018, 57.

11. Painter 1977.

12. Cox 2015.

CHAPTER 4

1. I am thinking here both of recent work that treats the speculative (and related ideas like Afrofuturism) as a topic (e.g., Eshun 2003; Schalk 2018; and Womack 2013) and work, especially in Black studies, that treats speculation (and related ideas like Afrofuturism) as a method and aesthetic (e.g., Best 2018 and Crawley 2016).

2. I want to be clear: I do not believe it is a requirement for Black Americans to name a desired alternative or possible solution when critiquing an outcome, institutional practice, or set of social relations that they deem unjust or inequitable. While many of the Black residents that I spoke with could and often did name such alternative visions, one of the fundamental claims of this book is that it would be okay if they didn't. That is what the backbeat means. "I don't like" carries value for learning even if we don't hear the other side. "We ain't that no mo'" carries value for knowing (e.g., identity formation, sense-making) all by itself. Paul Taylor (2007) discusses this idea in his essay "Post-Black, Old Black." In some instances, a refusal to name a thing, in this case a recommended alternative, could be born of a "deep skepticism about our ability to understand some unfolding state of affairs" (630). Here, Black folks don't say because they don't know. Or they don't say because they don't believe that one can know right now. In other instances, not naming could be a subversive performance (Hurston 1935; Robinson 2014; Quashie 2012), wherein Black folks know but don't say because there is safety or strategic significance in not saying. Finally, not naming could function as a "space-clearing gesture" (Appiah 1992)—that is, as a way to "make room for alternative approaches" and other possible recommendations. Here, Black folks don't say because they know they don't have to. They know that others will come along and say after them. So they just make room.

3. This term is most closely associated with the writing of Leon Trotsky and Marxist development theory (Ashman 2012; Smith 1984). In general, it refers to an emergent structural arrangement in which some nations or regional blocs grow, modernize, and accumulate wealth at higher rates than others, resulting in an unequal set of social and power relations. In some cases, less developed nations adopt or are subsumed under the economic and cultural traditions of their more "developed" counterparts. In others, developed nations exploit and seek conquest over their less developed counterparts. Woods (1998) adopts this term in reference to the continued rule of the plantation bloc in the Mississippi Delta into the twenty-first century.

4. While Clarksdale's blues economy is substantial—attracting more than 130,000 visitors and generating some $40 million (Henshall 2018) annually—the town's local blues community is small. Most of the local blues venues are concentrated on a five-block stretch of the downtown square; and most anybody involved with the local blues circuit (business owners, public officials, musicians, singers, festival organizers, etc.) knows

everybody involved with the local blues circuit. For that reason, I have opted to talk sparingly about my interactions with local singers and musicians—I talked with thirteen such people during my time in Clarksdale. Other than Pooh Baby, whom I mention the most in chapter 1, and Juwell Turner (chapters 2 and 4), I do not detail the demographic information of local blues folks and, save for the aforementioned examples and this note, I do not include quoted material from my exchanges with them.

I will note here that what I heard from the thirteen blues folks that I spoke with underscores what Rhondalyn said.

One person who had sung and played at multiple venues in Clarksdale and at venues throughout the Delta region shared two instances of being paid an amount that was less than what was agreed on beforehand. "Don't nothing I do be for the money," the person said. "The blues don't pay here." When I asked them to elaborate, they continued, "not how you think it might. . . . It's plenty money in [Clarksdale's blues scenes], but not for Blacks."

Another person who had sung and played in Clarksdale before, cursed about the reputation that one local venue had of "making you wait, for you to get paid the money you already played for. Already played. Already did your gig. . . . Where is the money, joker?"

A full discussion of the inner workings of Clarksdale's blues economy (i.e., how local singers and musicians navigate local blues scenes; details about the economic machinations of the town's blues venues and festival circuit; stories about the service workers at downtown businesses, restaurants, and blues venues, etc.) is beyond the scope of this story. This note offers at least a little context; and I have included in an earlier note an example of how the town's blues tourism apparatus brings benefits to local stakeholders (i.e., public officials, business owners, etc.) that do not trickle down to local folks and communities. For more on the local machinations of Clarksdale's blues economy, see Henshall 2018.

5. The belief that "race relations" are generally improving and racial inequality becoming less pronounced is a common view in modern American society, especially among white folks (Pew Research Center 2019). Most white people believe that the nation "has already" made or "will eventually" make the changes necessary for racial equality, thus pushing the specter of racism and the reach of racial discrimination further into the nation's past. This perspective colors how schools teach, to the extent they do, about American slavery and the civil rights movement. It underwrites critically acclaimed films like 12 Years a Slave and box office hits like Django Unchained. It colors public perception of federal policies, such as affirmative action and the Affordable Care Act. It is the guiding and organizing principle of public commemorative spaces (e.g., the National Museum of African American History and Culture and the Civil Rights Monument commemorating the admission of the first Black student at the University of Mississippi).

The pervasiveness and entrenchment of the racial progress story is not happenstance, mostly because it is not (just) a story but a tool. Like a trowel in the hand of a skilled mason or a broom caught in the bustle of household chores, progress helps smooth over and tidy up a national history that is otherwise messy, violent, and fraught. In Hope Draped in Black (2016), Joseph Winters writes eloquently on the national commitment to the progress story. He argues that the appeal of the progressive narrative lies in its ability to mediate guilt and engender optimism, in its ability to shapeshift. Sometimes progress is an emotional buffer, partitioning the nation's history into neat, easily digestible parts—the ugly past that "used to be" and the triumphant present that was always promised. Sometimes progress is a fire, a way to burn away (i.e., rationalize) the structural and historical foundations of contemporary patterns of inequality and clear space for a future freed from the burden of history.

6. For the Equiano quote, see Equiano 2015, 29. For the Douglass quote, see Foner and Taylor 1999, 188–206. The reference to Zora Neale Hurston alludes to her role in helping establish the literary magazine *Fire*, along with Langston Hughes, Richard Nugent, Gwendolyn Bennett, John Davis, and Aaron Douglas. The first issue was released in November 1926. For the Richard Wright quote, see Wright 2007, 3.

7. This is a reference to Henry's (2000) autobiography, *Aaron Henry: The Fire Ever Burning.*

8. It would be disingenuous to say that *every* decision and moving part related to Clarksdale's blues economy begins and ends with white elected officials, business owners, and public stakeholders, and *only* those white folks. While most of Clarksdale's elected officials (e.g., mayor, city commissioners, chamber of commerce) were white during the years that I spent time there (2014–2019)—as were a staggering majority of the town's blues-related business owners and, as I have documented at length, a staggering majority of blues tourists and enthusiasts—not *all* of them were. In fact, the town elected a Black mayor in 2017. Such exceptions do not negate what has been a two-century rule in the Delta: the *interests* of white planters rule the day, even when white planters don't seem to be ruling the day (e.g., present in elected office). There's quite a bit of writing on this (e.g., Cobb 1994; Hamlin 2012; Woods 1998). More to the point, the story of *I Don't Like the Blues* is a story of how Black residents of Clarksdale make sense of life in Clarksdale. A part of what they have had to make sense of is whether they feel like the town's blues development agenda considers them—their interests, their desires, their needs, their challenges. Time and again, their conclusion is that the town's blues development agenda does not; and that has been true regardless of the racial composition of the town's elected leadership.

CONCLUSION

1. Gwendolyn Brooks via Hunter and Robinson 2018, 13.

CODA

1. For a full account of the decision by W. S. Kincade, and the subsequent mobilization by Black Clarksdalians, see Hamlin 2012, 91–115.

A SPIRIT IN THE DIRT(Y): A METHODOLOGICAL NOTE

1. Carter and Little 2007, 1317.

2. For a review of constructivism and interpretive approaches to qualitative research, see Grbich 2013.

3. For some of the foundational work on grounded theory, see Glaser 1978; Glaser 1992; and Glaser and Strauss 1967. For more recent thoughts, see Charmaz 2003.

4. For some thoughts on what ethnography is (and should be), see Burawoy et al. 1991;

Fine 1993; Hoffman-Jeep 2005; Hurston 1942; and Van Maanen 1988. For some examples of ethnography in action, see Bettie 2003; Lareau 2011; Pascoe 2007; and Tyson 2011.

5. If you count the number of named characters in this book, you will count sixty-one; yet I have mentioned that forty-three people from my "analytic sample" are featured book characters. The explanation for the eighteen-person discrepancy is as follows: first, there are fifteen book characters who I mention because of their relationship to a person who was a part of my analytic sample, or because they were relevant to the story in some other way (This does not count the unnamed woman from the parade in chapter 2, Tee-Dy and the restaurant workers from chapter 3, the unnamed woman from the candlelight vigil in chapter 4, Boyce Shumpert's momma, or Cookie's two grandchildren). These characters include Himmens and Shelbie White, the tourist couple (chapter 1); the unnamed elected official who talked about the importance of blues tourism to Clarksdale's economy; Lashiya Hollinquest and Shalaya Johnson, daughters of Latoya Coleman; Rodrick Johnson, father of Shalaya; Mrs. Pearline and Mr. Jimmy, Eddie Kane's parents; Tyreek and Tyshaun Mayfield, sons of Shaunice McGee (chapter 3); John Doe and Porter Carrie, the two elderly white men at Woodlawn (chapter 4); Ty'wanna Montgomery and Clyde "Mr. Cee" Harrel, who worked at Woodlawn; and Mrs. Millie Monroe, whom many local residents honored at the candlelight vigil.

Of the remaining characters, three (n = 3) are "repeats," meaning there are three instances in which I have given the same person two different pseudonyms (put in yet another way, what appears in the book as six different people is really only three). The rationale for that is as follows: each of these three people are featured in multiple places in the book and, at one point or another, directly criticized one or more of Clarksdale's elected officials. I "repeated" these people in an effort to prevent the individuals who made these comments from being identified by their descriptions elsewhere in the text. To further detail the decision: let us say that Person A said Thing One about a local elected official in chapter 2; and Person A also said Thing Two in chapter 4. To prevent my description of Person A in chapter 4 from being used to triangulate the identity of Person A (for instance, by cross-referencing my description of Person A in chapter 2), I rendered Person A as two different people. Thus, when in reality Person A said both Thing One and Thing Two, in the book, Person A said Thing One and Person B (who is really Person A) said Thing Two. Thus, forty-three.

6. Following designations put forth by Lynn Reinschmiedt and Bernal Green (1989), the most straightforward and robust classification system that I have come across, I draw distinctions between "central" and "fringe" Delta counties. The central Mississippi Delta includes those eleven Mississippi counties "lying entirely within the flatland Delta region" of the state: Bolivar, Coahoma, Humphreys, Issaquena, Leflore, Quitman, Sharkey, Sunflower, Tallahatchie, Tunica, and Washington. Unless indicated, all data, including my own calculations in appendix table 2, reference social and demographic trends in these eleven central counties.

7. See Harding 2010, 253–70.

8. Emerson, Fretz, and Shaw 2011; Saldaña 2009.

9. See Abell 2004; or Agar 1980 for an explanation of the life history/narrative analysis approach. See Jacobs and King 2002 for an example of the life history approach in use.

10. For a discussion, see Goertz and Mahoney 2012.

REFERENCES

Abell, Peter. 2004. "Narrative Explanation: An Alternative to Variable-Centered Explanation?" *Annual Review of Sociology* 30: 287–310.

Adams, Luther J. 2006. "'Headed for Louisville': Rethinking Rural to Urban Migration in the South, 1930–1950." *Journal of Social History* 40, no. 2: 407–30.

Agar, Michael. 1980. "Stories, Background Knowledge and Themes: Problems in the Analysis of Life History Narrative." *American Ethnologist* 7, no. 2: 223–39.

Akinwumi, Akinbola E. 2005. "(Un)Making Place, Displacing Community: The 'Transformation' of Identity in a Russia-Poland Borderland." *Social & Cultural Geography* 6, no. 6: 951–56.

Amy, Jeff. 2015. "Miss. Hospital Whistleblower Gets $3.5M." *Hattiesburg American*, May 25.

Anderson, Elijah. 2014. "The White Space." *Sociology of Race and Ethnicity* 1, no. 1: 10–21.

Andrews, Kenneth T. 2004. *Freedom Is a Constant Struggle: The Mississippi Civil Rights Movement and Its Legacy*. Chicago: University of Chicago Press.

Aoki, Julia, and Ayaka Yoshimizu. 2015. "Walking Histories, Un/Making Places: Walking Tours as Ethnography of Place." *Space and Culture* 18, no. 3: 273–84.

Ashman, Sam. 2012. "Uneven and Combined Development." In *The Elgar Companion to Marxist Economics*, edited by B. Fine, A. Saad-Filho, and M. Boffo, 60–65. Cheltenham, U.K.: Edward Elgar.

Austin, Colin, John Cooper, David Dodson, Ferrell Guillory, Richard Hart, Megan Kauffmann, and Christina Rausch. 2009. *A Time of Reckoning: Testing the Will for Change in the Mississippi Delta*. Chapel Hill, N.C.: Manpower Development.

Autor, David H., and David Dorn. 2013. "The Growth of Low-Skill Service Jobs and the Polarization of the U.S. Labor Market." *American Economic Review* 103, no. 5: 1553–97.

Autor, David H., Lawrence F. Katz, and Melissa S. Kearney. 2006. "The Polarization of the US Labor Market." Working Paper 11986. Cambridge, Mass.: National Bureau of Economic Research.

Bacchi, Carol, and Susan Goodwin. 2016. "Making and Unmaking 'Places.'" In *Poststructural Policy Analysis*, 60–65. New York: Palgrave.

Bessman, Jim. 1993. "Ever-Growing Delta Blues Museum Keeps Music's History Alive." *Billboard*, December 4.

Best, Stephen. 2018. *None Like Us: Blackness, Belonging, Aesthetic Life*. Durham, N.C.: Duke University Press.

Bettie, Julie. 2003. *Women without Class: Girls, Race, and Identity*. Berkeley: University of California Press.

Birkeland, Inger. 2008. "Cultural Sustainability: Industrialism, Placelessness, and the Re-animation of Place." *Ethics, Place & Environment* 11, no. 3: 283–97.

Bonilla-Silva, Eduardo. 2019. "Feeling Race: Theorizing the Racial Economy of Emotions." *American Sociological Review* 84, no. 1: 1–25.

Brandfon, Robert. 1967. *Cotton Kingdom of the New South: A History of the Yazoo Mississippi Delta from Reconstruction to the Twentieth Century*. Cambridge, Mass.: Harvard University Press.

Bradley, Regina. 2017. *Boondock Kollage: Stories from the Hip Hop South*. New York: Peter Lang, International Academic.

Brown, Karida. 2018. *Gone Home: Race and Roots through Appalachia*. Chapel Hill: University of North Carolina Press.

Browne, Simone. 2015. *Dark Matters: On the Surveillance of Blackness*. Durham, N.C.: Duke University Press.

Burawoy, Michael, Alice Burton, Ann Arnett Ferguson, Kathryn J. Fox, Joshua Gamson, Leslie Hurst, Nadine G. Julius, Charles Kurzman, Leslie Salzinger, Josepha Schiffman, and Shiori Ui. 1991. *Ethnography Unbound: Power and Resistance in the Modern Metropolis*. Berkeley: University of California Press.

Carter, Stacy M., and Miles Little. 2007. "Justifying Knowledge, Justifying Method, Taking Action: Epistemologies, Methodologies, and Methods in Qualitative Research." *Qualitative Health Research* 17, no. 10: 1316–28.

Charmaz, Kathy. 2003. "Grounded Theory: The Logic of Grounded Theory." In *Contemporary Field Research: Perspectives and Formulations*, vol. 2, edited by R. M. Emerson, 335–52. Long Grove, Ill.: Waveland.

Coates, Ta-Nehisi. 2014. "The Case for Reparations." *The Atlantic*, June. https://www.theatlantic.com/magazine/archive/2014/06/the-case-for-reparations/361631/.

Cobb, James C. 1982. *The Selling of the South: The Southern Crusade for Industrial Development, 1936–1980*. Baton Rouge: Louisiana State University Press.

———. 1994. *The Most Southern Place on Earth: The Mississippi Delta and the Roots of Regional Identity*. New York: Oxford University Press.

Cosby, Arthur G., Mitchell W. Brackin, T. David Mason, and Eunice R. McCulloch. 1992. *A Social and Economic Portrait of the Mississippi Delta*. Social Science Research Center, Mississippi State University.

Cottom, Tressie McMillan. 2019. *Thick: And Other Essays*. New York: The New Press.

Cox, Aimee Meredith. 2015. *Shapeshifters: Black Girls and the Choreography of Citizenship*. Durham, N.C.: Duke University Press.

Crawley, Ashon T. 2016. *Blackpentecostal Breath: The Aesthetics of Possibility*. New York: American Literatures Initiative.

Crosby, Emilye. 2005. *A Little Taste of Freedom: The Black Freedom Struggle in Claiborne County, Mississippi*. Chapel Hill: University of North Carolina Press.

Dalaker, Joseph. 2019. *The 10–20–30 Provision: Defining Persistent Poverty Counties*. Washington, D.C.: Congressional Research Service.

Dawson, Michael C. 2011. *Not in Our Lifetimes: The Future of Black Politics*. Chicago: University of Chicago Press.

de Jong, Greta. 2016. *You Can't Eat Freedom: Southerners and Social Justice after the Civil Rights Movement*. Chapel Hill: University of North Carolina Press.

Delta Regional Authority. 2015. *Today's Delta: A Research Tool for the Region*. 2nd ed. Washington, D.C.: Delta Regional Authority.

Dittmer, John. 1995. *Local People: The Struggle for Civil Rights in Mississippi*. Urbana: University of Illinois Press.

Drake, St. Clair, and Horace R. Cayton. 1945. *Black Metropolis: A Study of Negro Life in a Northern City*. Chicago: University of Chicago Press.

Du Bois, W. E. B. 1898. "The Negroes of Farmville, Virginia: A Social Study." Bulletin. Washington, D.C.: U.S. Department of Labor.

———. 1899. *The Philadelphia Negro: A Social Study*. Philadelphia: University of Pennsylvania Press.

Edge, John T. 2017. *The Potlikker Papers: A Food History of the Modern South*. New York: Penguin.

Emerson, Robert M., Rachel I. Fretz, and Linda L. Shaw. 2011. *Writing Ethnographic Fieldnotes*. Chicago: University of Chicago Press.

Equiano, Olaudah. 2015. *The Interesting Narrative of the Life of Olaudah Equiano: Or Gustavus Vassa, the African, Written by Himself*. Scotts Valley, Calif.: CreateSpace Independent Publishing Platform.

Eshun, Kodwo. 2003. "Further Considerations of Afrofuturism." *CR: The New Centennial Review* 3, no. 2: 287–302.

Etheridge, Eric, Roger Wilkins, and Diane McWhorter. 2008. *Breach of Peace: Portraits of the 1961 Mississippi Freedom Riders*. New York: Atlas.

Falk, William W. 2004. *Rooted in Place: Family and Belonging in a Southern Black Community*. New Brunswick, N.J.: Rutgers University Press.

Fine, Gary A. 1993. "Ten Lies of Ethnography: Moral Dilemmas of Field Research." *Journal of Contemporary Ethnography* 22 (October): 267–94.

Foner, Philip S., and Yuval Taylor, eds. 1999. *Frederick Douglass: Selected Speeches and Writings*. Chicago: Lawrence Hill.

Foster, Catherine. 1991. "Making Green from Blues." *Christian Science Monitor*, January 23.

Frey, William. 2004. *The New Great Migration: Black Americans' Return to the South, 1965–2000*. Washington, D.C.: Brookings Institution Press.

———. 2014. *Diversity Explosion: How New Racial Demographics Are Remaking America*. Washington, D.C.: Brookings Institution Press.

Galster, George. 2012. "The Mechanism(s) of Neighborhood Effects: Theory, Evidence, and Policy Implications." In *Neighborhood Effects Research: New Perspectives*, edited by

M. van Ham, D. Manley, N. Bailey, L. Simpson, and D. Maclennan, 23–56. New York: Springer.

Gayarré, Charles. 1877. "The Southern Question." *North American Review* 125, no. 259: 472–98.

George, Nelson. 1988. *The Death of Rhythm and Blues.* New York: Penguin.

———. 2001. *Buppies, b-Boys, Baps & Bohos: Notes on Post-soul Black Culture.* Cambridge, Mass.: Da Capo.

Gieryn, Thomas F. 2000. "A Space for Place in Sociology." *Annual Review of Sociology* 26: 463–96.

Glaser, Barney G. 1978. *Theoretical Sensitivity: Advances in the Methodology of Grounded Theory.* Mill Valley, Calif.: Sociology Press.

———. 1992. *Emergence vs. Forcing: Basics of Grounded Theory Analysis.* Mill Valley, Calif.: Sociology Press.

Glaser, Barney, and Anselm Strauss. 1967. *The Discovery of Grounded Theory.* Chicago: Aldine.

Glasmeier, Amy K. 2019. "Living Wage Calculator." http://livingwage.mit.edu. Retrieved August 22.

Goertz, Gary, and James Mahoney. 2012. *A Tale of Two Cultures: Qualitative and Quantitative Research in the Social Sciences.* Princeton, N.J.: Princeton University Press.

Grbich, Carol. 2013. *Qualitative Data Analysis: An Introduction.* 2nd ed. Thousand Oaks, Calif.: Sage.

Griffin, Larry J. 2001. "The Promise of a Sociology of the South." *Southern Cultures* 7, no. 1: 50–75.

Gussow, Adam. 2017. *Beyond the Crossroads: The Devil and the Blues Tradition.* Chapel Hill: University of North Carolina Press.

Hall, Stuart. 1993. "What Is This 'Black' in Black Popular Culture." *Social Justice* 21, no. 1: 104–14.

Hamilton, William B. 1992. "Return of the Native Blues: In Clarksdale, Miss., an American Art Form Comes Full Circle." *Washington Post*, January 14.

Hamlin, Françoise N. 2012. *Crossroads at Clarksdale: The Black Freedom Struggle in the Mississippi Delta after World War II.* Chapel Hill: University of North Carolina Press.

Harding, David J. 2010. *Living the Drama: Community, Conflict, and Culture among Inner-City Boys.* Chicago: University of Chicago Press.

Hardwell, Byrd. 2004. "Mississippi Governor Signs Bill to Create Blues Commission." Associated Press. April 26.

Harrill, Rich. 2004. "Residents' Attitudes toward Tourism Development: A Literature Review with Implications for Tourism Planning." *CPL Bibliography* 18, no. 3: 251–66.

Hartman, Saidiya. 2008. *Lose Your Mother: A Journey along the Atlantic Slave Route.* London: Macmillan.

Henry, Aaron. 2000. *Aaron Henry: The Fire Ever Burning.* Jackson: University Press of Mississippi.

Henshall, John C. 2018. *Downtown Revitalisation and Delta Blues in Clarksdale, Mississippi: Lessons for Small Cities and Towns.* New York: Palgrave Macmillan.

Hobson, Maurice J. 2017. *The Legend of the Black Mecca: Politics and Class in the Making of Modern Atlanta.* Chapel Hill: University of North Carolina Press.

Hoffman-Jeep, Lynda. 2005. "Creating Ethnography: Zora Neale Hurston and Lydia Cabrera." *African American Review* 39, no. 3: 337–53.

Howell, Angela McMillan. 2013. *Raised Up Down Yonder: Growing Up Black in Rural Alabama*. Jackson: University Press of Mississippi.

Hunt, Larry L., Matthew O. Hunt, and William Falk. 2004. "Return Migrations of African-Americans to the South: Reclaiming a Land of Promise, Going Home, or Both?" *Rural Sociology* 69, no. 4: 490–509.

Hunter, Marcus Anthony. 2013. *Black Citymakers: How the Philadelphia Negro Changed Urban America*. New York: Oxford University Press.

Hunter, Marcus Anthony, Mary Pattillo, Zandria F. Robinson, and Keeanga-Yamahtta Taylor. 2016. "Black Placemaking: Celebration, Play, and Poetry." *Theory, Culture & Society* 33, nos. 7–8: 31–56.

Hunter, Marcus Anthony, and Zandria F. Robinson. 2018. *Chocolate Cities: The Black Map of American Life*. Oakland: University of California Press.

Hurston, Zora Neale. 1942. *Dust Tracks on a Road: An Autobiography*. Urbana: University of Illinois Press.

———. 1990. "Art and Such." In *Reading Black, Reading Feminist: A Critical Anthology*, edited by H. L. Gates Jr., 21–26. New York: Meridian.

Jackson, John L., Jr. 2005. *Real Black: Adventures in Racial Sincerity*. Chicago: University of Chicago Press.

———. 2010. *Racial Paranoia: The Unintended Consequences of Political Correctness*. New York: Basic Civitas.

Jacobs, Jerry A., and Rosalind B. King. 2002. "Age and College Completion: A Life-history Analysis of Women Aged 15–44." *Sociology of Education* 75, no. 3: 211–30.

Jazz News. 2006. "Haley Barbour Unveils First Marker of Mississippi Blues Trail." http://home.nestor.minsk.by/jazz/news/2006/12/1303.html.

Johnson, E. Patrick. 2011. *Sweet Tea: Black Gay Men of the South*. Chapel Hill: University of North Carolina Press.

———. 2019. *Honeypot: Black Southern Women Who Love Women*. Durham, N.C.: Duke University Press.

Johnson, Rheta Grimsely. 1998. "Can't Export the All-Feel Delta Blues." *Atlanta Journal and Constitution*, November 16.

Johnson, Kenneth, and Daniel Lichter. 2019. "Rural Depopulation in a Rapidly Urbanizing America." National Issue Brief 139. Carsey School of Public Policy.

Jones, David M. 2007. "Postmodernism, Pop Music, and Blues Practice in Nelson George's Post-soul Culture." *African American Review* 41, no. 4: 667–94.

Jones, Leroi. 1963. *Blues People: Negro Music in White America*. New York: William Morrow.

King, Stephen A. 2011. *I'm Feeling the Blues Right Now*. Jackson: University Press of Mississippi.

Lackey, Hilliard Lawrence. 2014. *Marks, Martin and the Mule Train: Marks, Mississippi— Martin Luther King, Jr. and the Origin of the 1968 Poor People's Campaign Mule Train*. Bloomington, Ind.: Xlibris Publishing Company.

Lacy, Karyn R. 2007. *Blue-Chip Black Race, Class, and Status in the New Black Middle Class*. Berkeley: University of California Press.

Lareau, Annette. 2011. *Unequal Childhoods: Class, Race, and Family Life*. 2nd ed. Berkeley: University of California Press.

Laymon, Kiese. 2013. *Long Division*. Chicago: Agate Bolden.

———. 2018. *Heavy: An American Memoir*. 1st ed. New York: Scribner.

Lemann, Nicholas. 1992. *The Promised Land: The Great Black Migration and How It Changed America.* New York: Vintage.

Lichtenstein, Nelson. 2014. "Today's South Is Boldly Moving Backward." *Reuters,* June 18. http://blogs.reuters.com/great-debate/2014/06/18/todays-south-is-boldly-moving-backward/.

Lloyd, Richard. 2012. "Urbanization and the Southern United States." *Annual Review of Sociology* 38, no. 1: 483–506.

Lomax, Alan. 2002. *The Land Where the Blues Began.* Revised ed. New York: New Press.

Lorde, Audre, and Cheryl Clarke. 2007. *Sister Outsider: Essays and Speeches.* Rpt. Berkeley, Calif.: Crossing.

McKittrick, Katherine. 2006. *Demonic Grounds: Black Women and the Cartographies of Struggle.* Minneapolis: University of Minnesota Press.

———. 2011. "On Plantations, Prisons, and a Black Sense of Place." *Social & Cultural Geography* 12, no. 8: 947–63.

McKittrick, Katherine, and Clyde Woods, eds. 2007. *Black Geographies and the Politics of Place.* Cambridge, Mass.: South End.

MDAH (Mississippi Department of Archives and History). 2003. "Governor Musgrove Announces the Mississippi Blues Commission." Press release, October 24. http://www.mdah.ms.gov/arrec/digital_archives/musgrove/pdfs/5229.pdf.

Moore, Wendy Leo. 2007. *Reproducing Racism: White Space, Elite Law Schools, and Racial Inequality.* Lanham, Md.: Rowman & Littlefield.

Morris, Aldon. 2015. *The Scholar Denied: W. E. B. Du Bois and the Birth of Modern Sociology.* Oakland: University of California Press.

Motley, Clay. 2018. "'Life Gets Heavy': Blues Tourism in Clarksdale, Mississippi." *Southern Cultures* 24, no. 2: 78–97.

Moye, J. Todd. 2004. *Let the People Decide: Black Freedom and White Resistance Movements in Sunflower County, Mississippi, 1945–1986.* Chapel Hill: University of North Carolina Press.

Munford, Luther. 1973. "White Flight from Desegregation in Mississippi." *Equity and Excellence in Education* 11, no. 3: 12–26.

Murray, Charles Shaar. 2001. "Friday Review: Highway 61 Resurrected." *The Guardian,* September 28.

Myrdal, Gunnar. 1944. *An American Dilemma: The Negro Problem and Modern Democracy.* Vol. 2. Piscataway, N.J.: Transaction.

Neal, Larry. 1972. "The Ethos of the Blues." *Black Scholar* 3, no. 10: 42–48.

Neal, Mark Anthony. 2002. *Soul Babies: Black Popular Culture and the Post-soul Aesthetic.* New York: Routledge.

Newkirk, Vann R. 2019. "The Great Land Robbery." *The Atlantic,* September. https://www.theatlantic.com/magazine/archive/2019/09/this-land-was-our-land/594742/.

Oliver, Sylvester W. 1980. "Local Folk Singer: An Unsung Legend." Clarksdale, Miss.: Carnegie Public Library.

Painter, Nell Irvin. 1977. *Exodusters: Black Migration to Kansas after Reconstruction.* New York: W. W. Norton.

Palmer, Robert. 1982. *Deep Blues: A Musical and Cultural History of the Mississippi Delta.* New York: Penguin.

———. 1988. "Muddy Waters' Imprint on Mississippi." *New York Times,* April 23.

Pascoe, Cheri J. 2007. *Dude, You're a Fag: Masculinity and Sexuality in High School.* Berkeley: University of California Press.

Peabody, Charles. 1903. "Notes on Negro Music." *Journal of American Folklore* 16, no. 62: 148–52.

Pew Research Center. 2019. "Race in America."

Pigee, Vera Mae Berry. 1975. *The Struggle of Struggles.* Detroit: Harlo.

Pike, Andy, Andrés Rodriguez-Pose, and John Tomaney. 2006. *Local and Regional Development.* New York: Routledge.

Powell, Richard J. 1989. *The Blues Aesthetic: Black Culture and Modernism.* Washington, D.C.: Washington Project for the Arts.

Purifoy, Danielle. 2017. "In Conditions of Fresh Water: An Artistic Exploration of Environmental Racism." Exhibit at Duke University Center for Documentary Studies, March 2–June 3. https://www.daniellepurifoy.com/in-conditions-of-fresh-water-1.

Quashie, Kevin. 2012. *The Sovereignty of Quiet: Beyond Resistance in Black Culture.* New Brunswick, N.J.: Rutgers University Press.

Reed, John Shelton. 2003. *Minding the South.* Piscataway, N.J.: Transaction.

Reese, Ashanté. 2019. *Black Food Geographies: Race, Self-Reliance, and Food Access in Washington, D.C.* Chapel Hill: University of North Carolina Press.

Reinschmiedt, Lynn L., and Bernal L. Green. 1989. *Socioeconomic Conditions: The Mississippi Delta.* Starkville: Department of Information Services, Division of Agriculture, Forestry, and Veterinary Medicine, Mississippi State University.

Ribas, Vanesa. 2015. *On the Line: Slaughterhouse Lives and the Making of the New South.* Oakland: University of California Press.

Richardson, Riché. 2007. *Black Masculinity and the U.S. South: From Uncle Tom to Gangsta.* Athens: University of Georgia Press.

Robinson, Zandria F. 2014. *This Ain't Chicago: Race, Class, and Regional Identity in the Post-soul South.* Chapel Hill: University of North Carolina Press.

———. 2018. "The B-Side of Blackness: Searching in Sound for the Loudness and Quiet of Mourning." *Believer Magazine,* August 1. https://believermag.com/the-b-side-of-blackness.

Rolph, Stephanie R. 2018. *Resisting Equality: The Citizen's Council, 1954–1989.* Baton Rouge: Louisiana State University Press.

Ruffin, Kimberly N. 2009. "'I Got the Blues' Epistemology: Jayne Cortez's Poetry for Eco-crisis." *MELUS: Multi-ethnic Literature of the U.S.* 34, no. 2: 63–80.

Rushing, Wanda. 2009. *Memphis and the Paradox of Place: Globalization in the American South.* Chapel Hill: University of North Carolina Press.

Salaam, Kalamu ya. 1995. "It Didn't Jes Grew: The Social and Aesthetic Significance of African American Music." *African American Review* 29, no. 2: 351–75.

Saldaña, Johnny. 2009. *The Coding Manual for Qualitative Researchers.* Thousand Oaks, Calif.: Sage.

Schalk, Sami. 2018. *Bodyminds Reimagined: (Dis)Ability, Race, and Gender in Black Women's Speculative Fiction.* Durham, N.C.: Duke University Press.

Shabazz, Rashad. 2015. *Spatializing Blackness: Architectures of Confinement and Black Masculinity in Chicago.* Urbana: University of Illinois Press.

Silver, Christopher, and John V. Moeser. 1995. *The Separate City: Black Communities in the Urban South, 1940–1968.* Lexington: University Press of Kentucky.

Slocum, Karla. 2019. *Black Towns, Black Futures: The Enduring Allure of a Black Place in the American West*. Chapel Hill: University of North Carolina Press.

Smith, Neil. 1984. *Uneven Development: Nature, Capital, and the Production of Space*. Athens: University of Georgia Press.

Sokol, Jason. 2008. *There Goes My Everything: White Southerners in the Age of Civil Rights, 1945–1975*. New York: Random House Digital.

Stack, Carol B. 1996. *Call to Home: African Americans Reclaim the Rural South*. New York: Basic Books.

Steele, Alysia Burton. 2015. *Delta Jewels: In Search of My Grandmother's Wisdom*. New York: Center Street.

Stewart, Steve. 2001. "Festival Is Evidence of Tourism Potential." *Clarksdale Press Register*, August 11.

Stolle, Roger. 2013. "In Memoriam: Frank 'Rat' Ratcliff (Riverside Hotel, Clarksdale)." *Blues Magazine*, March 29.

Sugrue, Thomas. 2005. *The Origins of the Urban Crisis: Race and Inequality in Postwar Detroit*. Princeton, N.J.: Princeton University Press.

Summers, Brandi Thompson. 2019. *Black in Place: The Spatial Aesthetics of Race in a Post–Chocolate City*. Chapel Hill: University of North Carolina Press.

Thomas, Lynnell. 2014. *Desire and Disaster in New Orleans: Tourism, Race, and Historical Memory*. Durham, N.C.: Duke University Press.

Touré. 2012. *Who's Afraid of Post-blackness? What It Means to Be Black Now*. New York: Atria.

Tracy, Kathleen. 2009. *Rosa Parks*. Newark, Del.: Mitchell Lane.

Tsuruta, Dorothy Randall. 1981. "In Dialogue to Define Aesthetics: James Baldwin and Chinua Achebe." *The Black Scholar* 12, no. 2: 72–79.

Twitty, Michael W. 2017. *The Cooking Gene: A Journey through African American Culinary History in the Old South*. New York: Amistad.

Tyson, Karolyn. 2011. *Integration Interrupted: Tracking, Black Students, and Acting White after "Brown."* New York: Oxford University Press.

Van Deburg, William L. 1993. *New Day in Babylon: The Black Power Movement and American Culture, 1965–1975*. Chicago: University of Chicago Press.

Van Maanen, John. 1988. *Tales of the Field: On Writing Ethnography*. 2nd ed. Chicago: University of Chicago Press.

Voth, Donald E., Molly Sizer, and Frank L. Farmer. 1996. "Patterns of In-Migration and Out-Migration: Human Capital Movements in the Lower Mississippi Delta Region." *Southern Rural Sociology* 12, no. 1: 1265–92.

Wald, Elijah. 2004. *Escaping the Delta: Robert Johnson and the Invention of the Blues*. New York: Amistad.

Walder, John C., and Allen D. Cleveland. 1971. "The South's New Segregation Academies." *Phi Delta Kappan* 53, no. 4: 234–35, 238–39.

Ward, Jesmyn. 2011. *Salvage the Bones: A Novel*. New York: Bloomsbury.

———, ed. 2016. *The Fire This Time: A New Generation Speaks about Race*. New York: Scribner.

Wilkerson, Isabel. 2011. *The Warmth of Other Suns: The Epic Story of America's Great Migration*. Rpt. New York: Vintage.

Willis, John C. 2000. *Forgotten Time: The Yazoo-Mississippi Delta after the Civil War*. Charlottesville: University of Virginia Press.

Winters, Joseph R. 2016. *Hope Draped in Black: Race, Melancholy, and the Agony of Progress.* Durham, N.C.: Duke University Press.

Womack, Ytasha L. 2013. *Afrofuturism: The World of Black Sci-Fi and Fantasy Culture.* Chicago: Chicago Review Press.

Woodruff, Nan Elizabeth. 2012. *American Congo: The African American Freedom Struggle in the Delta.* Chapel Hill: University of North Carolina Press.

Woods, Clyde. 1998. *Development Arrested: The Blues and Plantation Power in the Mississippi Delta.* New York: Verso.

———. 2005. "Do You Know What It Means to Miss New Orleans? Katrina, Trap Economics, and the Rebirth of the Blues." *American Quarterly* 57, no. 4: 1005–18.

Wright, Earl, II. 2016. *The First American School of Sociology: W. E. B. Du Bois and the Atlanta Sociological Laboratory.* New York: Routledge.

Wright, Richard. 1997. "12 Million Black Voices." In *Richard Wright Reader*, edited by E. Wright and M. Fabre, 145–241. New York: Da Capo.

———. 2007. *Black Boy: A Record of Childhood and Youth.* New York: Harper Perennial Modern Classics.

Yaeger, Patricia. 2000. *Dirt and Desire: Reconstructing Southern Women's Writing, 1930–1990.* Chicago: University of Chicago Press.

INDEX

Page numbers appearing in italics refer to illustrations.

Index

Made in the USA
Monee, IL
18 August 2023

41215263R00120